BE AUDACIOUS

Inspiring Legacy and Living a Life That Matters

MICHAEL W. LEACH

WESTWINDS
PRESS®

Library of Congress Cataloging-in-Publication Data

Leach, Michael W.
  Be audacious : inspiring your legacy and living a life that matters / by Michael W. Leach.
    pages cm
  Includes bibliographical references.
  ISBN 978-1-941821-72-5 (pbk.)
  ISBN 978-1-941821-93-0 (e-book)
  ISBN 978-1-941821-94-7 (hardbound)
  1. Young adults—Conduct of life. 2. Conduct of life. 3. Self-realization.
I. Title.
  BJ1661.L43 2015
  170'.44—dc23
                                        2015011455

Edited by Jennifer Weaver-Neist
Cover design by Brad Bunkers and Vicki Knapton
Interior design by Vicki Knapton

Published by WestWinds Press®
An imprint of

GRAPHIC ARTS
BOOKS®

P.O. Box 56118
Portland, Oregon 97238-6118
503-254-5591
www.graphicartsbooks.com

For the two people who keep my world spinning,
Kamiah and Amanda. Mahalo for your unwavering love,
for believing in this endeavor, and for always
having my back. You are my refuge.

CONTENTS

Foreword   9

Introduction   17

PART I: OVERCOMING ADVERSITY

1 Hardship Is Your Greatest Gift 25
- The BA Balance...27
- Physical Adversity 29
- Mental Adversity...31
- Spiritual Adversity..33
- Manage Expectations...37
- Practice Exercise: Belly Breathing.....................................39
- Closing Thoughts..42

2 Your Essence Defines Your Swagger 43
- Write a New Story 45
- Resiliency 46
- Mantra, Mantra, Mantra 49
- Scrappy and Undeterred 51
- Connection 53
- ODAAT 58
- Attitude, Character, and Integrity 60
- Practice Exercises: Positive Visualization 63
  - o   Exercise #1: Gratitude Windows...............................63
  - o   Exercise #2: Look, Plan, Act....................................64
- Closing Thoughts..66

PART II: LIVING AN AUTHENTIC LIFE

3   Lead from the Heart 71
     •   Becoming a Leader...73
     •   Uncertainty Scaffolding 80
     •   The Guts to Be Vulnerable...................................88
     •   Fight Fear and Shame..93
     •   Metamorphosis and the What Happened Bubble 100
     •   Core Values...106
     •   Practice Exercises: Change for the Better 110
         o   Exercise #1: Your Core Values 110
         o   Exercise #2: The What Happened Bubble 113
     •   Closing Thoughts 115

4   Embrace Criticism 117
     •   Flowing Waters, Open Roads.............................. 119
     •   In the Face of Dogma 125
     •   The 30 Percent Rule 130
     •   Swagger versus Peer Pressure 132
     •   Swagger versus Arrogance 136
     •   Belonging and a Thick Skin 138
     •   Your Personal Mountaintop 143
     •   *One* Tribe: Local and Global............................. 146
     •   Armor and Training 154
     •   Practice Exercise: The Three Rs........................... 158
     •   Closing Thoughts 162

PART III: UNCOVERING PURPOSEFUL PASSION

5   Harness Your Potential 167
     •   Change Happens.. 170
     •   The Remake 172
     •   Purpose and Permapassion 173
     •   Legacy Work 178
     •   Fire Plus Vision 185
     •   The Time for Purposeful Action............................ 188
     •   The Waters of Personal Growth 191
     •   A Word of Caution: Recover and Recharge...................... 193
     •   Practice Exercise: Exploring Your Passion(s).................... 197

      o   Session #1: *I Am Passionate About*........................ 197

      o   Session #2: *I Admire* 198

      o   Session #3: *I Can Make an Impact By* 200

  • Closing Thoughts.. 202

PART IV: DEVELOPING YOUR VISION

6 Think Big and Dream Even Bigger................................207

  • Get Up and Try..209

  • Fall In Love with "Impractical" 211

  • Avoid Dream Stealers 215

  • The Nutrients to Stay the Course........................... 217

  • Plan for Your Vision 220

  • The Handful 223

  • The *All In* Mantra..225

  • Practice Exercise: Your Mission and Vision Statements 230

      o   Session #1: Noodling...............................230

      o   Session #2: Committing to Paper 231

      o   Session #3: Making It Official 232

  • Closing Thoughts..235

7 Weather the Storm, Face Your Fears..............................237

  • Resiliency Reservoir: Part I 240

  • Change Your Narrative.....................................243

  • Resiliency Reservoir: Part II 245

  • Brush with Eternity 252

  • Aftermath...257

  • Love, Balance, Gratitude..................................260

  • Practice Exercise: A Gratitude Journal 265

  • Closing Thoughts..268

In Conclusion: Your Legacy—A Life That Matters   269

Acknowledgments   275

Notes   279

Foreword

Audacious. It is such a powerful word that has had a major impact on how I want to live my life. I was first introduced to it by Michael Leach when I was a senior in high school, and I am going to share with you my side of the story—how I have been inspired to be audacious and how it has affected my life. There is so much to tell! Just let it be known that Michael Leach is an extraordinary person who is deeply committed to sharing his bold passions and inspiring knowledge.

Back when I was a senior, Michael was the assistant coach for the Lady Bruins basketball program in Gardiner, Montana, and I was one of two senior captains on the team. The instant Michael came into the gym, I knew my life was going to change—both on the court and in my heart. Michael spoke a truth and passion about basketball, and he made me dig deeper to find how it fit into life. He became my mentor and friend, inspiring me with the fire he had in him.

One night, when he could not make a basketball game, he gave the other senior captain and me a list of quotes that we were to go through as a team before the game started. It was Michael's way of starting a strong and thoughtful tradition that I was proud to have implemented. From then on, every night before battle, we read quotes from Henry David Thoreau, E. E. Cummings, and people of the like, but what struck me most that night was a quote Michael composed himself:

> If you have the courage to be authentic and original,
> you can therefore be audacious—and thus beautiful.

I was blown away by such simple yet magical words: all I really needed to be was *me* in order to show other people what I was capable of. It led me to believe in myself and to have one of the best games of my career. "Audacious" was a word that changed my perspective and gave me a desire to live by its definition—to be bold, courageous, and without fear.

As the years have passed, I have watched Michael grow into his life and reach goals he'd set for himself before he even met me. I like to think, though, that I was one of the first to help inspire his vision of spreading the idea of being audacious and sharing his passions with the rest of the world!

I saw a handful of Michael's talks when he worked as a bear education ranger, wearing the green and gray for Yellowstone National Park. His ways of captivating an audience seemed so effortless for him. Once I saw his swagger and stage presence, combined with his in-your-face facts and authentic sense of place, my view of Yellowstone changed forever. Michael was dubbed "The Rev," not only because he preached about the wonder and glory that is Yellowstone but because he showed reverence in his heart and in his words. I can still picture him in front of a fascinated audience, quoting Terry Tempest Williams.

He shared his passion for the last free-ranging bison and the controversial politics that surround their wanderings; his concern over the clearcutting effects in the Greater Yellowstone Ecosystem; how the grizzly bear is the umbrella species of Yellowstone and an integral aspect of the Ecosystem, as well as the spiritual connection he has to the land. Michael has four generations of history in the tri-state area (Montana, Idaho, Wyoming) and grew up bubbling with excitement about Yellowstone, which he also translates through pictures. His slideshow that focuses on the wondrous places of Yellowstone—as well as the dangers and threats to the area—encourages you to search within yourself to find out why Yellowstone is special to you.

Beyond its formal definition, I learned that if you want to show other people how to "be audacious" then you should live with humility and compassion, and be a leader who fights for the things you believe in. During Michael's presentations, he did nothing but that, and it truly motivated me to strive to live my life that way too.

After leaving the Park Service, Michael's idea of starting a nonprofit called Yellowstone Country Guardians (YCG) became a reality. Determined to continue his Yellowstone sermon, he wanted to pursue the dream of putting youth into action, "Inspiring a New Surge" (his manifesto) of environmental activism in the area. Though his thirst for change made him vulnerable to the naysaying public, nothing was going to stop him. If there were one point in time that I would say Michael was at his most audacious, it would have been at this time. To take an idea so fresh and young, and then build it into what Yellowstone Country Guardians eventually became is incredible.

I wanted to invest in Michael's journey and participate in any way possible because I knew that he was paving the way for something big. Ideas for advocacy projects started to bloom, including outreach and education programs. Utilizing everything he knew about Yellowstone and the politics that thrive in the area, Michael wanted to take activism and environmentalism to the next level, getting youth and communities more involved. The Yellowstone Leadership Challenge (YLC) became the first vehicle, and I volunteered to be a counselor.

Michael's ambition to promote what is good about Yellowstone Country was fostered by his commitment to fuel a new conservation movement. With programs such as the YLC, the baby steps toward changing the hearts and minds of the people began. Michael expressed his mission like this:

People want to believe in something and they want to believe in something profoundly. What better to believe in than the land and waters that sustain us all?

I have never seen anything like the interaction and motivation that Michael shared on these three-day weekend adventures; the teens that participated in the Yellowstone Leadership Challenges changed my life. Michael encouraged *all* participants—mentors and guest speakers included—to be appreciative and excited about the place in which we live. Though it is the norm for the locals to see bison meandering through town, and the Yellowstone River swelling and receding with the seasons, our passion should never falter. Michael inspired us all to take pride in this beauty and showed us what makes Yellowstone *Yellowstone*. He rejuvenated what we had lost, and he established ideas that penetrated the heart. He taught us how to be audacious: to be independent leaders, to share our opinions and to respect the opinions of others, and to have passion for life and passion for self. He ignited the flame in all of us—the audacious goal he'd set out to achieve.

In the midst of all the Yellowstone Country Guardian action, Michael kept at his busy pace with the Gardiner basketball program, now heading up the high school boys' team. My younger brother, Kyle, was in high school then, and I could not have been more excited for him to experience what I had experienced with Michael. I knew that Kyle was going to benefit and change in a profound way too.

Michael started the season with an "On a Mission" packet that included goals and visions of how he wanted the season to go, as well as the correlating attitudes he wanted the team to strive for (such as positively representing the Gardiner school and community). He wanted them to embody strength and courage toward opponents and people in general, and to be proud of who they were and where they came from. He wanted to turn boys into men.

As much as Michael's time was about drawing out plays and making the boys run 20 in 20s (twenty suicides in twenty minutes), his teachings were about much more than basketball: he taught his team to create goals and dreams for *life*. Michael wanted the boys to find what was important, make their mark, and always be remembered.

As a spectator to all his endeavors, I could not have been more proud of how Michael encouraged the boys—especially my brother—to be independent and to work on self-transformation. Of course, they all worked on their skills as basketball players, but they worked on skills to better their attitude overall. Kyle developed a strong mental focus and found his sense of self—things he had always struggled to accomplish. I saw Kyle climb mental mountains and grow into an incredible young man; the goals of the team were also achieved for him in the classroom, in his relationships, and personally. Kyle indeed learned how to be audacious, and then some.

I can also say these things about my dad, Wade, as he was Michael's assistant basketball coach for two years. My dad became more invested in his emotions, which helped him discover a part of himself—an attitude— I had never really seen before. Dad began to be more expressive, carrying himself with a bolder presence. Michael showed the boys a lot of love, but that was even *more* true with my dad. Preaching basketball knowledge was definitely important to Michael (who was a standout basketball stud in high school), but he also brought about what he called "core values." They were concepts that provoked change and ambition: *Humility, Love, Compassion, Respect, Passion*, and so on. To this day, my dad and brother live by them.

From that paper filled with quotes to watching Michael's impeccable presentations in Yellowstone to volunteering as a mentor for YCG, Michael has changed my view on life and given me strength I never thought I could have. I have watched and participated in practically every YCG program and endeavor, and could not have found a better way to spend my time and to learn about life. I have also been a spectator, watching my family and others convert to Michael's way of being audacious, putting their own spin on it.

In the winter of 2011, after earning my degree in education, I had the opportunity to choose what I wanted to do with my time before I got a teaching job. I had always dreamed about traveling, so I signed up with a nonprofit organization called Cross-Cultural Solutions. I chose to go to Salvador, Brazil, purely based on instinct—from that feeling inside my heart that told me that was the place. It was my first-ever huge solo trip, and I spent those precious six weeks working with amazing women in a *favela* (poverty-stricken) preschool. The adventures I went on and the knowledge I gained about being a traveler, an activist, an educator, and all-around better person kept reminding me what being audacious is all about. I adopted what Michael had taught: my goal was to not only inspire the people I met in Brazil but to be the inspiration for others back home. And I'd like to think I did just that.

Now it is time to spread the word to more people. Since 2012, when I began my teaching career, I have been passing on the "Be Audacious" principles and values to the next generation. But being audacious cannot flourish when only practiced in the rural communities of Montana; it has to be shared globally. It is a concept that will promote all that is good in this world, all that is good in the communities in which you may live, and all that is good within your very own heart. I guarantee that becoming audacious will change your life.

Be audacious,
—Heather Laubach, age twenty-six
January 2015

If you'd like to learn more about my adventures in Brazil,
please visit my blog from the trip:
beingaudaciousjourney.blogspot.com.

Introduction

Do you believe there is a unique greatness within you that is simply waiting to shine? I assure you, I wouldn't be embarking upon the intimidating, frightening, and often daunting journey of writing this book if I didn't already know the answer to that question. I wouldn't take time away from the rivers and mountains that fill my spirit, the advocacy work that represents my commitment to wild places, and the family and friends that embody my bedrock and foundation if I didn't believe that *you* have the ability to discover meaning and purpose—and change the world in the process. You, my friend, represent *my* hope for the future.

Knowing the value of your time and energy, and the vast array of distractions, pulling at your attention, I've purposefully kept his book tight, passionate, edgy, and on point. We live in an era where Facebook posts, tweets, Instagram and blogs consume the vast majority of our ability and willingness to sit down, pay close attention, and read. But there is tremendous power in the word. *Unmatched power.* The words we play and replay in our minds have the potential to enslave us, trap us, and limit our potential—or they have the ability to set us free, to pave our own unique path, and to help us find purpose and meaning in our everyday lives. Living an extraordinary life doesn't take a graduate degree, a PhD, endless time sitting idle in meditation, or a rare opportunity; it takes *audacity*—that bold willingness to put yourself out there to find the extraordinary within.

Life is complicated—full of struggles, heartache, hardships, setbacks, and failures. But life, *this* life—*your* life—is the most beautiful piece of art you will ever create. You are the canvas. Regardless of your circumstances, you have the power to choose your own palette of colors; you choose your outcome. And while this book will not uncover all the answers to the questions you have or erase your fears, your doubt, your anxiety, and your uncertainty, the simple but powerful tools and stories that unfold here—if adopted and embraced—can become a foundation upon which you face and ultimately embrace what the world throws your way. They can unharness your courage to break from the pack and live a life that is uniquely yours.

I've always told the remarkable young people I've had the privilege to work with that my word is my bond. No matter which hat I'm wearing—coach, wilderness guide, nonprofit director, motivational speaker, father—I say what I mean and mean what I say. So let's make a few things clear from the get-go:

1. I haven't created a *magical* formula that will ensure that you tap into your truest self. I recently celebrated my thirty-fifth birthday and am still on a constant quest to tap into my potential by deepening my awareness, knowledge, mindfulness, compassion, courage, and grace. We all walk our own path at our own pace.

2. I'm not going to bullshit you by telling you that I'm some kind of self-help guru whose words will change your life if you simply take the time to read them. The walls of my home are not covered in PhDs or other "expert" accolades. I'm a college graduate and writer

turned Yellowstone ranger and advocate; turned speaker, coach, and dad. I am not immune to questions of self-doubt—a challenge that is an innate part of our human experience. But the fire that's in me to make a difference in your life and in this world burns bright with authenticity and lived experience. I only ask that you read my story before you pass judgments on whether or not I "deserve" to put my thoughts to paper. It takes guts to be vulnerable and to be real, and this is something I promise to always be as I share this time with you. It is my hope that, in this way, I can earn your respect so we can walk this audacious journey together.

3. I also promise you that I'm not going to dummy things down; I'm going to write the way I speak—passionately, with a lot of love and a little bit of swagger. Each word is written from the heart, going with the flow in the only way I know how: fingers dancing across the keyboard, laying it down like the Macklemore of the motivational world.

4. If you have the audacity to join me on this journey—with an open heart and a fertile mind—the content laid out in the following pages can and will profoundly impact your walk upon this Earth.

Time is the greatest gift we are given on this journey, and you are your own greatest asset. *Right now* is the time for you to begin living a life that matters. But living a life that matters doesn't simply happen; and inspiring a legacy doesn't occur by simply being, dreaming, or hoping. Neither one is a fate reserved for the affluent or the gifted. Inspiring a legacy and living a life that matters is a choice that you make each and every day, and this choice takes a bold and daring individual.

You might think to yourself, "I'm not bold, so I might as well put this book down"; but that would be a great mistake that could change not only the fate of your life story but, ultimately, the fate of the planet. I know without question that *every* person has the ability to "be audacious."

In my work, I've chosen to focus my efforts and energy on young adults because energy and time are finite resources that I want to maximize in my own pursuit of inspiring a legacy and living a life that matters—all the while working to be the best damn single father walking this Earth. Big goals? Yep. But I once read that "big thinking precedes great achievement."[1]

It is difficult to inspire change in matters of the heart and mind after getting stuck in the typical "real world" rut that captures so many adults. And I've always thought it's a cop-out when people tell me, "Michael, if you affect the life of one young person in your work, you've accomplished something great." I'm not buying it. This is actually one of the great *failures* of our current culture: *we don't think big enough.* We don't dare to dream the wildest dream imaginable. But I've spent the last decade (all of my twenties) working in Yellowstone, the wildest place left in the lower forty-eight, and it has taught me many lessons—perhaps none more important than the power of shooting for the stars and believing in your own wild spirit; the "knowing" that nothing is impossible.

Of course I'm delighted when I inspire *any* number of people to take action and find the courage to do the extraordinary. But I strive to move and inspire *every* kid I coach, *every* member of an audience I speak to, and yes, *every* single reader taking the time to read this book, even though it may not be statistically possible. (I've never been a big math guy, so what do I have to lose?) Will I succeed? Probably not! Will it stop me from trying? Hell no. Striving is what matters when living audaciously.

I've worked with enough remarkable people of all ages to know that every one of them yearns to be inspired—to discover how they can pursue greatness no matter how many times they've revolved around the sun. Still, I've chosen to focus much of my motivational work on young adults and twentysomethings because I know how remarkably fertile these young minds are for new ideas and thoughtful change. Frankly, I'm not that far removed from walking in their shoes, and I'm still throwing off the shackles of our societal norms in my quest to find meaning and fulfillment—to live an authentic life of nonconformity. I've also witnessed firsthand, with countless young people, the power of the simple and potentially transformational message that I've outlined in the pages ahead—yet I trust its universal appeal.

I'm fully aware that a plethora of self-help books abound on the market (I know because I've been reading them for fourteen years), but far too often, I find that these books complicate what I believe is a relatively simple game plan to success: having the audacity to overcome adversity (part I), live authentically (part II), uncover your purposeful passion (part III), and develop your vision (part IV). In addition, I've included practice exercises near the end of each chapter to aid you in your BA journey. From a simple gratitude journal to mapping out your life's mission and vision, each exercise represents another tool that helps to keep you on your path—the roadmap to your deepest potential. Period.

The Be Audacious movement is all about breaking free from a culture that tells you how you need to dress, talk, walk, and act. It's about creating a new social paradigm that doesn't dictate what kind of education you need, what kind of job will bring you status, what kind of car will make you happy. It's about embracing a path and life of nonconformity, authenticity, courage, and confidence while blazing new trails and charting new waters as you pursue your passion. But the Be Audacious movement also extends beyond *you* and the uncovering of your true self; it takes your bold courage to positively impact our society, our world, our communities, and our environment.

We only get one time to walk this Earth. *Now* is your time to explore and ultimately decide what you want your walk to be all about.

I look forward to sharing with you in this Be Audacious journey. *Game on—let's do this!*

With nothin' but love,
—Michael W. Leach

PART I

OVERCOMING ADVERSITY

1

Hardship Is
Your Greatest Gift

*The ultimate measure of a man is not where he stands
at times of comfort and convenience, but where he
stands at times of challenge and controversy.*
—Martin Luther King Jr.

Have you have ever walked into a doctor's office and been told something that would change the trajectory of your life? Have you have ever felt so dejected or depressed, so down and out, that it was difficult to find meaning in your life? Have you ever discovered a passion that burns so deeply that it consumes all of your waking thoughts and occupies your most vivid dreams, yet there seems to be no room for it in a traditional nine-to-five world? And lastly, do you strive or even yearn to live a life that matters but are paralyzed by the thought of exploring the road that leads you there?

Why, you might wonder, would I open the first chapter of this book with these downer questions? The answer is simple: these are experiences I've endured and questions I've asked myself, not just in adolescence but also in my walk through the often daunting world of being an adult. During times of hardship it's natural to feel isolated, but I'm here to tell you: while your path may be your own, you are not alone.

A teacher of mine who has profoundly impacted my journey—from a young man struggling to hold water in what we call my "vase of self-worth" to a resilient dude no longer blown around like garbage in the wind of what others think—is fond of flipping his hand from front to back, alternately showing the palm and the backside, reminding me that there are positives and negatives to every decision and challenge a person confronts. I've adopted this simple yet effective teaching tool with my basketball teams, with my daughter, and most importantly, in my own life; because there is no way of avoiding hardship without living in a Pollyanna bubble. Life is hard—it is full of heartache and heartbreak. But it is also full of love, beauty, and power.

Most straightforward adults—those who are not caught up in delusions of grandeur (perfect job, perfect house, perfect car, perfect family)—will admit that high school is one of the most challenging times of self-discovery. The path through this intimidating, adolescent forest (from day one of freshman year to graduation) is far from clear, as the trail is often muddied by uncertainty, and rutted by peers venturing this way and that in their own search for the elusive map to a life of meaning and purpose.

Then, for those whose next chapter leads them to college, it doesn't take long to experience the complete opposite: a newfound freedom from parental control and high school drama, both of which can weigh down one's shoulders with burdensome expectations. This time offers a significant window—one full of promise—that ushers us from our late teens to our early twenties. But it is also full of distractions: an overload of classes, next-level love, managing a landlord and a roommate who parties too hard, fifteen pounds that come outta nowhere. This isn't exactly the "freedom" we anticipated.

Even so, we may journey through our college experience and arrive fairly unscathed to those first few years post academia—years that present a rare opportunity for personal transformation; a spiritual catharsis and awakening as we learn about the endless possibilities and uncharted waters that lie ahead.

But don't be fooled by anyone telling you that the path suddenly becomes as smooth as a treadmill once you venture out of that tender, undergrad habitat you've known, eager to find your place in this big, wild, and often rugged world. Emerging from that youthful cocoon as enlightened, grown folk who are ready to take on the world simply isn't a formulaic process; it doesn't work that way. *You will face adversity.*

Adversity is inevitable for all of us, but in particular, it will challenge those of us who keep chasing that dream of becoming our truest self—our *best* self. It is a critical ingredient to growth and transformation—the boulder in the river that teaches you to flow a different way. Adversity is also what drives you to go *against* the flow; sometimes, *you* are the rock that challenges the norm for the better. And that leads to living a life that matters—a life that makes a difference.

Ultimately, that is the quest: a meaningful and purposeful life lived in accordance/union with our core values and the principles that serve as our foundation. And for each of us, this recipe looks different. Though some of the more universal ingredients will undoubtedly be the same (love, a home, fulfilling work), the story you ultimately tell will be as unique as your DNA. It will be all yours.

You forge the path. *You* blaze the trail.

But while no two paths will look exactly alike (and I hate to harp on this), one of the few absolutes in this world is this: as long as you keep striving to change yourself and the world for the better, adversity will be an element for you to overcome *and* (here's the kicker) embrace.

THE BA BALANCE

Before I go any further, I want to introduce an impactful ingredient in the

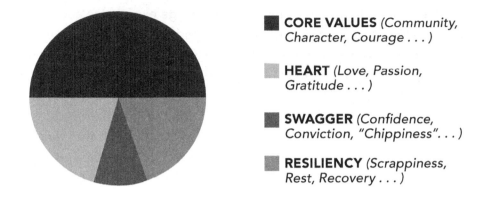

CORE VALUES *(Community, Character, Courage . . .)*

HEART *(Love, Passion, Gratitude . . .)*

SWAGGER *(Confidence, Conviction, "Chippiness". . .)*

RESILIENCY *(Scrappiness, Rest, Recovery . . .)*

recipe of being audacious and living a BA life—one that will serve you throughout this book's content and beyond: the BA Balance.

Whether in our own lives, our immediate communities, or the diverse ecosystems making up our wild and watery planet, *balance* is key to durability and sustainability. Without balance to ground us, we are susceptible to venturing far off our course when pursuing a life of meaning and purpose. For each individual, this balance will look different, but this simple chart can serve as a little reality check and compass to help navigate the uncharted and oftentimes choppy waters that accompany the BA path.

You'll find that your core values (a topic we will explore in chapter 3) make up the majority of the balance, and as such, are positioned like an umbrella that protects the other key pieces of the formula. Your core values will be uniquely your own but are likely to include characteristics such as character, community, courage, integrity, honesty, gratitude, tenacity, respect—this is where you hang your legacy hat. Then heart, a slice of swagger (see my definition on page 132), and resiliency make up the rest of the balance wheel to support you and your mission

For example, some of you may be heavy on swagger and light on community, spending too much time focused on "you" and not enough energy on the greater good. If it's all about you, your swagger may be beyond palpable, and it's time to put the spotlight on core values like humility and grace. Remember, our mission here extends far beyond personal growth and the pursuit of your passion; it's about the bigger picture of living a life that matters—one that positively impacts the world around you.

On the other hand, some of you may have the community piece nailed but struggle with your swagger barometer, needing to turn up the swaggage to increase your confidence and effectiveness in your work and personal life. Perhaps you are an individual who lives your life from the heart but crumbles in the face of criticism or hardship. Then it's time to further develop your resiliency reservoir. Or maybe you are very resilient, but you go about it by keeping your cards too close to the vest—too guarded and stubborn to show your heart and be vulnerable.

While the percentage of each piece of the pie will be different for each person, depending upon your individual qualities, the BA Balance can serve as a life raft and map to forward progress, keeping your eyes on the prize in periods of turmoil—when you're treading water. It can also serve as a friendly reminder of why you're doing what you're doing during times of prosperity, keeping your advancement (evolution and growth) steady, honorable, and sustainable.

However you implement the BA Balance in your story is ultimately up to you; tweak it, adapt it, customize it as you see fit. But by all means, use it as another tool to support your personal metamorphosis and your mission. Keep the "BA" in "balance."

PHYSICAL ADVERSITY

While no one relishes the heartache and despair that comes with immense struggle, there is no doubt in my mind that the strongest, most resilient and impactful people are those who have endured and struggled the most. One of the adjectives that I would least like to have associated with the man that I am would be "average" or "boring." Who could possibly embrace these labels?

I vividly remember a cool autumn day when I was lying in agony in my bed in an old single-wide trailer not far from the banks of the Bitterroot River. I had just graduated from North Idaho College in my birthplace of

Coeur d'Alene, and I was in the middle of my first semester at the University of Montana as a "nontraditional" junior. I say nontraditional because I was a twenty-four-year-old junior. School never came easy to me, but now I was finding my groove after graduating from NIC on the dean's list—largely because of a newly discovered passion for a subject matter that would consume my college existence, my decade of work postgraduate, and (I'm firmly convinced) the rest of my life.

I had just finished my second summer season as a ranger in Yellowstone National Park and I was high on life, ready to take the University of Montana and its environmental studies program by storm. Just five years earlier, months after my nineteenth birthday, I had been diagnosed with ankylosing spondylitis (AS), an autoimmune disorder that completely changed my life's direction; but with scrappy grit, I had weathered that storm, uncovered a new passion, and remade myself into the young man that I had become. (You'll learn more about this in the next chapter.) Life was good. Life was rich. Life was exciting and simply bountiful.

But there I was, bedridden, tossing and turning in a heap of pain and frustration. I'd had a remission of my AS, which had allowed me to pursue my outdoor passions; but now, the inflammation had returned with a vengeance. Instead of living my beloved new life, I was only dreaming of running rivers, bagging peaks, scaling canyon walls. Despair over my circumstances consumed every waking thought: I was going to be forced to allow my body time to recover from the flare-up as well as a severe reaction to an off-label prescription medication. I had no other choice.

Sitting beside my bed, within earshot of the slowly meandering Bitterroot, my mom, whose graceful wisdom knows no bounds, shared with me a simple yet powerful statement that would change the way I looked at hardships in my life.

"Mike, I know you are in the middle of an all-consuming struggle that simply feels like too much to bear," she said softly, rubbing my head like she used to when I was a child and suffering a migraine. "But people who haven't struggled bore me."

I want you to reread and memorize that last sentence: *people who haven't struggled bore me.* Now imagine a life story without bruises and bumps, adventures and dead ends, good times and bad times; imagine stopping just when the plot gets intense and all hope seems lost. Who wants to participate in a story in which things always go perfectly or according to plan? What about the mystery, the foe, the chance to turn things around?

This moment—the one you're in—is influenced by where you've been, and it's full of potential because you're still here plugging away. Despite your war wounds, you've made it this far; what about tomorrow and the next day? Don't you want to see the light at the end of this tunnel? As the artist—the storyteller—of your own life, *you* control the narrative that guides the outcome.

People who haven't struggled bore me. These words guided me through that ankylosing spondylitis relapse and a plethora of hard times since. And in the past eleven years, I've shared my mother's words (a celebrated author and master storyteller) with thousands of students across the country.

Good or bad, *now* is a moment you won't get back. How will you write it into *your* next chapter?

MENTAL ADVERSITY

Some of you may relate to what I'm about to share.

Though many of you are gifted with academic prowess, that isn't the case for *all* of us. School was always a struggle for me. To this day, I vividly remember the feelings of inadequacy that ravaged my spirit and grew more pervasive with each barely passing grade. For me, school was simply something to endure. I was a hoopster—a pretty damn good one. I had skills on the basketball court and much swagger to boot. I knew my ticket to college life was on the hardwood with a rubber ball in hand. Because of that, I adopted the mind-set that I merely needed to stay eligible—*just pass* the SAT, in other words—to get by.

This worked fine through middle school and my first two years of high school, where my basketball skills were on full display, but by my junior year, my hoops dreams began to unravel. Love (in the form of a high school sweetheart), injuries, and an adversarial relationship with my coach were the ingredients for two years that spiraled out of control. In the blink of an eye, my plan, dream, and vision of a successful college basketball career had been shattered.

By the time I reached North Idaho College, my confidence regarding my prowess and ability in the classroom was that of a beaten-down, stray dog. The fear of failure was all-consuming, and the belief that I could succeed in an academic setting was as dry as an empty well.

But sometimes, all it takes is that little taste of success to make us question that pesky voice in our head that says *I can't*. After over a decade of feeling *stupid* and inadequate, I realized I simply needed to tap into my own brilliance. And I don't say this with arrogance or even swagger, as "brilliant" is an adjective I'm still unsettled by whenever anyone associates it with the likes of me. That said, when one grasps the magnitude and biochemical complexity of the human brain (which, according to physicist Sir Roger Penrose, is more complex than a galaxy, enabling superior cognitive ability while representing a vast frontier of uncharted terrain),[1] it is hard to downplay the utter magnificence of our most glorious organ.

The key to success lies in unlocking that part of your brain that works best for you. Knowing that the DNA in our brain cells is identical to that in our heart, is it possible that this relationship might also shed light on the manner of thinking and learning that is unique to us? For it wasn't until I unearthed my passion for the environment—passion that can't exist without heart—that I unlocked what I was good at on a cerebral level.

And for me it was memorization. Discovering this was a total game changer. Though I had to put in four hours of studying for every two my friends and classmates put in, once I finished my first semester of college with a 4.0, that success became addictive. I wanted more.

With a lot of grit, hard work, and perseverance, I went from rags to riches—from a junior college hoopster fraught with angst over making the grade to a graduate of two institutions who not only made the dean's list but did so with high honors over the course of five years. I had discovered my key to success in the classroom. Later, as a ranger in Yellowstone National Park, I became a guru of bear and Yellowstone information—a living encyclopedia spitting mad game to visitors from all over the globe. I freely dispersed my Yellowstone knowledge after countless hours of reading, highlighting, and rereading everything on Yellowstone that I could memorize.

I learned that struggling in a classroom setting didn't mean I couldn't succeed in academia; it did, however, require that I *learn* to adjust, adapt, and reload. (Remember that adversity boulder in the river?) Similarly, success in life is largely about our ability to embrace uncertainty while learning the art of adapting to the cards we are dealt. No matter the cards, we must learn to play them to the best of our ability.

SPIRITUAL ADVERSITY

I learned to fully appreciate the storm and the struggle when I moved to the Garden Island of Kauai in the middle of one of the most challenging times in my adult life. I'd hoped to use this new adventure to reconnect with my core mission—pursuing my passion and living a life that matters—but I was relegated to a walking boot cast for most of the calendar year due to a hotly inflamed Achilles (one of the symptoms of my tendon-assaulting autoimmune disorder, which had worsened through a series of sports-related overuse injuries). Forced to adapt my passion for exercise and my *need* for dopamine, I had taken up swimming to facilitate the flow of endorphins I require to function in this highly complex and competitive world.

It was a beautiful day with a bright blue sky, mild trade winds, and temperatures in the mid-80s. A northeast swell bombarded the east shore of the peaceful island that served as the backdrop for one of my all-time favorite TV shows, *Lost*, and that I was now attempting to make my home. The surf was up, and I was consumed with grief as I watched it roll in. After moving 3,000 miles from my Montana home to one of the most remote archipelagos in the world, I'd had the vision of daily *Saltwater Buddha* (a book that fed my soul) surf sessions that would fuel my writing. And here I was, once again, laid up in a boot cast.

We have two choices during times of despair, and they are pretty simple: we can either wallow in a puddle of self-pity, or we can turn our focus from our pain and heartache to what we *can* control and do. This is one of many practices I share throughout the pages that follow—but it is easy to say and hard to do. Focusing on the negative in our lives is effortless; the difficult and audacious work is focusing on that which is good.

One of my great mentors, the brilliant Dr. John Wimberly, often told me, "Acceptance is allowing reality to be as it is without requiring it to be different." Perhaps this is just a philosophical way of saying it is what it is, yeah? But one thing was very clear: I had spent enough time mourning my physical ailment that day, enviously watching two dozen surfers and paddleboarders shredding up the perfectly arching waves, cleanly breaking just 100 yards from Kealia Beach.

It was time for a "mini vacation."

No matter your age, learning the art of the mini vacation is a masterful skill that, once tapped into, can facilitate powerful medicine, helping us stay sane during the most challenging of times. Each person's mini vacation will look different, taking form in the shape of a car ride, a movie, music, yoga, a book, exercise, mediation, or countless other avenues. For me, it has always been exercise: a few hours chasing waves on a paddleboard; hammering my legs while pounding the pedals of a big climb on my road bike; a laptop sabbatical with fly rod in hand while wading knee-deep in a river, pursuing an encounter with a finned friend; an afternoon spent scaling rock walls, completely immersed in the simplicity of my next foot- or handhold; dancing down a steep slope of powder on fat-planked skis; shooting baskets, rhythmically listening to the snap of the net (music to my ears); or simply busting out a full-body blast in the gym. These simple acts of endorphin-releasing pleasure have served as my bedrock and foundation, providing both a sense of self and the chemicals my brain needs to thrive.

But I was on the beach in a walking boot cast, frustrated by an ailing

Achilles and an aching wrist awaiting surgical repair. (I'd torn my triangular fibrocartilage complex [my TFCC, oft known as the Achilles of wrists] in a bike accident). With injuries to both lower and upper extremities, my options were limited.

Before the move, I had taken up long drives on the highways and back roads under Montana's big sky as my go-to mini vacation, but after two months on the island of Kauai, where one road circumnavigates a landscape obstructed by the Pacific Ocean along its coast and a thick, mountainous jungle on its interior, the redundancy of vehicle travel had lost its charm.

It was time to swim.

While I had been swimming on a daily basis for most of the year (the one cardiovascular activity my wrist and Achilles could routinely tolerate), my swims had taken place in the comfort and safety of a pool. I had only attempted a handful of ocean swims, which, for this boy from the mountains of the Northern Rockies, was more than a little intimidating. But as my audacious boy Scotty B Black would say, the brain train had left the station and my mind was running like tape loop on repeat. I needed a change of scenery—a mini vacation to turn the focus of my overly active brain.

Two weeks earlier, I had attempted my most ambitious and intimidating open-ocean swim on a magnificent bluebird day, and I was richly rewarded with one of the most amazing wildlife experiences of my life (which is saying a lot after a decade of working in the wildlife mecca otherwise known as Yellowstone National Park). I encountered not one, two, or three but *seven* massive sea turtles in the crystal-clear, turquoise waters of Poipu (our home beach), on Kauai's south shore. But these waters on Kauai's east side were unfamiliar.

Pushing through the break, weaving my way through the body boarders and surf lineup proved easier than I'd anticipated, though I swallowed my fair share of salt water with each pounding wave. Once beyond the break, the water looked glassy within the jetty, where I intended to swim parallel to the shore in eyesight of a cadre of lifeguards.

I hadn't been swimming ten minutes when I realized that something wasn't right. While I'd planned to swim in a straight line, staying within the relative safety of the bay, the ocean water around me grew darker with each stroke. I was no longer in shallow water. When I popped my head up, it was clear that I was in a spot of bother (a phrase I absolutely love as a road-bike junkie and have borrowed from the European world of Tour de France cycling analysts, who use it to indicate when a rider is in trouble on a big climb). A mini riptide had pulled me several hundred yards off my route of travel—past the jetty and into open water—and I was now caught in it.

My mind raced with scenarios. I remembered a story my physical therapist had told me about the unbreakable nature of many of the island's most powerful riptides, some of which he insisted could easily drag an unknowing swimmer miles to sea, spitting them out en route to Japan.

Instead of fighting the current, I simply tread water long enough to take five deep breaths as I drifted farther from shore. This simple act of taking five deep, lung-filling breaths activates the parasympathetic nervous system, calming anxiety while sharpening focus, which allowed me just enough headspace to reject the *Oh shit* part of my brain and find a solution. Raising my arms and waving them to solicit a rescue from the lifeguards would be my last option, as I had experienced too much racial tension as a *haole* (white mainlander) on the island to be "that guy" who needed to be rescued by the *kama'aina* (the locals). So I did what any of us should do when we are in a spot of bother (not yet fucked but definitely in a precarious position): I tread water long enough to let the eye of the storm pass, and then moved into a place of action.

As an avid paddle surfer I had learned enough about ocean dynamics to keep myself from panicking when multiwave sets pummeled me after crashing off a wave, and similarly in this situation I knew I couldn't fight the unrelenting tide. And while every fiber in my being screamed to turn my head toward the shore, thrashing at the water in hopes of reaching the safety of the beach packed with Saturday-afternoon *ohanas* (families), those five deep breaths allowed me to go from worry mind to wise mind. With a shake of my head, I pointed my shoulders north, parallel to the shore but into open ocean water—as I was well beyond the comfort of the rocky jetty—and calmly but strongly began a freestyle stroke, swimming perpendicular to the tide that pulled me to sea. While the tide was sure to pull me farther from shore, this is always the best bet for finding an exit. Fatigued, I swam until I no longer felt the riverlike tension tugging against my body. It had spit me out. I was overwhelmed by a sense of relief. No embarrassing rescue, and I didn't drown. Pretty good ending if you ask me. Now, with visions of an afternoon of building elaborate sandcastles with my daughter, I leisurely swam to shore.

The moral of this story: sometimes we simply need to weather the storm, but at some point, we have to move beyond treading water into action.

MANAGE EXPECTATIONS

Don't put pressure on yourself to *always* be productive. If you just got dumped by your longtime boyfriend or girlfriend, didn't get into the college you'd set your heart on, received word that you didn't get your dream job, or are dealing with a major family shake-up, give yourself time to mourn. No matter what the circumstances—a daunting health ordeal, emotional struggle, personal loss—there are many times in our lives when treading water is the best we can do.

We must not underestimate the power of finding the courage to *simply* tread water in the eye of the storm. The storm will pass—trust me, it always does. But I know this is hard to believe when we are in the midst of the shitstorm. I've been through enough raging hurricanes, spinning tornadoes, and tropical storms where I couldn't see my way through— couldn't see an end to the onslaught—and began to despair. Yet I've always come out the other side. *So will you.*

Give the storm time to pass. And remember that it's not unusual for one powerful surge of emotion to be followed by another. But energy is finite, not infinite—it will pass. Still, remember not to pick up the broken pieces the moment the skies clear. Take a look first at the weather forecast to avoid having your reconstruction project devastated once more.

I love this analogy. It has helped me through many days of heartache and anguish. I've learned the hard way the pain that comes from trying to rebuild too soon, without adequate time to heal and *feel* the loss. It's okay to rough it for a while—to live in a metaphoric tent as a wanderer and nomad until the seas calm, the winds become a gentle breeze, and the sun shines again on your life. During these hard times, take your mini vacations and utilize the tools—the positive coping skills that you've acquired over the years—in your toolbox. Simply *endure*.

While noodling ideas for this book one day over the phone with my Portland-based editor, she shared with me a simple exercise that gave her much peace during times of gloom. The simple act of writing "I have something to say" on a sheet of paper was enough to provide some comfort.

Don't overthink the struggle; the storm will pass when it passes. You will overcome.

Once it is clear that the storm is over, however, it's time to make a choice: Do you begin to reconstruct after the devastation? Or do you resign yourself to a shelter-less life of bare-bones survival? Either are viable options. I know many who thrive in the Burning Man culture of vagabonds. But remember: striving and surviving are two vastly different ways to live. If you believe, as I do, that most of us ultimately want to live a life that matters, you must keep striving.

There will inevitably be moments of peril for everyone—periods where survival is the best you can do. But merely surviving is not a path to a purposeful life of meaning and intention. Our journey of self-discovery and self-acceptance leads us to a higher purpose—a karmic adventure of paying it forward, leaving smiles and goodness in our wake.

In the end, it is not about the things we acquire, the cars that we drive, the clothes we wear, or the money we make. It is about *love*. It is about *people*. It's about our sense of place and advocating for a healthy and verdant environment. It is about overcoming adversity with character and courage as we shower the world around us with a humble grace.

Practice Exercise:
BELLY BREATHING

In the midst of hardship, struggle, and adversity, it is easy to become overwhelmed with anxiety. Some of you may have heard the term "paralysis analysis." When the brain train leaves the station and really gets spinning, it is very common to become frozen, unable to even see the next move. Try not to fret when overwhelm or anxiety takes over; there is nothing wrong with you. You are simply a thoughtful human *striving* to find your way in a big, wild, rugged, and challenging world. If you are striving, there will be moments of overwhelm. If you are enduring hardship or battling through adversity, anxiety will almost surely come knocking on your door. Remember, while far from pleasant, this is all to be expected!

You have all heard the phrase "too much of a good thing." Though it seems paradoxical, this idiom holds much truth. Take this moment in my world, for instance. I've spent much of the last year battling and scrapping my way through storm after storm—a season that has raged on far longer than I could have imagined. My spirits have been ravaged at times; but through it all, I've kept my head up, eyes forward, and feet moving—grinding my way through four surgeries, a painful divorce, a brush with eternity, and a journey of discovery in my attempt to be the best supa-dupa "Dadda" I'm capable of being. It has been a period fraught with angst: *What if I can't write this book? What if my first book,* Grizzlies On My Mind, *is a bust? How am I going to pay the bills? How am I going to put enough money away to pay for my daughter's education? What if I have to go get a nine-to-five?* But through it all, I went *all in* on my Be Audacious endeavor. In fact, I would venture to say that doing so—diving into the BA movement—is what got me through the hurricane, earthquake, and subsequent tsunami.

And now, here I am, writing the first chapter of this book only two weeks away from the release and publication of *Grizzlies On My Mind*, an intimate memoir written from a place of great vulnerability. Things are looking up. I'm booking speaking engagements and book signings in Denver, San Francisco, Berkeley, San Jose, Boulder, Grand Junction, Moab, and throughout the Idaho, Montana, and Wyoming region. I'm living my dream, yeah? And yet I'm overwhelmed as hell just trying to keep my ducks in a row, head above water, dotting my i's and crossing my t's in hopes of pulling it all off. While I have anticipated this moment for years—the time of my book release, the speaking tours, the celebration—right now it feels like a little too much of a good thing.

So, how do I do it? How do I keep it together and still manage to get my daughter to bed on time, make her bomber breakfasts in the morning, and send her to school with tightly braided hair and a clean crisp outfit (with much style and swag, I must say)? How do I manage that while trying to cocreate a speaking tour with my publicist, working my part-time gig, rehabbing my broken body, rebuilding a basketball program, and writing this book?

I breathe.

Remember: the very act of deep breathing activates our parasympathetic nervous system, facilitating our return to a balanced state of homeostasis. Our busy, overstimulated lives tend to be dominated by the sympathetic nervous system; but unlike the sympathetic nervous system, which awakens our fight-or-flight response and causes that frazzled appearance so familiar on the road to total burnout, the parasympathetic nervous system enables our bodies to rest and recover in a more peaceful and balanced state.

How do we get there? The exercise below is easy, effective, and impactful, representing a stealthy arrow in your quiver of tools to overcome anxiety and overwhelm.

Here's how you do it:

1. Find a quiet space where you can sit comfortably.

2. Position yourself upright in a chill posture, allowing your body, chest, shoulders, and jaw to relax. Close your eyes if you wish.

3. Be intentional—in the moment—focusing on your breath.

4. Inhale deeply through your nose, filling and expanding your belly (hence the common name for this exercise: abdominal breathing), drawing air into the bottom of your lungs as you breathe in.

5. Hold your breath for a two-second count, then slowly release it through your mouth. You have just completed the first repetition.

6. Placing one hand over your navel can help to guide the depth of your breath to ensure that you are expanding your belly.

7. Repeat this six to twelve times, at least one to three times daily.

Practice this belly-breathing exercise as many times a day as you can. But by all means, *practice it!* The likes of Damian Lillard, Maya Moore, and Stephen Curry didn't groove their shot by waiting for a pressure-packed free throw in the closing seconds of the NBA/WNBA finals. They practiced it hundreds of thousands of times. Next time you find yourself in a stressful situation, give this a try and observe the difference the simple act of intentional breathing can make in your ability to overcome the overwhelm and anxiety that you inevitably feel when facing adversity.

CLOSING THOUGHTS

My mom is fond of sharing a quote from Philip Yancey during hard times: "Pain is the gift that no one wants." I find this to be a beautiful oxymoron. Karl Marx tells us that the path to peace and self-awareness comes when we uncover the courage to go through the wound. While painful and uncomfortable, there is tremendous power and perhaps unmatched opportunity for personal growth and transformation when we face, embrace, and tolerate the periods of pain and heartache that will undoubtedly come as we journey through life.

So here is my wish for you: May your journey of self-discovery be twisted, confusing, and arduous; weaving soulfully through life's river valleys, deserts, coastlines, and forests; ultimately leading you to the most rewarding and fulfilling mountaintop vistas you will ever experience on your walk across this Earth. Like a saying on a T-shirt I once read in Telluride, Colorado, *may your journey be your destination. . . .*

2

Your Essence Defines
Your Swagger

Difficulties strengthen the mind, as labor does the body.
—Seneca the Younger

*We could never learn to be brave and patient if
there were only joy in the world.*
—Helen Keller

Life is a grind filled with good times and bad—there is no way to avoid this. But I'm convinced that the biggest difference maker between those who ultimately succeed in their walk upon this wild and watery planet and those who let their potential slip away is *resiliency*. For some, being resilient is perhaps in their DNA; for others, it is a trait acquired through overcoming difficulty and challenge.

At the age of nineteen, I had my life taken from me—or so I thought back then. School had been a struggle of seemingly epic proportions since my earliest memories, but I had always been a standout athlete. Playing basketball was my passion, my identity, and what I did best. After battling my way through a tenuous relationship with my high school basketball coach the last two years of high school, I found myself attending a small junior college north of Seattle, where I had been invited by a legend of the Pacific Northwest hoops world to walk on to the team. Both he and I assumed I would eventually earn a scholarship—I had high hopes of redis-covering my prowess on the hardwood (and therefore, my purpose in life). I started school with big dreams of two successful years as a Triton fol-lowed by a prosperous Division I career, and then a lifetime of competition through triathlons and other strenuous athletic pursuits.

As a young man, I was never comfortable with the unknown; I always needed a plan. Athletics represented both my future and my source of refuge. When running, competing, and pushing myself to my physical lim-its, I could calm my overly active mind enough to feel purpose and mean-ing in my life—something I had yet to discover outside of the athletic arena. But two weeks before the start of my freshman season, I was rear-ended in a car accident. The accident itself wasn't severe, but the back pain following the collision forced me to take a hiatus from the team.

Without basketball, I was a mess. My already below-average grades suffered, and I became disengaged and angry at the world.

After squeaking by in my first year of college, I made plans to rejoin the team and recapture my dream of playing college basketball. But some-thing just wasn't right. After twelve months of physical therapy, MRIs, and countless visits to specialists, there were no answers; and my pain had worsened. It became clear that my back was not ready to withstand the rigorous demands of a basketball season, so I made the decision to take a break from school—and basketball—until I could figure out the next move.

I was nineteen, lost, and desperate for answers.

Ankylosing spondylitis. I will never forget those two hard-to-pronounce words.

One bright and sunny day in the Emerald City, I visited a rheumatol-ogist who would break the news that the pain I was experiencing was caused by an often debilitating autoimmune disorder—a systemic rheumatic disease that affects the entire body. There I was, a healthy, fit young man about to turn twenty, with a dedicated girlfriend, an amazing family, and a long life of adventure ahead of me. But with two words, my entire world was flipped upside down.

According to the doctor, I presented the classic symptoms of this relatively rare arthritic condition that most often rears its ugly head in young men between the ages of eighteen and thirty. The jolt of the car accident almost two years earlier had ignited the (until then) dormant flame within my body, drastically altering the path I had planned to walk on my life's journey.

As with everything in my life, I fought. I fought the diagnosis, continuing to work out each and every day, bound and determined to return to the hardwood, and believing in my core that the only way I would ever find happiness, self-worth, and a life worth living would be through heroic feats of athleticism.

I had no idea what my future held—no idea what kind of work I could pursue. I had told myself a story about who I was on so many occasions that it had become ingrained in my core beliefs, ultimately becoming my reality. I was an athlete, and with the vulnerability I felt because of my learning disability, I couldn't fathom how I could possibly get through college without the support that athletes far too often receive. I was adrift in every way.

WRITE A NEW STORY

It really doesn't matter what your story is; whatever you decide is "true" for you is going to be your reality. But when the story you repeat to yourself is bound by a negative or deflating narrative, what you believe to be true will ultimately trap and limit what you can become.

So, what's the answer? What ultimately helped *me* to move forward from this life, this place in which I had never dreamed of living, much less accepting?

I wrote myself a new story.

As many times as we've told ourselves our old story, we can always write a new story—*if* we find the courage and the stamina to do so. We have to let go and move *beyond* the life we had envisioned in order to grow, evolve, and transform. Only then can we discover the meaning and purpose that is innate to our human experience.

Adapt, adjust, reload, and repeat—that is the formula. And to follow this, we have to be *resilient*.

RESILIENCY

Resiliency is an ever-important—dare I say *critical*—trait often lost in a culture that hypes up the importance of fairness. We live in a world where fairness is almost always held in higher esteem than toughness. But let me break it down for you in a typically blunt and honest "Coach" style: *To hell with fairness!* Life ain't fair. Life is hard as hell, confusing, scary, and sometimes devastating. That is what it is.

That said, there is no excuse for kicking the downtrodden or feeding stereotypes that hold back *anyone's* ability to be his or her best self. We, as a culture, can no longer accept a world that lacks compassion. In order for us to foster an environment where everyone can thrive, we must hold compassion in high esteem. We should always stand up for equality—be unwilling to tolerate it when a person (including oneself) is not treated justly because of gender, sexual orientation, skin color, a learning disability, the side of the tracks one lives on, the way one walks, the way one dresses, or any other reason that may be outside modern society's standards and circle of influence.

But life is unfair, right? How are we supposed to navigate being both resilient and compassionate?

When we master resilience—when we tap into our personal reservoir of toughness—we can recoil and bounce back from any heartache life presents. This goes for ourselves and for every living thing around us. Whether it be the neighborhood tree slated to be cut down for development, a crew of construction workers harassing an attractive woman walking by, or a dog lost and weaving its way through traffic, we can exercise our resiliency reservoir by taking action that expands our circle of influence. We can use our resilience to level the playing field even when some circumstances appear out of our control.

Someone asked me recently how I endured a health saga that nearly took my life last winter, and my answer was really straight: I'm a gritty, scrappy, tough, and resilient dude with a lot of love in my heart. That's it. No matter how hard life gets, there are things we cannot control and things we can—and the latter is where we need to focus our energies. We cannot control what others think, for example, so why get caught up in their perception of who we are and what we are about? More often than not, they are the ones who don't have a clue. We're better off "killing them with kindness," as my mother always says, sending a little love their way in an audacious gesture of forgiveness—and then letting it go.

Perhaps you are familiar with the beginning of the Serenity Prayer: "God, grant me the serenity to accept the things I cannot change, the courage to change the things I can, and the wisdom to know the difference." You could just as easily swap the word "strength" for "serenity," as it takes heavy lifting to journey into this realm of personal growth.

Whether you are a teenager striving to become a strong, resilient, character-driven young man or woman; a twentysomething traveling through the uncharted waters of new adulthood; or you are already grooving your path in your 30s, 40s, or older, this is the beauty of being grown: you get to make your own choices. While some of us are forced to become resilient and tough by necessity, resiliency and toughness are not characteristics exclusive to those who have been through shit. I firmly believe that these characteristics can be acquired by choice. (Remember the BA Balance wheel in chapter 1?) Regardless of how independent you are in your life right now, in this moment, there are important choices you get to make every day. You get to wake up each morning, look at yourself in the mirror, and decide what your attitude is going to be.

I first read this quote by Charles R. Swindoll on the wall of a counselor's office: "Life is 10 percent what happens to me and 90 percent how I react to it." The essential life lesson here is that *we*—and *only* we—get to choose what our attitude will be. In a world where much of our life is out of our control, this is one solid lifeline we can grasp on to.

A word of caution: don't get discouraged when your good attitude or your resiliency falters from time to time. Some days, we simply don't have the energy or mental fortitude to be tough and courageous. That's okay. Call in sick that day. Play hooky. Take a mini vacation as suggested in chapter 1. Do what you need to do to nurture yourself in a healthy way, whether that means watching a movie; taking a nap; reading a book; listening to music; or going for a walk, a swim, or a hike. Take care of *you* in whatever way feels right to you. Nurture yourself on the days when you feel weak, tired, and broken. Remind yourself that, while tired in this moment, you are *far* from feeble and broken overall.

How could I know that you are not weak and broken without knowing you and your struggles? I know this because I've been there—in that dark place of false belief—far too many times to count. As long as we are still breathing and battling, we are bravely enduring. We must not let the struggle of the moment define us. No matter how broken or inadequate we feel at any given time, it's important to recognize that our perspective is clouded when our sense of self is under assault. As a single dad, enduring my own struggles as I navigate the world of parenthood, I've learned that life's hardships are in many ways similar to potty training a child: they're full of hits and misses. Oftentimes, we overthink the process, getting stuck on what we perceive to be right and what we believe to be wrong. It's not until we begin to trust ourselves as parents, letting go of expectations, that the desired result manifests. Let it go and let it flow; mastery of our emotions is a process that will come when it comes.

The German philosopher Albert Schweitzer once said, "One who gains strength by overcoming obstacles possesses the only strength which can overcome adversity." When we *embrace* the reality that life is full of adversity, and build our repertoire of tools to help us overcome the perils and pitfalls that stand to trap us in a place of inaction and despair, we truly begin to harness our fullest potential, tapping into our vast well of resiliency—the waters that provide strength during hard times.

I cannot overstate the importance of developing tools. So, let me share another tool that can help guide you when you find yourself in the heart of a storm or struggle. I not only use this technique myself but have seen many of the young people I work with benefit from it.

MANTRA, MANTRA, MANTRA

The tool I encourage you to adopt, acquire, and sharpen—by repeated use!—is the simple yet profound practice of crafting or finding a mantra. It doesn't have to be elaborate, nor does it have to be something you come up with yourself. In fact, one of my favorite mantras has always been the oft heard "it is what it is." However, one memorable adventure during my first autumn at the University of Montana prompted me to expand on that popular saying. And it definitely helped to get me through a storm—literally.

I vividly remember the day. It was gloomy, late September. The leaves along the Bitterroot River were losing their luster, their pigment changing from a rich green to varying shades of yellow and orange as summer daylight and overnight temperatures faded into fall. I had been planning to attempt a solo climb up the tallest mountain in the Bitterroots—the gnarly, seriated Trapper Peak, which, at 10,157 feet, juts up and towers above the valley floor. The temperatures were in the mid-40s; and there was a bone-aching dampness in the air, snow on the ground, and starkness to the uninhabited wilderness.

I had heard about Trapper Peak since my early childhood, as my father and uncle made it a tradition to climb it every February. It had become an annual rite of passage for them—and now it was my turn. But I knew better than to wait until the bitter Montana winter to earn my stripes. I had also endured far too many injuries over the course of the previous five years, so I had to get after it while the getting was good.

I had long recognized that my insatiable thirst for adventure (when my body allowed it) ultimately led me to put too many miles on my legs, adding wear and tear that often required a lengthy recovery. But nothing was going to halt my summit attempt on this day—not even the snow that was deepening with every hundred feet in elevation I climbed. By the time I reached the rocky scree field, I was beginning to post-hole to my knee— about the same time that the demarcation of fog enveloping the mountains swallowed me up.

With a tinge of anxiety, I had a decision to make: *Do I bag my summit attempt and live to fight another day; or do I roll the dice in hopes that my meager compass skills guide me back through the fog to the tree line and trail after reaching my destination 6,000+ feet above the valley floor?*

Young and full of backcountry swagger, I opted to journey through the thick mist that limited visibility to fifteen feet but periodically opened up enough to allow me to find a route across the sketchy scree field. On multiple occasions, my foot punched through a patch of hollow snow, and I'd end up jammed thigh-deep between jagged boulders, my forward momentum threatening to hyperextend my knee (the results of which could have been disastrous in a remote wilderness setting).

I pushed onward to the summit. After a brief ceremony atop the Bitterroot's highest peak, I started back down; but I quickly realized it would be a bigger challenge than I thought to find my way. The trail was still consumed by fog, which was thickening below. Anxiety filled my belly as the viscous vapor swallowed me up, forcing me to take short breaks with the compass to ensure I was on the proper bearing. With the cold, wet air biting through my Capilene, I couldn't help but think of the worst-case scenario. With much more momentum going down than I had on the way up, I remained cautious. Yearning for the warmth and safety of the truck, I found myself speaking out loud:

"It is what it is."

Then, almost instinctively, I added three more words:

"You got this."

Time after time, I repeated it: *It is what it is. You got this.* And each time I uttered these simple words, my racing mind calmed enough for me to find my focus. Soon, I'd guided myself to the safety of the thick lodgepole forest—and then to my truck. I had accomplished my own rite of passage.

It is what it is. You got this.

When we combine the power of deep belly breathing (our exercise from chapter 1) with this tool—a meaningful mantra—we've developed a potent recipe for building up our resiliency scaffolding and ability to face adversity. I've grown fond of telling my high school basketball team here in Montana that "we are what we are." No matter how much time I spend wishing I were six foot seven, I'm never going to be taller than six foot one. And for all of the time spent lifting in the weight room, I'm a gym rat with a tight, lean, and sinewy build. Getting big just isn't in the cards; I am what I am.

Adversity will keep coming at us as long as we have the privilege of awakening each day. And it is a fact that life is harder for some than others. For whatever reason, some face more daunting challenges than others.

It is what it is. You got this.

This mantra is gold for me. It has gotten me through some major challenges in my life, and sometimes that—just getting through—is accomplishment enough.

But we needn't settle for "just getting through" when times are tough. If we think big and dream even bigger—and remain tenacious and resilient—we can shoot for more. *Much more.*

SCRAPPY AND UNDETERRED

Last spring, I journeyed to Denver, Colorado, for one of the most meaningful days of my life. Five days later, I was still riding the high. After nearly a decade of plugging away on my memoir, *Grizzlies On My Mind: Essays of Adventure, Love, and Heartache from Yellowstone Country,* I was in the Mile High City for its official release.

But I had also been asked by the Sierra Club to be the closing speaker at their Denver rally to protest the Keystone XL Pipeline, in hopes of my firing up the crowd. And fire up the crowd I did. With a passionate call to action, I threw white gas on the fire that had been brewing in the bellies of the protesters all day. The response was visceral and powerful—*electric*. And the weather was glorious. There I was, speaking to the Northern Rockies chapter of one of the most powerful environmental organizations in the country, standing on the front steps of the Colorado State Capitol and flowing—a modern-day Earth warrior. And a moment for the memory bank.

Then, less than an hour later, I was heading across town to the legendary indie bookstore Tattered Cover for my first book event. For fifty-seven minutes, I shared a passionate presentation to a standing-room-only audience at the bookstore of bookstores. I couldn't have dreamed of a better launch.

A couple days later, I got a call from one of my best friends from college. He had chauffeured me for my thirty-two-hour, whirlwind book launch.

"Mikey, I've been through some shit in my life. But I've never seen anyone who has gone through more than you have the last two years on so many levels. I can't begin to express how inspiring it was for me to see you rise above all you've been dealt to reach this moment in time. Seeing you in all of your glory this past weekend inspires me to reach my own personal mountaintop."

I share this for a reason. It had been the year from hell for me—actually, *two* years. And though the journey of seeing my first book to publication was also a grind, that Saturday in mile-high country represented the power of purposeful passion (PPP)—what we can accomplish when we think big and dream even bigger while remaining undeterred in defense of those dreams. Even in the midst of heartache and heartbreak, depression and despair, we can accomplish and achieve greatness.

Right, wrong, or indifferent, some face more adversity than others. Again, it is what it is; we are what we are. And while there are numerous negatives to hardship, there are always positives as well. We may not be able to change who we are (our experiences, where we come from, our DNA), but we sure as hell can change what we're about. And that is perhaps the greatest gift of adversity: it forces us to dig deep, ask the uncomfortable questions, and grow from within.

The most resilient people are those who have endured the most. You either break or you don't; and for those who survive the onslaught of challenges innate to our human experience, we come out the other side with an enlightened perspective of what really matters.

CONNECTION

Working as a motivator, advocate, and coach, I've gained much experience with young people in the midst of challenging times in their lives. And as the founder and director of a nonprofit organization that worked with a high percentage of at-risk youth, I had hopes of inspiring a future generation of guardians to Yellowstone Country. For five years, I brushed shoulders with juvenile probation officers, school counselors, and local police officers in my quest to provide a platform where local teens could thrive. Many of these inspiring young people had been through the full gamut: broken homes, trouble with the law, foster homes, the devastation of meth and alcohol, and the everyday struggles of survival in the conformist setting that often pervades our public schools.

Midway through the recent health saga that led to my brush with eternity, I found myself visiting a blood specialist at the University of Utah in Salt Lake City for a very rare blood disorder I had been diagnosed with. As fate would have it, a sibling of one of the young men I once had the privilege of coaching was in the intensive care unit at the university hospital, recovering from her own brush with eternity.

I've said it before and I'll say it again: *life is hard.* And being a teenager / young adult trying to find your place in a confusing, complex, and challenging world can present what may appear to be insurmountable odds. In fact, this is true at *any* age, and I'm sure many of you have been there at some time in your life—in a place of quiet desperation, desolation, and depression; a time when it is immensely difficult to see beyond the clouds to recognize that no matter how big, dark, and daunting the storm is, it *will* eventually pass.

According to a 2012 Centers for Disease Control and Prevention survey, nearly one in six high school students have seriously contemplated suicide, while one in twelve have actually attempted to end their life.[1] Though it may seem simplistic, this following statement rings true: suicide is a *permanent* solution to a *temporary* problem. And yet, for the fifteen- to twenty-four-year-old age group, suicide is the third-leading cause of death. It's not uncommon for there to be as many as 1,700 teen suicides a year in the United States.[2]

This both scares and saddens me—and I say this without judgment. None of us knows what it's like to walk in another's shoes. Tragically, and far too often, suicide is seen as the only option to escape the pain and anguish of depression. Largely because of an unfounded shame associated with depression and thoughts of suicide, those struggling must dig deep to find the courage to seek support and help. Until we can foster a more empathetic, enlightened, and understanding dialogue surrounding the topic of depression and suicide, this will remain a cultural crisis.

I've lost two friends to suicide. And I've witnessed the profound heartbreak and guilt that is left in the wake of tragedy when someone takes his or her own life. For those left behind, there will always be questions: *How did I not see this coming? What more could I have done for him/her?* I often wonder how the suicide victims' lives would have turned out if they could have endured the darkness long enough for the pain to dissipate, allowing their loved ones to shine light on the one-of-a-kind potential their life represents. One cannot help but to be haunted by the question "What if?"

I've shared moments of inconsolable desperation with friends who simply couldn't bear the thought of living another day in the desolate darkness of depression, unable to see the light at the end of the tunnel. They falsely believed that their only remaining option was suicide—to end their pain and to remove the burden they placed on their loved ones. But oftentimes, those struggling with suicidal thoughts—as well as those who succeed—are viewed as "less than," weak, or selfish because they can't hack it. *This couldn't be further from the truth.* Depression is far too complex and widespread to be whittled down by such one-dimensional thinking.

I often reflect on the severity of the pain my friend must have experienced to be driven to leave his beautiful wife and radiant children far before his time. I cannot look at my friend's boys without wondering about what could have been. I know they will be more than okay because they are surrounded by the boundless love of their unwavering mother and grandparents, but my heart aches that they won't experience their father's adventurous spirit and love. My heart aches that he won't be able to share in the ups and downs of their life journey and his journey through fatherhood. That unknown of the lives of those lost to suicide is what saddens me most.

So when I received the news that this beautiful young lady's attempt to end her life had not succeeded, my heart soared with hope. She was alive. She had endured. After exchanging text messages with her brother while en route to Salt Lake City, I asked if I could drop by with flowers and give him a hug. In response, he asked if I would consider talking with his sister as well—to, in his words, "do what you do, Coach."

Four hours later, after I had been through a slough of tests and a series of doctor appointments in which I repeatedly received the sobering news that I was "lucky to be alive," it seemed an opportune time to get outside myself and do something to positively impact someone else. With a deep breath and a sense of reprieve, I limped my way through the hospital to meet up with a young man whose sister was enduring far more than I could imagine.

After shaking everyone's hands and giving the girl's mother a big hug, we sat down and spoke about the young teenager we had all come to support. Thirty minutes later, her mom and aunt also asked if I would speak to her. Honored and touched, I simply said, "When the time is right, I would love to meet and speak to Naomi." I was more than a little taken aback by their response.

"How about now?"

I hadn't prepared anything; and I was still reeling from an intense morning of doctor appointments after a white-knuckled drive through a blizzard over two passes before sunrise. But *carpe diem*, yeah?

Minutes later, I was being escorted through the halls of the ICU. Only two months removed from my own six-day, six-night stay in the hospital, witnessing the tubes coming out of each patient I passed—many teetering on the brink of survival—took my breath away. That was, until I walked into Naomi's room.

It really doesn't matter the magnitude of the struggle; there is something profound about enduring difficult times that binds survivors together. You see it in the cancer community—a sense of kinship that connects those who have withstood the onslaught of a vicious disease. What a beautiful reminder that there are pluses to even the most devastating of experiences.

Seventeen years old and less than seventy-two hours removed from her suicide attempt, Naomi was radiant, with dark skin, flowing chocolate hair, and bright eyes that lit up the room. It was clear from the first time our hands touched that this young lady had an indomitable spirit. She had endured more than the vast majority of young people her age, and yet, with tubes coming out of her nose and arms, she greeted me with a glorious smile.

Though we had just met, the atmosphere was comfortable and real. And I launched into a forty-five-minute speech in which I hardly took a breath. Knowing the magnitude of what Naomi had experienced, I bared all. I shared my own stories of struggle and survival, and spoke about weathering the storm of high school—of simply getting through that challenging time. A firm believer that we are all writing our own life stories each and every day, I emphasized that this is just one chapter in her journey—that in her seventeen chapters (years) so far, this may be the most important yet. But it is only *one* chapter, and there are so many more to write.

"We can't pick up a book at chapter eighteen and have it mean much," I said. "Moments like this are important to remember; but now you get to turn the page and begin the next chapter."

I emphasized the importance of not spending any more time worrying about what her classmates think of her, as it simply isn't relevant: "The ones who are with you will be with you, and the ones who aren't—well, to hell with them."

We had both been gifted with something bigger than the hardships we had both suffered.

We had connected.

Attempting to endure the eye of a storm without connection is akin to going into battle without armor or standing in the middle of a field as the tornado barrels down, without taking cover. With connection—to a person, place, pet, passion—we can weather the most daunting of storms. Developing, nurturing, and fostering connection should top the list of tools we stockpile for when the storm comes.

According to sociologist Brené Brown, "Connection is what gives purpose and meaning to our lives." Consider it a vital part of your survival kit; because, like it or not, living life is no different from calling a place like the Caribbean home: it's a beautiful landscape with much potential for rich and meaningful encounters, but hurricanes will undoubtedly flatten the islands from time to time. So, you might as well be prepared, as you never quite know when the storms will hit.

One positive that can be uncovered following an attempted suicide is that it brings people together. Through hardship, we form bonds that are stronger than any other—but only if the fertile ground of connection has been sowed. When I walked into that ICU waiting room, I witnessed a concerned but *united* band of brothers, aunts, cousins, and parents. Though they had endured unfathomable heartache in recent days, a beloved member of their *ohana* (their family) was in stable condition, and their sense of relief and gratitude pervaded the room.

This is the power of the human spirit; this is the power of connection. Connecting on an intimate level with another human being, with a beloved pet, with a sacred place can serve as the foundation for our resiliency reservoir.

But connection doesn't just happen. Fostering connection is similar to planting and nurturing a garden: you have to put in the work and time in order to have a harvest; you have to uncover the courage to be vulnerable. It takes guts to be vulnerable—to open up and share your heart, your demons, and your skeletons. When you find the audacity to embrace vulnerability, however, you are able to share your true self, creating the most fertile soil possible for a bountiful crop of connection and intimacy.

Can *you* embrace the concept that we are what we are? Are you willing to share your story in order to connect with others on an intimate level? If so, you are on the path to connection.

Our lives are finite, and in the end, our personal story is all we truly have. So make it count, and tell it well. Enduring hardship, adversity, and struggle is an integral part of the plot. And while it may be far from comfortable to walk across the hot coals of adversity (much less share the experience with others), these moments of despair and seeming desolation represent the building blocks of the most important intangible element we can hope to foster on our walk upon this Earth: *character*. The loving footprint of legacy.

ODAAT

Many days during my time living on the Garden Island of Kauai, relegated to a walking boot cast for my ailing Achilles while also nursing an injured wrist, the idea of jumping into the cold water of the local YMCA—a pool I'd coined "liquid gold" for its pristine and effervescent water—felt like too much to bear. I had journeyed to one of the most remote archipelagos in the world to surf, not to swim in an outdoor pool with temperatures that plummeted when the winter clouds and monsoons descended upon the island. The water seemed to drop a degree for each day the sun failed to shine. But I needed the endorphins and dopamine that I had grown accustomed to after twenty years of daily exercise. If cold water is all you've got, you better start swimming.

This unexpected experience with water molecules in a pool over 3,000 miles from Montana has provided a powerful metaphor for other challenges in life: once you've experienced, faced, and ultimately overcome adversity, you build up your resiliency reserves—your stamina—so the icy-cold water seems a little less daunting the next time. So it makes sense to embrace adversity as an *opportunity* to grow, training your resiliency muscles by doing the heavy lifting now, ultimately preparing yourself to endure the storms to come.

Another mantra that has helped me during times of overwhelming adversity might seem overly simplistic if it weren't so brilliant:

ODAAT. One day at a time.

Think about it for a minute: what happens when things get really hard? We tend to prognosticate. We look ahead through a lens clouded by overwhelm, fear, distress, and depression. Though it's difficult for us to recognize at the time, we usually aren't seeing things very clearly. Of course, the same can be said about the really positive moments and experiences in our lives.

After I spoke in front of that standing-room-only crowd at Tattered Cover, I felt like I could take on the world. Bumping The Notorious B.I.G.'s "Juicy" en route to the Denver Airport (a cut from my youth where one of the freshest rappers of that era flows about making it against all odds) and on my flight back home to Bozeman, Montana, there was zero doubt that I was going to make it in this writing and speaking world.

The truth is, just like in the rap game—or in that of an actor, musician, or any other artist—there is no such thing as a sure thing, a can't miss. But after one magic day, I was seeing the world and my career through rose-colored glasses.

That's okay. These natural highs can provide comfort during the times when we are feeling less optimistic about our future. Still, these aren't the best times to make big life decisions. Hell, if I could have found a bank willing to give me the loan when I touched down just after 11 PM that night, I might have easily purchased a house and car far beyond my means the next day, so strong was my optimism for my future.

But I know better. For one thing, I've learned that money and material possessions aren't what make us truly happy, nor what make us our best selves. My hope is that you, too, will learn to keep things in perspective when you are feeling really low—or high.

These two concepts—that of embracing hardship as an opportunity to do the heavy lifting as well as that of recognizing what type of lens we are seeing the world through—are two lessons Dr. John Wimberly, one of my mentors, shared with me. They have served as what I like to call "break-through concepts" during my own periods of challenge and adversity, because there are really only two ways to deal with life's challenges and problems: we can either be proactive and change them (which represents the best approach, when viable), or we can learn to accept that which we cannot control.

Acceptance is allowing reality to be as it is without requiring it to be different—remember this lesson from chapter 1? If we learned to embrace this straightforward yet profound concept, how much would our suffering be lessened?

When changing your circumstances isn't an option, we must make the ever-important choice to *choose* acceptance. Though change is rarely easy for any of us, for those of us who are stubborn, thickheaded, or simply have a propensity to fight like a caged lion in defense of what we believe to be *right* or *meant to be* in our lives, acceptance can prove a Herculean feat. But I will promise you this: when we truly embrace the concept of allowing reality to be as it is without requiring it to be different, we unleash our true self—our *higher* self—and our ultimate potential.

ODAAT. One day at a time, you will endure whatever life throws at you.

ATTITUDE, CHARACTER, AND INTEGRITY

When shit hits the fan, it can be a monumental challenge to keep your head up. If you believe the Swindoll quote that I shared earlier in this chapter—that "life is 10 percent what happens to me and 90 percent how I react to it"—you will quickly come to recognize the power of attitude; attitude is the game changer. Attitude can make or break a team, friendship, relationship—even a business. And the beautiful thing about attitude is that it's completely within our control: it's the most important choice we get to make every day.

I don't believe any human qualities are more important than character and integrity. Character is defined by *Merriam-Webster* as "the way someone thinks, feels, and behaves," where integrity is defined as "the quality of being honest and fair." Ultimately, I believe our character and integrity are what define us. It's not the way we look, the activities we pursue, the car we drive, the house in which we live, or the money we make. It's not our education, our looks, our charisma, or our charm. It's character and integrity that make us rich.

When someone finds the courage to face adversity with a positive attitude—without being pie-in-the-sky or Pollyanna—you are witnessing character in action. In this chapter's practice exercises, I'm going to challenge you to harness a positive (or improved) attitude through the power of visualization.

To be clear, there is a big difference between positively visualizing your life and maintaining delusions of grandeur. I'm not asking you to blindly adopt some baseless bullshit, but I *am* hoping you'll at least open your mind to the potential of positive attraction. While I don't fully embrace the law of attraction (which states that "like attracts like," meaning positive thoughts yield positive outcomes and negative thoughts bring about negative results), I do believe there is something to be said about this theory that fills the pages of the best-selling self-help book *The Secret* (a book that has sold more than nineteen million copies and has been translated into forty-six languages). However, I sure as hell don't believe that meditating under a banyan tree on your desire to acquire a banana is going to yield a ripe piece of fruit to quench your hunger. Nor do I believe all the meditation and positive visualization in the world is going to produce all of your desired results.

Positive visualization without *action* is passive and short on backbone.

The idea that there is always a link between adversity and our choices in life is preposterous. True, some choices may cause problems for us. Who you spend your time with has the potential to drag you down into a muck of problems, for example. Our choices—when not made from a place of character, integrity, and self-awareness—can lead us down a path of destruction. But are millions of people diagnosed with cancer each year because these people have failed to lead a virtuous life or have allowed negative thoughts to permeate their mind? Are thousands of young people sexually abused each year because they succumbed to negativity? Of course not! Inevitably, bad things happen to really good people.

It's true that we must take ownership of our decisions, but far too often, the shame we feel while facing adversity is unwarranted, illogical guilt. I learned this the hard way after years of self-deprecating talk—what I like to call "Piece of Shit-itis" (or POS-itis). Unless you are a narcissist (I doubt you are, as you probably wouldn't be reading this book if you were), you are likely to experience Piece of Shit-itis to some degree from time to time. It is the nature of being an imperfect human in an acclaim-driven society—one that emphasizes unrealistic expectations of what it looks like to be *worthy* of success and praise. We're taught from an early age to question our self-worth with fears of not being good enough.

Still, if we want to achieve a specified goal, *action is critical*. No matter how much a high school basketball player positively visualizes being an All-Conference player, if he or she doesn't put in the time, energy, and effort during the off-season, working on skill development, the dream is nothing more than a fantasy. Can you imagine how one would fare on the SAT if, instead of studying, one simply sat and visualized a spectacularly high score, day after day? The answer is clear: you must *first* commit to putting in the work to achieve your goals. Once you've done so, there is tremendous power in visualizing the desired outcome.

Practice Exercises:

POSITIVE VISUALIZATION

So how does this positive visualization thing work? It's really pretty simple. There was a time not long ago when scientists and doctors believed that our mind and body were two very different, disconnected elements. But over the course of the last half century, the scientific community has clearly proven a mind–body connection that represents a very complex and capable ecosystem of sorts. As such, in addition to getting regular exercise, adequate sleep, and eating healthy, nutritious meals, it makes sense to nurture our mind–body connection with positive images of our hopes and dreams.

The following exercises should take no more than a couple minutes each morning and night—but I'm going to ask you to take it a step further. After focusing on gratitude (an essential core value to adopt and master), take three to five additional minutes to take things to the next level.

EXERCISE #1: GRATITUDE WINDOWS

First and foremost, when things are tough, it is essential to focus on what is going well in the world and in our lives. But life gets busy, yeah? Before you know it, another day is done, and your mind is already spinning with the next day's tasks. How the hell do you focus on anything when you're already tapped out and exhausted?

Use the short but profound windows of time as you are laying your head on your pillow each night and rising each morning to focus on gratitude. I call these gratitude windows.

1. Go to bed each night reflecting upon what you are grateful for. (Your list can include the everyday [a sale on your favorite mac-n-cheese] and the bigger picture [the loved ones around you]).

2. Put a limit on your list so that you can really consider these things before you drift off to sleep. (I like to name five things.)

3. Keep expectations out of it. The point is to get in a space of gratitude as you close the day.

4. Wake up each morning asking yourself what you are thankful for. You can repeat the list from the night before or start with something new. (As before, put a limit on your list, remembering that there are no right or wrong answers.)

5. And if you are feeling particularly audacious, ask yourself, *What can I do to add beauty to the world today?* (This can be as simple as complimenting a perfect stranger, opening the door for someone, or helping an elder at the store with his groceries.)

You don't have to move mountains in these gratitude windows; there is power in simply thinking these thoughts. The practice enables you to create positive space in your mind, nurturing the soil that will provide nutrients for a verdant yield throughout the day and beyond.

EXERCISE #2: LOOK, PLAN, ACT

Every morning for a week—or better yet, a month—I encourage you to lie in bed for five minutes after you awaken to engage in the following practice. (It's the ideal time to create space for positive visualization, before your morning routine distracts you.)

1. Utilizing your belly breathing, take five deep breaths, once again

activating your parasympathetic nervous system (see the exercise in chapter 1).

2. After five deep breaths, take a journey through your day's itinerary, focusing your attention on the parts of your day that could prove particularly challenging. (This may be a test, an encounter with an ex-boyfriend, girlfriend, or spouse, a job interview, a trip to the dentist, or any spectrum of anxiety-inducing events.)

3. Now I want you to visualize a positive outcome—the optimum results—if you were able to orchestrate them.

4. Get up and *put your plans into action!* Don't rely on or settle for visualization alone, as action is always the key. That said, there is absolutely no doubt that imagining ourselves in an anticipated situation helps to prepare us for the day ahead.

As a basketball coach, I wouldn't just throw my kids into the fire and expect them to pull off miracles. We practice every situation we can imagine in hopes of preparing for the worst-case scenario. And when I am amping up for a big keynote presentation, I practice until I have my material completely dialed in. I can't shoot for a win without first putting in the work.

Then the night before any game or presentation, I spend a few minutes in positive visualization mode, envisioning my desired result. I review what I'm grateful for—like the opportunities to coach and to speak—and I shut out the light on a positive note. Both exercises help me sleep while keeping my perspective in check, giving me the best opportunity to be as sharp as possible the next day.

Positive visualization is yet another tool that builds up our resiliency reservoir. Whether it involves looking back through gratitude windows (exercise #1) or planning ahead for potential challenges (exercise #2), it is a reliable support during times of adversity and fair weather alike.

CLOSING THOUGHTS

I don't share the stories in this book to wow you or to boost my ego; I simply wish to remind you of what is possible when we remain resilient. And whether or not we're lucky enough to have some of it in our DNA, resiliency *can* be cultivated and strengthened.

There was a time in my life when I was unable to accept the reality of my fight with ankylosing spondylitis. Truth be told, it is still a struggle to wrap my head around the fact that my legs simply don't work the way they once did. But in the past, every time my Achilles flared and I found myself relegated to the walking boot cast, a cloud of unwarranted shame washed over me. The boot cast was my kryptonite. And when you consider the fact that I own *four* different boot casts that have been used and abused walking through airports, riding road bikes, wading rocky river bottoms, it's safe to say that "the boot" ignited many formidable flames of depression and dread. The loss of activity resonated so deeply within me, but it was also the onslaught of questions regarding why a young, fit, and seemingly healthy man—supposedly in his prime—was once again limping in a knee-high boot.

Eventually, I learned to accept my reality for what it is. (*Acceptance is allowing reality to be as it is without requiring it to be different.*) Even today, after extensive hip surgery and a series of experimental procedures on my Achilles (all treatments I've endured in hopes of returning to the activities that fuel my spirit), I have to accept the little hitch in my giddyup that comes with the constant flare of my Achilles. But with time, I've come to realize that it is not my body; my outdoor pursuits; or any heroics on the bike, in the mountains, or on a stand-up paddleboard that define my worth. It is my character, my heart, and my core values—that's what I'm all about.

I may walk with a limp, but it is my essence *that defines my swagger.*

When things are tough (an inevitability of being a person *striving* in a challenging world), it's more important than ever to focus on gratitude—on what we *can* do. If we are experiencing loss of any kind (boyfriend or girlfriend, husband or wife, family member or friend, pet, physical change), it is essential to uncover the courage to embrace the pain instead of running from it. *Let yourself hurt.* Acceptance of a shitty situation doesn't have to be passive. We don't have to like it—in fact, we can have utter disdain for the cards we've been dealt. But we can't let ourselves get stuck in the mud of life—not when we live in a world so big and full of possibility and potential.

To live a life that matters, we must face adversity, become resilient, and harness our own scrappy spirit. We all have our limp, our Achilles heel. The key I've discovered is not to fight it. Accept it, embrace it, and then pursue what you love with a religious fervor. Be audacious—develop your own personal "swaggage"—but always remain humble, grateful, and compassionate.

This is the recipe for uncovering that which you wish to become.

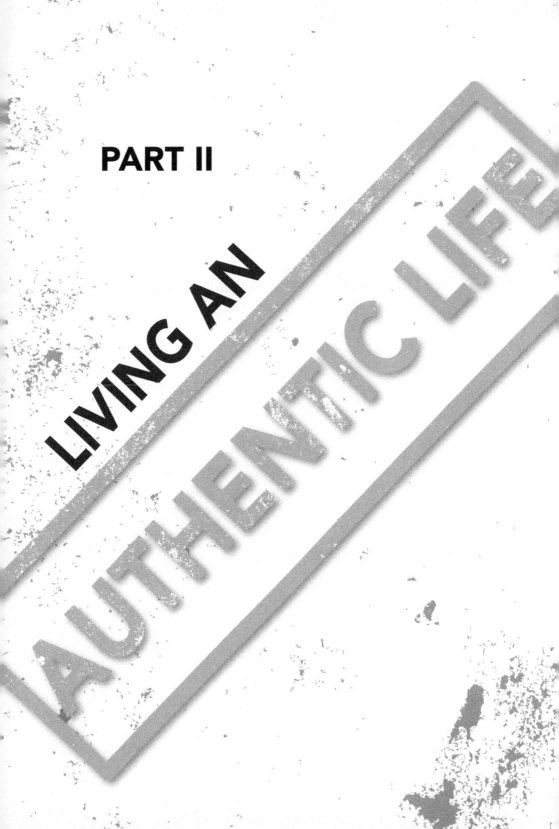

PART II

LIVING AN AUTHENTIC LIFE

3

Lead from the Heart

*To be yourself in a world that is constantly trying to make
you something else is the greatest accomplishment.*
—Ralph Waldo Emerson

These brilliant and profound words from the legendary Ralph Waldo
Emerson speak to the heart of what it looks like to live and love authentically. In a world dominated by Twitter, Facebook, and Instagram, there
has never been a more challenging time in the history of human civilization
to stay true to the power of authenticity. Thus, ironically—as far as I'm concerned—Emerson's words ring truer today than when they were written
near the end of the nineteenth century.

Why is it is so hard to be authentic? To answer that question, we
must first understand what it *looks like* to be authentic. Authentic is

defined as "real or genuine; not copied or false" (per *Merriam-Webster*). So in the real world, I would say it looks like someone who stays true to their core values; who is unwavering in their convictions; who stands up for what they believe to be right; who doesn't blow around like trash in the wind of popularity or what others think.

A true original doesn't let the number of followers on Twitter or the number of likes on Facebook determine the worthiness of their endeavors, the validity of their journey.

Young people experience more peer pressure than ever to look, act, dress, and live a certain way—but this burden bleeds into the adult world too, from lofty expectations regarding body composition to family dynamics and professional success. In the pluses and minuses equation, it sucks at *any* age; but flipping the hand over and looking at the positive side of things, there has perhaps never been a time where the soil has been more fertile for a person to do their *own* thing than in the here and now. The question becomes: *how resilient are we willing to be?* (The BA wheel from chapter 1 reminds us that resiliency is key.) Being authentic in a society of sheep, where conformity is the norm, presents an extremely daunting challenge.

In his groundbreaking book *The Art of Non-Conformity*, Chris Guillebeau shares stories of people who have bucked the norm to follow their own path and chart their own waters. Guillebeau masterfully threads stories of those who have successfully blazed their own trails while sharing his own adventure of unconventional prosperity. However, as romantic and inspiring as these stories are, we cannot overlook two important components of authenticity embodied by the people Guillebeau profiles: *audacious determination* and the *unwillingness to settle* that accompany the accomplishment—the *nobility*—that comes with living authentically.

It takes a gritty, tenacious, and tough spirit to break away from the pack in pursuit of a life of purpose, conviction, and authenticity. Perhaps that's why there are far more followers than leaders in our world. It is much easier and more convenient to be a member of the crowd than it is to have the guts to change direction and take charge of our lives—to go that extra mile and *lead*!

I believe that all great leaders have one thing in common: a sincere and genuine desire to positively impact lives and the world around them. *Always* be authentic—true to your own self—when you choose to lead in the lives of others and, perhaps more importantly, in your own life.

My work has provided me a platform to lead on numerous occasions. And while wearing the leadership hat may come naturally to me, leading is never easy. Doubt, for example, can sabotage anyone's ability to become a leader. Yet doubt is a natural part of any daring or worthwhile endeavor. I'm plagued with doubt each time I embark upon a new path, but the potential success—the potential to live a life that matters—quickly consumes that spark of uncertainty with each step forward.

Don't let doubt stop you; *accept* that anything new and worth pursuing is likely to make you feel uncomfortable and scared at first. This is natural when stepping outside of the box. Remember that those you look up to—those who have impacted and inspired you—have also experienced doubt, anxiety, and fear; but they went ahead and took the leadership leap anyway. Doubt just comes with the territory whenever we attempt anything that triggers our emotional immune system to kick into high gear.

Now that we have an idea of what being authentic looks like, let's take a closer look at how it can (but far too often does *not*) play into becoming a leader.

BECOMING A LEADER

According to *The Oxford Dictionaries*, leadership is "the action of leading a group of people or an organization." Not only do I think that's too simple a definition, I also believe there is a big difference between traditional leadership and what I like to call *authentic leadership*. Authentic leadership encompasses far more than one's ability to lead a team or army of believers. Whether it be starting a business, running a nonprofit, or simply embarking upon a journey into uncharted waters, going at it solo takes guts and, ultimately, some form of leadership.

I've often heard young people I work with insist they don't have the desire to be a leader, and yet they, like all of us, yearn for something more meaningful and fulfilling in their lives. Perhaps a lack of confidence is causing them to sell short the value of leadership; or perhaps they don't actually see the power of simply leading by example. As I said, going at it solo *takes guts*—especially when *no one* is behind you.

The difference between traditional leadership (which many millennials do not aspire to) and authentic leadership (which is within the grasp of every person) is a matter of the heart. When we uncover the courage to lead from the heart, we unleash our highest potential for impactful, authentic, and meaningful work. *You* can become an authentic leader! Even those of you who have never before aspired to it.

It is time for us to redefine what leadership looks like.

The traditional leadership model has always placed a special emphasis on *leadership presence*, an intangible "something" that a very small percentage of people seem to have. Often, people fail to try on a new hat out of a fear of the unknown and a fear of failure. I believe this is a major factor when people of all ages insist they have no desire to lead. If you're five foot two, slow, without coordination, and missing a jump shot, why try out for the varsity basketball team, yeah? If you don't have what you perceive to be the *traditional* traits of a leader—what society has demonstrated to you—why even venture down that road?

This limited definition of leadership, the traditional view, has resulted in a society lacking in leaders but brimming with followers. It is a society, as a close friend of mine once described it, "churning out young people to become cogs in its corporate-driven, money-making wheels." Without a catalyst to change—without leaders young people can relate to, look up to, and *believe* in—these teens and early twentysomethings become firmly stuck by the time they've become adults, playing the role far too many of us accept without questioning: that of followers.

Full of Heart

Now I don't want to be a downer here with my observation that we live in a society dominated by people unwilling to lead, but remember: I'm not going to be bashful. And I'm sure as hell not going to be Pollyanna—I'm going to tell it like I see it.

So, why do you think I choose to focus so much of my work on young adults (millennials) versus the general population? Whether it be my basketball players; a group of inner-city teens from Atlanta, Dallas, Boston, or Los Angeles; or the beautiful young people I had the opportunity to mentor and teach through my nonprofit organization Yellowstone Country Guardians, for me, there is one universal that bridges the gap between environmental education, motivational work, and leading a basketball team: HEART. *Young people see through the pretentious crap that far too often pervades our culture.* They want to be the change, not talk about it. They want to live their dreams, not just dream. They are fresh, alive, empowered, and full of heart.

It makes sense for all of us to gravitate toward an arena where we know we are good at what we do and are reminded that we've got game— where we *resonate*. One of the reasons I believe my work with young people has been so meaningful and successful is because of how I choose to lead: authentically and from the heart. Repeat after me: *from the heart*. Young people know when someone is living from the heart and when someone is trying to bullshit them. And they respond to what comes from the heart.

Indeed, I am inspired by young people—by their open hearts and minds, their willingness and desire to uncover meaning and purpose in their lives; and their unquenchable sense of wonder and ability to hope for a better world. But my reason for choosing to work with young people extends beyond all of this too. My concern for our wild world—for our planet in peril, where an estimated 200 species per day are going extinct— is another reason I choose to work with the up-and-coming generation. They are our hope—our *only* hope—for the future of our wild planet and species like grizzly bears, wolves, bison, wild trout, sharks, whales, and an estimated 8.7 billion other species who call the Earth home.

According to the brilliant ecologist Carl Safina, our current extinction rate is one thousand times what it would naturally be without our insatiable appetite for economic development and our no-limits approach to population growth.[1] I share this as an example because I have a passion for wildlife and wild places, for conservation, and for preservation—and as a result, for inspiring the future guardians of our environment. *Passion and leading from the heart go hand in hand.* I also share this because there is no arena in greater need of leadership from young adults and generation Y than the field of environmentalism. This is the only planet we have, and now, more than ever, we need audacious individuals willing to speak out and up for the issues that matter most. I can think of no issue of greater relevance than the fate of our planet.

It doesn't matter where you live, what your background is, how much education you have, how impressive you look, or how charming or charismatic you are; issues pertaining to our environment are fair game for *everyone*. We have a moral and ethical responsibility to advocate on behalf of our planet to ensure that the next generation (and the two hundred thereafter) has the opportunity—if they so choose—to shoulder a pack twenty miles into the Yellowstone backcountry and enjoy a sleepless night with grizzlies on their mind. We must ensure that the next generation has clean air to breathe, clean water to drink, and a wild world to explore. We must confront the challenges and reality of climate change, demanding an impactful shift in policy. And this dream of mine will only be a reality if enough young people *make the choice* to become authentic leaders.

But I want to be clear: the message here isn't about the most pressing *environmental* issues on the planet; it is about the most pressing *human* issue. I believe that the single most important piece of habitat left on our wild planet is that of the human heart—we only fight to save what we love, and we only love what we know. My mission is to spark that gritty determination and heart to explore all that *you* may become when you throw off the shackles of our societal norms—the "programming" that attempts to tell you whether you are cut from the leadership cloth or not. It's your life and no one else's—*your* walk, *your* journey. You get to define your own style of leadership, and the world benefits from your audacity when you do. Never underestimate the power of *you*.

The Power of You

What is *your* dream? What kind of mark do you see yourself making on this world?

When we share our authentic selves with others, we are bestowing upon them the greatest gift we can offer. There are certainly times in your life when you need to fake it till you make it; but when you learn to hold fast to your authenticity through whatever life presents you, you unleash the power of *you*—you are on your way to becoming a leader. No matter what happens, if you can honestly say that you hang your hat on your authenticity, you are already winning the battle and leading a true life. And what could be more valuable than that?

And here's the beautiful thing about being an authentic leader, someone who leads from the heart: *anyone* can do it! There is no cookie-cutter approach. You don't have to be cut from that traditional leadership cloth, have leadership lineage, be rousingly articulate and overtly charismatic, or have the desire to stand on a stage to address a crowd. That is *old-school* leadership. Twenty-first-century leadership is about positively impacting the world around you by doing it *your* way. The authentic leader simply needs to make the choice to lead from the heart, whether it's in the environmental arena, engineering, sports, music, computers, politics—you name it. *Whatever* fuels your heart, identify it, nurture it, and lead with it. Just make the commitment—make that heartfelt choice—and then forge ahead in the best way you know how. Lead by the power of *you*.

An Open Heart and an Open Mind

For four years, as the head boys' basketball coach at Gardiner High School (in a small, rural, and sometimes desolate Montana town), I coached a group of young men that would have walked through fire or charged through a brick wall for "Coach." By leading from the heart, with nothing but love and a willingness to share tears and vulnerability, I earned the trust, respect, and love of my players. This was also an important component to the early success of my fledgling nonprofit organization, because I was an outsider who dressed like a city boy; talked with an urban accent; loved wolves, bears, bison; advocated for the environment and Yellowstone Country; and voted for Obama. In a community where many of the townspeople hated the very things I embodied, it was an audacious and steep climb to say the least! But because I had earned the trust of my players and their families, we were able to recruit an impressive number of students for our first Yellowstone Leadership Challenge and River Guardian Fly Fishing School. In fact, having my players at those first two programs laid down the foundation for what our organization and programs would be all about: heart, passion, and love.

The reason for our success? It wasn't that these young men came in with a take-charge leadership attitude; the reality was quite the opposite. My boys simply intermixed well with the other students from bigger towns downriver and up the road, many of whom came from challenging family situations and were what many organizations would classify as "at risk." Though the players from my team came from a relatively insular community (presenting a different set of challenges), they were unfazed by the diverse range of students from Livingston and Bozeman, who had clearly endured their fair share of adversity.

During one of the exercises on the first evening of the program, we went around the room and everyone shared why they were present for this three-day leadership challenge. To call my boys sheltered would be a gross understatement, so I was more than a little concerned about how they would react when the other students discussed their encounters with marijuana, alcohol, meth, physical and sexual abuse, and law enforcement. While their parents would likely have been horrified by what their sons were being exposed to, the boys simply rolled with it the way they did when we played the more physical team from Twin Bridges.

The Gardiner basketball players may not have been the toughest bunch of kids, but over time, we developed a scrappy, gritty, and determined resiliency that allowed us to compete every night we stepped on the hardwood. And on one glorious weekend—with a team that had graduated our six-foot-seven, three-time All State stud and was picked in the bottom half of our preseason bracket—our acquired toughness allowed us to share two nights none of us will ever forget: first we knocked off the number-seven team in the state (and our archrivals at home) in front of a packed house on Friday night; and then we journeyed west into the hostile confines of the Twin Bridges Falcons, where we played in a dirty scrum of a bloodbath (blood was literally pouring from the nose of one of my players) and knocked off the defending state champs, ending their twenty-three-game home-winning streak.

What does this story have to do with authentic leadership? *Everything.* We weren't the most talented bunch and we sure as hell weren't the toughest, but each member of this outstanding group of young men met me each day on the practice floor, on the bus, and in the locker room with an open heart and an open mind. I challenged them every day for four years to make the choice to be tough, tenacious, together, and resilient. And over time, that is exactly what they chose. This group wanted more out of their lives, and they recognized the tremendous power of *now.* They knew they weren't going to get this time back, so they made the choice to become resilient and unwavering, even when we got down ten or when another team made a run. They kept scrapping, clawing, and fighting until they got back into the game. And if we lost on a given night, it wasn't going to be from a lack of effort.

We did have one guy—PG3, Bennie B.—who was the undisputed leader of our team, but every other senior on the team led in his own way. For example, while affable and having a smile that could light up any gym, bravado simply wasn't Michael's style. I called him The Man-Child, as he was built like a grown man and had freakish athletic ability. But he wasn't your traditional leader; he led by his actions—by being deliberate, durable, and dependable. Then there was Jacob, Michael's frontcourt mate, who had started for me on our varsity squad since his sophomore year but hardly ever uttered a word. He was a silent assassin. Burly, built like a brick, always eager to please, and willing to put his body on the line, Jacob was the consummate teammate. Last but certainly not least was Special K. Kyle wasn't the fastest, strongest, quickest, or most prolific of our starters, but he is a testament to the power of now and the power of making positive choices. Bighearted, soft-spoken, and kind, Kyle went through a complete metamorphosis his senior year—he became a beast. He didn't handle the ball overly well and his shot was often sketchy, but his spirit overflowed. Statistically, he was the least significant of our five starters, but he had become the undisputed heart of our team.

How does that happen? How does a young man go from struggling on junior varsity to being a major contributor on varsity in one year, without putting in loads of off-season work to better his skills? It's simple: *by choice.*

Kyle was the last kid I would have expected to become our leader, as he seemed unmotivated and out of shape, and simply didn't appear to be "all in." But something changed in him his senior year. He still wasn't the fastest guy on the team, but he busted his butt at practice, making the allotted times in our suicide sprints (something he was unable or perhaps unwilling to do his first three seasons); he dropped thirty pounds; and he went through emotional changes too. Did I motivate him? Yes, to the best of my ability. Was that the catalyst for change? Not in the least. The change occurred the day Kyle looked himself in the mirror, didn't love what he saw, and decided he would take charge of his own life. It was the day he decided he would be audacious, become a leader in his own world, and ultimately, with much spirit and passion, shower his teammates with his authentic self. Kyle had discovered who and what he wanted to be and tapped into that sense of authentic self to positively impact his community of teammates, inspiring all of us to reach our own personal pinnacle of success. That is what authentic leadership looks like.

UNCERTAINTY SCAFFOLDING

I've observed similar transformations in my work with students on a very different but equally powerful platform. During my time serving as the founder and executive director of Yellowstone Country Guardians (YCG), my passion was all about the programs. While we didn't wield a mighty sword in terms of the number of programs we ran each year, I took great pride in our two flagship programs: the River Guardian Fly Fishing School and our Yellowstone Leadership Challenge (YLC). One of my goals with these two programs was to replicate the team environment we built with the basketball squad. But I knew from the get-go that this would be easier said than done, as we didn't have the opportunity to spend six days a week together, two of which included nighttime battles on the hardwood as we represented our community—a combination that ultimately formed bonds that transcended the sport we played.

While the time wasn't as substantial with my YCGers, our immersion in each program was focused, intense, and intentional. We may not have been battling it out against rival towns to become or remain the pride of our community, but battle we did, in a different—and perhaps more profound—way.

What could possibly be more important than joining forces in hopes of inspiring guardians, ambassadors, and champions of our environment? This was YCG's core mission. In a world where traditional environmentalism is seen as played out by most young people, we were striving to foster commitment to a wild Yellowstone by developing programs that spoke to every young person's need to feel purposeful and connected to *something* that matters. We became known for our energetic, nonconventional programing and fresh approach to environmental education—an approach that resonated with youth. Perhaps this edgy style contributed to the undeniable edge, both visible and audible, in the young people who exited our programs as fierce guardians of Yellowstone Country.

Two students who really stand out in this regard are Kelly and Cameshia.

Kelly and Cameshia attended the same high school and were in the same grade, yet they came from two vastly different environments. Kelly came from a stable home, was very shy, and didn't appear to have much in the way of confidence. Cameshia, on the other hand, had enough swaggy attitude for both of them. She lived with her grandma and rocked a very punk style. One of these young women was sheltered whereas the other had seen way too much for her age. One carried herself as an altar girl while the other was grinding her way through the juvenile probation program. One appeared to have few experiences with rebellion while the other had experimented with drugs. Nothing about these two indicated they would get along when they entered their first Yellowstone Leadership Challenge—let alone become leaders. But they joined me nonetheless, with an open heart and an open mind (as I'm hoping you are doing by reading the pages of this book).

One of the things I appreciate most about the young people who participate in a program like our three-day Yellowstone Leadership Challenge is the guts it takes to embark upon a journey with peers into the unknown. YLC participants were willing to throw caution to the wind and leap. Uncertainty is one of the biggest stumbling blocks we two-leggeds face in our journey to uncover meaning and purpose; very few worthwhile endeavors come without hardship and heartache, and sometimes heartbreak too. It simply comes with the territory of personal growth when slaying the dragons of uncertainty.

As a teacher of mine taught me, authentic leaders have the ability to build up *uncertainty scaffolding*. Uncertainty causes so much angst that it often paralyzes us, preventing us from pursuing what could be a meaningful and life-affirming endeavor. But it's only through having the balls to face the unknown that we can build the uncertainty scaffolding that ultimately allows us to weather the risk-taking storms of challenge and disappointment.

Perhaps it was having my basketball players in attendance the first year that set the tone, or perhaps it was simply the raw power of experiencing Yellowstone—a landscape like no other—but it was clear from the beginning that the young people in our program were yearning for a purposeful existence and something they could identify with on a visceral level. Each and every student embraced our program's core values: passion, attitude, courage, compassion, love, and respect.

Throughout the course of our multiday programs—immersed in a wilderness setting, exploring trails, walking rivers, whitewater rafting, and giving back through service projects that enhanced students' understanding of the natural world—a palpable sense of wonder pervaded the group.

While the ultimate goal was to provide a platform that would inspire passionate guardians of our wild rivers, wild mountains, and wildest species, the programs were about more than the environment and stewardship: the programs were about nurturing each student's sense of self while expanding their belief in what was possible. And it was clear from that first weekend that something transformative had taken place with Cameshia and Kelly. I could see immediately that they were both all in.

At the conclusion of that first YCG program, Cameshia gave me a massive bear hug with tears in her eyes. She had been profoundly touched, and vowed to participate in the River Guardian Fly Fishing School the following summer. This wasn't the first time I had seen a transformation like this; and though a multitude of students talked a good game about returning, I had more than my fair share of doubts about whether this young lady could hang with our five-day river school that was still months away. Even when Cameshia was the first to turn in her scholarship application the following spring, I still wavered in my belief that she would really push herself that far out of her comfort zone.

But she proved me wrong. The first day of the program, when one of our camp counselors came rolling into the Gardiner school parking lot with a Suburban full of Park High students, my eyes immediately locked with Cameshia's through one of its windows, smiles hijacking our faces.

For the next five days, an unwavering Cameshia pushed herself mentally, emotionally, and physically, wading rivers, hiking trails, learning to cast a fly rod, landing and releasing fish, immersing herself in watershed ecology—all the while demonstrating heart, perseverance, and perhaps the most authentic form of leadership I have witnessed in my work with young people on any level. I would say it was a profound experience for both of us; and to this day, Cameshia and I remain in contact.

She recently shot me this note on Facebook:

Hey, I hope you and your daughter are doing wonderful. I just ran into the core values from YCG while I was packin'. It made me realize how far I've come and how far I will go. Coach, you helped me grow into the person I am today. You brought me to the last step of changing my ways. You will always be my hero, not because of how many you helped or how many you will have the opportunity to help; but it will matter in the end who you helped. Honestly, I have no idea where I would be without YCG. Every time I set out my line or tie a fly to my rod, I lose myself in the river. I am more connected to my surroundings and always remember to give back. You showed me the qualities of who I really am. YCG will be in my blood and branded on my heart, along with the memories I shared. Thank you for everything.

> *Much love,*
> *Cameesh*

Cameshia didn't fit any predefined model of what someone participating in a youth fly-fishing school should look like. Quite the opposite. A grungy, rocker type with lots of swagger, tats, and 'tude, she was probably the antithesis of what one would expect of a student participating in a nature-based program—much less one focused upon fly fishing. But I'm not sure anyone got more out of their experience than Cameesh.

That is, with the exception of Kelly.

Quiet, shy, and unsure of herself, Kelly's high school journey didn't look like leadership was going to be in the cards. While book smart, she didn't participate in any sports (a big leadership factor in countless small towns across the country) nor did she gravitate toward the other traditional leadership roles within her school. During her first River Guardian Fly Fishing School, Kelly seemed to sit back and take in the experience. I wasn't entirely sure what to make of her reaction to our program, so you can imagine how shocked and stoked I was to receive the following testimonial from her:

Before I went to River Guardian Fly Fishing School, I really didn't like fishing because I thought it was boring and a waste of time; and I didn't know hardly anything at all about the watersheds of Montana, or the fish and bugs that inhabit it and are so very important to its livelihood. I also wasn't very motivated to keep the fish populations and the waters healthy or unpolluted. I just really didn't care. But after spending a week with one of the most influential, passionate, inspiring, special, and outstanding people I have ever met, Coach Mike, I now feel an unbreakable bond between myself and nature. I now am motivated completely to do my part to teach others about how to keep the watersheds of Montana and the world, and their populations of organisms, healthy so that the generations of people that come after us can also do their part—and hopefully the cycle will continue.

I also had the great opportunity of experiencing a whitewater rafting trip down the Yellowstone, I learned how I could enjoy a new hobby (fly fishing), I got to meet tons of fantastic people that I was beginning to think didn't exist anymore, I got to spend an entire day floating and fishing the Yellowstone River with an awesome professional guide, and I got to have some genuine fun.

When we arrived at the Gardiner school on Monday morning and Coach started talking to us, my brain felt so flooded at first that I was afraid I either wouldn't remember everything or that my brain wouldn't hold that much. But after a while, and with some practice, everything Coach told us started to make sense; and I found I could remember most of it. And when that happened, all I wanted to do was learn more—absorb more. I am so very thankful to God that He has blessed me with all the things in my life, that He blessed me with the opportunity to become a Yellowstone Country Guardian, and for our super Coach. Thanks, Coach!

Simply taking the time to write something so meaningful, powerful, and full of heart says everything about this young lady's character. But I still wasn't sure how far she would move into the role of being an authentic leader. By the time the next Yellowstone Leadership Challenge rolled around in October, ten weeks following her first YCG program, Kelly arrived at our retreat site with something she didn't carry two months earlier: confidence. She had conquered the dragon of uncertainty and was clearly ready to continue her journey of discovery and personal growth. Not only did she participate in the next year's programs, she ultimately became a force of positivity, gracefully impacting her peers and representing the core values of our organization.

Following her second River Guardian Fly Fishing School, Kelly shared these words:

> This being my second year at the River Guardian Fly Fishing School, I had kept some knowledge of what we learned and did last year with me; but I went with an open mind nonetheless, and learned all of what I had last year—plus one hundred times more. I met new people that I hadn't spoken to before, though we go to the same school. I branched out in my tastes in music, and I learned that it isn't right to judge someone on their clothing or their actions. (Just get to know them and you'll see a completely different person than you thought they were.) Who knows how long I would have gone on judging people if I had never met Coach; or if I hadn't decided to put on my brave face and go to these programs (when, secretly, I was kind of shaking inside), and be audacious enough to step outside of my comfort zone to try something I didn't think I would have any interest in.
>
> This River Guardian Fly Fishing School and the Yellowstone Leadership Challenge have been something to look forward to in the tumultuous (seemingly so) and unexciting life of going to Park High School every day while watching the snow fall gently on the lawn outside. These programs and Coach inspire me

*greatly to be someone I thought I could never be; to speak out
and not let other people run my life or my world; to realize that
I have a voice and that it is up to me and my peers to protect
the beautiful whitefish, Yellowstone cutthroat trout, the stone-
flies and mayflies, the plants that keep the rivers healthy, the
grizzly bears, the bison, the ecosystems in the world and the
lives that exist in them.*

*Coach has taught me actual respect for the life of every
organism. Whether it be a grizzly bear, whitefish, grasshopper,
rattlesnake, bison, or ant, I now have the utmost respect for all
life. Before I had the opportunity to participate in the RGFFS or
the YLC I had no idea what passion, attitude, love, compassion,
respect, or any of the YCG core values actually meant. I thought
I did, sure, but Coach has taught me what they mean; and now
I realize how closed-minded I was.*

To my surprise and delight, in the months following the program
that inspired Kelly to write the words that would serve as confirmation that
I was indeed on the right path, Kelly and Cameshia would join forces, and
without my knowledge, schedule a meeting with their principal to discuss
the formation of a new Yellowstone Country Guardians after-school program. We called them *El Presidente* One and Two. They were YCG's first
presidents, and they fought all odds by meeting with the higher-ups at
their school to establish a nontraditional after-school program in a very
traditional educational setting.

The metamorphosis of Kelly and Cameshia is a testament to what we
can become when we choose to be audacious—choose to buck expectations and shred the box society wants to place us into. No two students
were more unlikely trailblazers than Kelly and Cameshia, but in the end, no
two students had a greater impact on our organization, their peers, and
their community. They looked doubt in the face and took timid steps until
their stride strengthened, and the first layer of their uncertainty scaffolding was built. Already, these two young women have left an inspiring

legacy in the wake of their actions—and they're just getting started. *That's* authentic leadership in action.

THE GUTS TO BE VULNERABLE

Traditional leadership has always placed a special emphasis on personal growth to benefit oneself, but I would argue that authentic leadership is all about the onion approach: growing from the inside out in order to positively impact your community and then the world around you. This is my biggest issue with traditional self-help books: they often promote our "me" culture. Authentic leadership promotes the "we" culture, enhancing our sense of community and our ability to become difference makers while building prosperous, durable communities.

It doesn't matter what you are working toward; by all means, work toward *something* bigger than yourself. Whether it be a social, environmental, or political cause; an adventure; an entrepreneurial endeavor; or a team goal, find something that matters to you and has the potential to positively impact those around you.

I firmly believe one of the most overlooked characteristics of leadership—and a cornerstone of authentic leadership—is the ability to be vulnerable. You cannot be effective as an authentic leader if you don't embrace vulnerability. Though it is most often seen as a weakness in the traditional, old-school leadership model, finding the audacity to be vulnerable can serve as a potent difference maker when we move beyond the fear of judgment

How can your peers or those you are striving to connect with—and perhaps inspire—trust your intentions if you are guarded, reserved, and unwilling to express your fears and inner emotions? Regardless of the type of platform or cause, you will be ineffective in your mission if you don't get those around you—your peers, your teammates, your family, and your community—to believe in you as a leader. Without a cadre of dedicated cohorts who *truly* believe in the mission at hand, it will always be a long shot (not impossible but certainly beyond challenging) to inspire impactful and lasting change as a one-man or one-woman show. And while passion is a critical link to facilitating others to believe in whatever cause, mission, or program you are working to impact, vulnerability is the straw that stirs the drink, maintaining authenticity without getting caught up in the desired outcome.

It takes guts to be vulnerable. I can think of few characteristics that better represent what it means to be audacious than the willingness to be vulnerable. It's not easy to expose yourself to your peers; it's far easier to posture and keep the fear of failure bottled up. And that's fine if that's what helps you to endure the challenges that come with being a fallible human in a daunting world. But to truly inspire others and, more importantly, to become comfortable in your own skin, embracing vulnerability is one of your most powerful tools.

This, like so many other personality traits, comes easier for some than others. I've grown fond of saying my mouth's filter is very porous. Others would argue that I'm lacking a mouth filter altogether. From the onset, I tell all the young people I have the privilege of working with that my word is my bond; I say what I mean and mean what I say. It may not always be pretty, politically correct, or popular, but I believe this is what it looks like to lead from the heart. *I say what I mean and mean what I say*—it's a powerful mantra that can give you peace when things get dark.

Nobody wants to feel like a coward. Deep down, we *want* to stand up for something we believe in. If you take on this mantra—*I say what I mean and mean what I say*—you, too, can discover the power and sense of peace that comes with walking your talk and leading from the heart. But to do this authentically, you must adopt a willingness to be vulnerable.

Courageous and Beautiful *You*

During my first winter as a girls' high school basketball coach, I wrote the following on a chalkboard in the locker room: "If you have the courage to be authentic and original, you can therefore be audacious—and thus beautiful." That's what it looks like to be beautiful in my book. It's not about the perception of others, your hairstyle, your body composition, or your attire. These elements are, in many ways, out of our control. Are there things that we can do to enhance our appearance? Of course. But on many fronts, we are what we are.

I'm a six-foot-one, 160-pound gym rat who has obsessively worked out and pursued adventure since I was a boy. In the weight room (a place I love to grind), no matter how hard I get after it, I'm never going to be jacked and 220 pounds. I'm never going to be six foot four or look like a Greek Adonis—it's just not in the cards. This is my DNA, and I'm okay with that.

An audacious woman and friend recently shared a vulnerability that has caused her to struggle with self-esteem. In her early thirties, Sarah has taken up exercise for her release and sense of self. She is beautiful, lean, strong, and full of grace; and her spirit radiates authenticity and good-ness—a young woman that anybody would be blessed to know. While most people would look at her and see someone who is clearly very fit, like most of us, she struggles with one part of her physique: her thighs. It doesn't matter whether her concern is grounded in reality or not because this is what she believes. But the simple fact that she had the guts to share this with me impressed me tremendously.

Leadership has never been a quality Sarah would associate with her-self, but that hasn't stopped her from practicing the art of vulnerability. Instead, she's facing her fears and innermost demons by donning bike tights and, with a microphone to cheer on her students, leading a group of fitness enthusiasts as a spin instructor. Until recently, she had never worked out at a gym. She doesn't even own a road bike. She struggles with her body image (something that is common for men and women alike) and has a deep fear of speaking in public, but she decided to become a spin instructor anyway. And as her class increases in size each week, the grow-ing confidence in and acceptance of the body she was blessed with has been a beautiful thing to behold. Simply thinking about this always makes me smile. *Sarah is audacious as hell.*

The lesson here is simple: when we learn to accept who we are and what we are about, we truly begin to maximize our potential for living a full, meaningful, and spirited life.

I once wrote, "We can't change who we are, but we sure as hell can change what we're about." There are things about our past, our DNA, and the way our brain works that—like it or not, for better or for worse—simply make us who and what we *are*. But we can *always* change what we are *about*. And in the end, this is what truly matters anyway.

The young people I work with call me "Coach" as a term of endearment. Whether it be a group of inner-city teens, rural youth, basketball players, or participants in a leadership seminar, I go about coaching them up the same way each and every time: from the heart, with emotion, with sincerity, with vulnerability, and with nothing but love.

Humble, Approachable, and Real

I know I might sound like a broken record, revisiting the importance of vulnerability over and over, but the reason for this is two-fold. The first is pretty straightforward: I've always gravitated toward sharing my vulnerabilities in life and in roles of leadership. I find that it makes us humble, approachable, and real. If we ever hope to wear the leadership cap in life, we must embody these characteristics; otherwise, we are dictators—dead in the water.

When I stand up in the locker room after a tough loss and am willing to cry in front of my team—*with* my team—I'm taking the risk that some of them might see me as weak. But this is certainly a risk worth taking.

In the cost–benefit analysis that drives so many business endeavors (those driven by traditional leadership), the greater the risk—the vulnerability—the less sound the investment; but the two are separate when it comes to authentic leadership. In this case, the reward lies in being vulnerable, and it *far exceeds* the risk. When you share your emotions, you experience the joy, sense of peace, and fulfillment that comes with living authentically. And if someone thinks less of you for sharing your heart, to hell with them, as they aren't worth the salt in your tears.

For some of us, sharing our vulnerability comes naturally. I'm not sure if it's my DNA, genetics, or simply the way that I was raised, but I've always been an open book, wearing my emotions on my sleeve and sharing some of my heaviest demons, even with people I've just met. Right, wrong, or indifferent, that is simply me. So perhaps I have a vulnerability bias, but I've witnessed firsthand the potential, power, and potency that comes from exposing one's true self to others. A willingness to express vulnerability is a major step in what it looks like to be audacious.

The second reason I push the importance of vulnerability is because of the sagelike sermon of Brené Brown. Her TEDxHouston Talk, "The Power of Vulnerability," is one of the top-ten viewed TED Talks in the world.[2] In twenty minutes and sixteen seconds, Brené shares one of the most poignant speeches I've ever witnessed. She debunks the "suck it up" and "git 'er done" bullshit that is so pervasive in today's society—a society that seems to value the ability to "pull yourself up by your bootstraps" above all else. These idioms are not only preposterous but have likely caused more undue shame than any other accepted norms in our culture. Sometimes we are dealt a shitty set of circumstances that we *can't* grit and grind our way through without the help and support of our friends and family. It's more than okay to lean on the shoulders of those near and dear to us when the going gets tough; it's forward thinking and wise. And it's a key ingredient of the vulnerability recipe.

As I hammered home earlier, there is great importance in building up your uncertainty scaffolding, and having a willingness to expose yourself emotionally is a strong start. The *last* thing you want to do is succumb to society's false expectations by feeling shame for your struggles. *Your hardship is your treasure—your greatest gift*. As such, you do need to be aware of who you are showing your "gold" to and only trust responsible innkeepers. But how are you going to learn who is and who isn't a responsible innkeeper without first taking a risk?

Until we are ready to embrace the tremendous power that comes with being vulnerable, we will remain stuck in a place of inaction.

I spent the first thirty years of my life believing the world is black and white. In my own self-righteousness, for the vast majority of my life, I believed in right or wrong, good or bad, beautiful or ugly. I was the *king* of definites and absolutisms. Only when I embraced the tender soil of vulner-ability and a willingness to explore my own psychology did I begin to understand that there is *a lot* of gray in our world—that, in fact, most of life *isn't* definite or absolute.

We tend to make things definitive and absolute as a defense mecha-nism, because it allows us to avoid the vulnerability that comes with the uncertainty around us. This is a classic means of protecting ourselves from the uncomfortable and painful nature of vulnerability—a nature that can leave us feeling helpless and adrift.

While it is smart to have your guard up if you know you're about to get sucker punched, you must not let the few cowards who throw unan-nounced blows force you into living a guarded life. I cringe when I hear parents say to their kids, "suck it up" or "don't be a baby." Unintentionally, these parents are teaching children from a young age that it's not okay to be vulnerable. And while we can't blame parents for adopting a cultural norm without an understanding of the psychological implications that the "toughen up" / "git 'er done" mind-set inevitably leaves in its wake, we sure as hell can begin to challenge the societal norms that foster a society of fol-lowers who are not only insensitive but too afraid to be audacious and walk the path of an authentic leader. The first step in debunking this archaic mentality—a mentality that inspires this lack of empathy that plagues our society—is a desire to learn, adopt, and embrace the art of vulnerability.

To be vulnerable is to be authentic. To live vulnerably is to live authentically. It takes courage and audacity to embrace vulnerability and choose the path of authenticity. But first, we must be willing to enter a street fight with the demons of fear and shame.

FIGHT FEAR AND SHAME

Fear is a powerful, instinctual driver. It kept our ancestors alive during the Pleistocene period, when saber-tooth tigers, wolves, short-faced bears, and mastodons roamed the landscape. But in the twenty-first century, this response is more often than not overactive. Our fear today is that of failure, which is unlikely to result in our bodies being recycled into the food chain via the digestive tract of a hungry carnivore. The fear of shame is such a pervasive force that we are often paralyzed by it, unable to act intentionally and purposefully even if we wanted to. Though our inner voice may speak clearly of our purpose and mission, this fear of "not good enough" keeps us from pursuing the path that we know, deep inside, we are meant to follow. Our inability to slay the dragons of fear represents the ultimate killer of dreams.

To live authentically and with vulnerability, we must harness the power of intention. Only when we learn to live intentionally can we uncover the power of now and navigate the treacherous waters that encompass our fear of failure and our shame at not being good enough. This is the only way to unharness the reality of who we are and what we hope to become. But the fear of experiencing shame is so strong that we will go to polar extremes to avoid this messy encounter. I'm sure you've all heard of the term "conflict avoidance." Well, I would like to introduce you to a similar concept: shame avoidance.

Shame Avoidance

Everyone deals with shame and guilt in their own way, some healthily and some not. Sadly, escaping shame and guilt in the form of drugs and alcohol is commonplace in our culture. As someone who has struggled with "not good enough" syndrome and Piece of Shit-itis (POS-itis) over the years, I'm very aware of the pervasive and overwhelming nature of shame. Rather than turning to drugs and alcohol, however, I've always turned to exercise and outdoor pursuits in the form of the gym, bike rides, backcountry hikes, and river escapades. Perhaps my unquenchable thirst for exercise and adventure—an "addiction" that has put excessive wear and tear on my joints—has been driven in part by shame avoidance.

Why is shame such a powerful force? First and foremost, we need to acknowledge that it is not unusual to experience shame, so don't trip. Shame is completely natural—something we all feel—unless one is a narcissist or sociopath, who lacks the ability to experience empathy or connection to others. In the positive-negative equation (front of hand, back of hand—from chapter 1), the negative is that uncomfortable feeling of shame or guilt; the positive is that you likely aren't a narcissist or sociopath. For those of us who have a conscience (which is the vast majority of our society), shame is triggered when we act in a way that is not in alignment with our core values, our beliefs, our character—that which we know to be "right," or just.

That said, I speak to the power of shame from the heart and with humility. For much of my life, a fear of facing shame represented a formidable foe, having a crippling effect at times. It wasn't until I met my Socrates, Dr. John Wimberly, and uncovered the guts to sit down in his counseling office—and "guts" is not too strong a word—that I began to unearth the root of my shame.

My editor teasingly refers to me as her "Favorite 'Adequate' Author," an endearment that came about during our work together on *Grizzlies On My Mind*. While I can now smile as I write this from the roost of my favorite coffee shop, where I sit each morning for my daily writing sesh, this wasn't always the case. The very idea that my writing skills are beyond an "adequate" level—a barely average, treading-water level of talent—is still something that I wrestle with, even after publishing many articles, my first book, and now my second. How could a guy like me get from a serious learning disability to *this*?

I recognize now that my learning style simply wasn't a good fit for our traditional cookie-cutter approach to academia. But at the time, having a learning disability that required a different approach to learning just meant I was probably "less than" or lacking in intelligence—a truth I used to believe. Early testing (in first grade) erroneously concluded I did not have a learning disability, so my struggles in school seemed to be without explanation. And "just try harder" wasn't really an option, as I simply wasn't learning at the same pace as my fellow classmates.

Fortunately, more advanced testing during my junior year of high school revealed that I not only had a learning disability but one that was no joke. As an eleventh grader, I had the reading comprehension of a third grader. While the diagnosis explained my struggles in the classroom, the damage to my confidence and self-esteem had been done. Mix in my shattered dreams on the basketball court, and there was a time when it took every fiber of resiliency I could muster to avoid disappearing into shame and despair altogether.

After enduring many ups, and downs, I ultimately found my way to college and earned—believe it or not—two degrees, graduating with high honors on the dean's list from North Idaho College and the University of Montana. These degrees paved the way for my growing interest in advocacy, writing, and speaking. And over the course of the last decade, I've written dozens of articles, essays, and op-ed pieces for regional and national publications. I've witnessed my first book reach number one on the best-seller list of a bookstore that was recently ranked number fourteen on a list of the top independent bookstores in the world. I've founded and run a nonprofit organization and given over a thousand presentations all over the country—most often without the aid of notes. How are these achievements possible for someone who spent the vast majority of his life convinced he was intellectually inadequate?

Whenever I feel my confidence wavering, I try to remember: *our inability to slay the dragons of fear represents the ultimate killer of dreams.* And this life of speaking, advocacy, and yes, writing, is the dream I want to claim as my own. So, I live *with* my demons instead of allowing them to dictate my future. I acknowledge that I may *always* struggle to believe that I am worthy of the testimonials I receive about my ability to inspire, but I've learned to embrace the gift that these testimonials represent. Even after I signed my first book deal, when speaking over the phone with the editor my publisher assigned me, I exposed my vulnerability by sharing my fear about whether or not my writing was good enough; in fact, I shared this with her multiple times through the editing process. But after reading my book (and falling in love with it, I might add), she concluded: "You can most certainly write, my man. In fact, you have become my Favorite 'Adequate' Author."

Unjustified Shame

Let's return for a moment to the issue of the classic brick-and-mortar education model.

Our traditional classroom setting likes to pigeonhole students based on whether or not they fit a preconceived "model" of how students should learn and how they should then be judged (graded) within this inflexible structure. This is not only outdated but *asinine*. I don't want to lay the blame on teachers, but I *will* put it on the system. Something is clearly wrong when it's the *students* who are made to feel stupid because their learning style isn't conducive to a formulaic prototype. I'm thirty-five years old—clearly not a kid anymore—and even now, I struggle with the shame from bygone school days, wrongfully falling back to the "less than" story I so often told myself simply because I didn't get math or learn verbally.

Last year, after I spoke in front of a packed house at *the* bookstore of Montana bookstores, Country Bookshelf, my father overheard one of the audience members say, "Can you believe he just spoke for over an hour without any notes and without once uttering an 'uh'? He was flawless." Yet the fallout from our traditional learning system still made me question my cerebral prowess and ability to make it in the author/speaker world. That is messed up. If it weren't for my scrappy, gritty, and resilient personality (and the unwavering support and confidence of my family and friends)— if I had listened to the voice of shame alone and not had the audacity to duke it out with vulnerability—I sure as hell would not have accomplished what I have today.

The traditional education model is just a microcosm of a much larger picture: a culture fueled by conformity rather than freedom, fear rather than courage, boxes rather than horizons. How can a limited set of standards even *begin* to measure a student's immeasurable potential? Can the extent of Yellowstone's beauty, biodiversity, and grandeur be captured in a postcard? The results of today's rigid and standardized testing represent little more than a snapshot of human potential in a system that fails to adapt to a diverse population of learning styles. Armed with this understanding, it would behoove you to refuse to let anyone or anything define that which you are capable of. Your potential is only bound by your imagination and belief in yourself.

Dr. Wimberly has helped me to recognize what he calls "justified" and "unjustified" guilt, and I would add shame to this equation. My high school basketball team played in a tournament last summer, and the fact of the matter is that we aren't very good. We've gone from a state title contender to a 2-18 record in just two years. And this year's prospects aren't all that promising, but we are young and continue to keep our eyes on the prize, getting better each day we hit the hardwood. With that said, I've never hollered at my boys in the locker room after a game for falling short on the scoreboard; that would be like you beating yourself up for not being six foot if you are five foot three. That is out of your circle of influence—out of your control. I believe the same can be said about my basketball team. If we lose a game because we shoot 30 percent, that is simply because we don't shoot the ball worth a lick. But that is very different from losing a game because we aren't putting forth the effort.

One of my players was frustrated after one of these losses because he shot the ball poorly throughout the game. He apologized, clearly feeling shame for his dismal shooting percentage. My response was easy:

"Did you try to miss those shots?"

Befuddled, he replied, "Of course not, Coach."

"Did you try to make each shot?" I pressed.

"Of course I tried to make every shot, Coach."

"Well, my man," I said, "it sounds like you have absolutely nothing to apologize for. Let it go, big boy."

He was experiencing unjustified shame.

Effort and skill/ability/giftedness are very different things. I won't hesitate to light into my boys if we aren't getting after the 50/50 balls (what we call loose balls that are up for grabs), hustling, or giving maximum effort. But what kind of coach would I be if I chewed them out for struggling to score the ball? I don't think it would be any different from faulting a kid for being thick boned, light skinned, or short in stature—characteristics beyond his or her control.

If I, as a father, let my daughter stay up late on a school night so I can watch a basketball game or hang with friends, then I have a justified reason for feeling shame if she's dragging and cranky the next morning. If you blow off a friend in need so you can go kick it with your crew, you have reason to feel guilt. If you sit by idly while a peer is bullied, you have enough justifiable reasons for shame to fill your belly. If you fail to speak up and out as a voice for the voiceless, then your shame is valid. But shame caused by what others think or perceive of us is the demon we must come out swinging against.

Tests kicked my ass in school, for example. No matter how prepared I was, I struggled (and truth be told, I rarely prepared in high school out of a fear that to do so and fail would just prove my inadequacy). Nothing pushed my panic button more than preparing for a test and feeling like I had things dialed in only to see the questions in a different format than what I had studied (actually, *memorized* would be a more accurate description). What may have been a little curveball for other students was enough to send my mind spiraling into a cascade of self-doubt and POS-itis.

It wasn't until I was a thirtysomething man battling an ailing Achilles tendon—in limbo, fighting both the wear and tear I had put on my body and the often crippling nature of ankylosing spondylitis—that I reached out to Dr. Wimberly. Through his sagelike wisdom and laid-back style, "Wimbo" would ultimately have a profound impact on my journey and my sense of self. He showed me that it took courage to seek out a counselor because I had to admit that I couldn't navigate the tricky and sometimes treacherous waters of self-discovery myself. And while those who are closest to us may be able to provide empathy, compassion, and support, it doesn't mean they are equipped with the right tools to fix the leak in our vase of self-worth. The opinion that one is weak if they need to speak with a psychologist is not only played out but destructive—unjustified shame.

Fortunately, I suspected then what I now know: the idea that we can always pull ourselves up by our bootstraps and get through life on our own is overhyped, misinformed, and quite frankly, bullshit. Though we live in a society that values the story of heroism, where a person can overcome all odds by digging deep and getting it done, the story seldom plays out so simply in the real world. These tales cherry-pick the heroic segments and leave out the vulnerability, the imperfection, the struggle. And far too often, this emphasis on going it alone lends itself to a culture where we are discouraged to open up (wear our hearts on our sleeves) and made to feel weak if we seek help from others—be they family, a friend, or a counselor. It is long overdue that we debunk this myth.

METAMORPHOSIS AND THE WHAT HAPPENED BUBBLE

My sense of identity, purpose, and what others thought of me was rocked to the core that summer I was relegated to a walking boot cast for the fourth time in seven years. Friends often referred to me as the "Guru of Go" for my propensity to work ten- to twelve-hour days (eight hours of which were spent rowing the waters of the mighty Yellowstone as a fishing guide), followed by a massive climb up from Gardiner to Mammoth Hot Springs on my bike. Losing the ability to do the work caused a crushing identity crisis in itself. At the same time, I was unable to pursue the activities that fueled my soul, provided spiritual sustenance, and released the endorphins that allowed me to function at a high level—leading hikes, facilitating environmental education in Yellowstone, guiding people on fly-fishing trips, giving high-energy presentations, coaching kids up with passion and zeal. The most challenging component of my physical struggles during this time was how deeply my sudden lack of mobility changed my sense of self. But I also knew that, even though the physical struggles were out of my control, I could eventually learn to master the art of acceptance with the guidance and coaching of someone solid.

We all go through a metamorphosis at some point; this is just how life works. But I had been forced into transformation and catharsis more dramatically and unexpectedly than most people my age—at least that's how it felt. This, however, is one of the gifts of adversity: it opens up the window of awareness and inspires metamorphosis. Regardless of how shitty the hand we've been dealt, *the ultimate measure of our character is how we choose to respond in the face of adversity.* And I knew during that tough time that if I had any chance of finding acceptance of my situation, I needed a damn good coach to guide me.

One of the most powerful tools that Wimbo shared with me during our odyssey together is the "What Happened Bubble," or WHB. (You'll get a chance to practice this yourself in one of this chapter's exercises.) It's pretty simple, really; but like so many things that are simple, the results are quite profound. Here's where the first bubble ("What Happened") begins:

Largely because I grew up consumed by our sports culture, where one's ability to "suck it up" and "push through pain" is what it looks like to "be a man," when I lost the ability to power through, I encountered my own demons of self-worth. While I don't think it's admirable or courageous *now* when I hear about a muscle-head hockey player finishing his shift with a punctured lung, concussion, or broken femur (machismo behavior that is ultimately self-destructive), throughout my teens, twenties, and up until my perfect storm of physical ailments, I prided myself on my ability to push through more pain than the next guy.

With the exception of the little hitch I have in my stride (following a sports-related hip surgery last year), you wouldn't peg me as someone who has anything wrong physically. I'm lean, fit, and full of life. And yet, for most of the last decade, I've battled the aches and pains that come with a rheumatoid arthritic condition. The clients I've guided, the kids I've lit up in the gym, the friends who've lagged behind on a climb, and the people I've passed in a bike race would probably never know that I do what I do in *a lot* of pain. I've simply become accustomed to its companionship.

To do the things I love, I've been forced to grit my teeth and get in Zen mode to overcome the sometimes-piercing agony that screams at my body to stop. This is part of the reason I've always taken a sick day following any particularly grueling endeavor. The adventure itself may be a ball buster, but combined with the pain, I'm more often than not forced to deal with the consequences the following day. But this day of rest, in and of itself, always causes another struggle for me: rather than feeling a sense of pride for doing what I do with a pain level that could justifiably keep me on the sidelines, I've beat myself up for needing to restore myself—unjustifiable guilt and, quite frankly, machismo stupidity in action. With time, however, I've come to better understand the essential importance of rest, relaxation, and recovery.

So when I was forced to pull the plug on a summer full of speaking, guiding, and environmental education gigs because of that ailing Achilles tendon that has become my "Achilles heel"—literally and metaphorically—the storm of POS-itis came crashing in with a vengeance. I liked to call it "Tropical Storm Achilles," and destructive it was. (You've heard me talk of this several times already.) But anytime we experience something that alters our quality of life and ability to pursue that which fill us up, there is bound to be fallout.

I didn't know then and still don't know now what the future of my legs looks like. But I can say, with coaching from Wimbo, that I've changed the way I think about the uncertainty, no longer snowballing and catastrophizing the future, and have developed the ability to turn my focus to what I *can* do and control instead.

Not too long ago, my beautiful six-year-old daughter, Kamiah—my world and my mission—pointed her little index finger at Sinopah, a powerful peak in the Two Medicine region of Glacier National Park, where we had been camping for the weekend. I had climbed a neighboring peak years earlier, and I shared with her the fact that I had planned a summit attempt on my birthday (in October) two years earlier—just months before an Achilles flare that would be followed by the discovery of a labrum tear in my left hip and femoroacetabular impingement syndrome (FAI), requiring surgery in both hips. It had been torn cartilage in my right wrist that had sent me on an escapade of peak-bagging adventures to begin with, as the injury prevented me from rowing for fly-fishing clients the remainder of that fall.

I had climbed five ten-thousand-plus-foot peaks during the month of September, and Sinopah would have been my last big climb of the season.

But snow flurries and icy terrain kept me from attempting a summit bid that day. Since then, my desire to reach the summit of the peak held sacred by the *Amsskapii Piikunnii* (Southern Piegan of the Blackfoot Confederacy) has haunted me, as I could never have known when I opted to play it safe what would unfold over the course of the following two and a half years.

When my daughter suggested we come back to climb Sinopah for my birthday this year, I had to be very honest, as I always am. I don't believe I need to shelter her from life's difficulties when I have the great opportunity to teach her about resiliency—an opportunity where she can witness the man she loves most in this world enduring challenges with what I hope she one day sees as grace. So I told her that my legs aren't up for a big climb right now.

With a saddened look on her face, she asked, "Dadda, when are your legs going to work like they used to?"

Not an easy question to answer with Sinopah stoically standing in full view.

"Kamiah," I answered, "I'm not sure my legs are *ever* going to work like they used to. I don't like that and I know you don't like it either, and that's okay. But I'm killing it as a dad, yeah?"

"Yes," she nodded. "You are the best dadda in the world."

I went on to explain that while I'd been dealt some challenges, what is most important is *not* how we carry ourselves during good times—times of abundance—but how we carry ourselves during the hard times.

"And think about this, Kamiah: we are finding new ways to explore the wild country we both love. Heck, you've now camped in Grand Teton National Park, Yellowstone National Park, and Glacier National Park—our nation's three greatest national parks—in the past two weeks! I'd say we are adapting just fine and with much panache."

As always, Kamiah's smile lit my heart afire.

So what does all of this have to do with metamorphosis and the "What Happened Bubble?"

When we recognize that it is not *what* happens to us that matters but how we react to these happenings, our perception changes. When we begin to embrace the power we have within us to *choose* how we are going to look at life, we revise the script and tell a vastly different story.

Dr. Wimberly often spoke to me about the lens through which we see life. When we are sleep deprived, sick, tired, stressed, and worn-out, our lens is fogged and darkened; we cannot see our reality clearly. And we have to recognize and acknowledge this—*accept* it. During these adverse times, we have to work that much harder and be that much more intentional if we hope to become an authentic leader.

The power of the "What Happened Bubble" is in both its simplicity and its universal reach. Regardless of your challenge, the "What Happened Bubble" can help you deal with it in a positive manner. You can either write it out or visualize in your mind. Here's how it works:

1. The first bubble represents what happened in your life—the facts.

2. The second bubble, on the outside of the first, represents your reaction to the "What Happened Bubble"—the feedback from your emotional mind.

3. The third bubble, beside the second and on the outside of the first, represents your thoughtful interpretation of what really happened— the feedback from your wise and logical minds. (And by the way, the key that unlocks the power of the "What Happened Bubble" is found when we tap into the wise and logical minds.)

Through my studies and hard work with Dr. Wimberly, I've come to understand that we have an emotional mind, a wise mind, and a logical mind. Because of the passionate, unfettered nature of the emotional mind, it behooves us to tap into the wise and rational minds—our grounding minds—as often as possible, especially in the midst of challenging times. But this is much easier said than done. Most of us get so wrapped up in the spiral of our emotions—our immediate reactions— during times of angst that it can be hard to step outside the cyclone to access our wise and rational minds. With focused practice, however, we can get there.

I'm going to use my basketball team as an example of a time I've used the WHB to help a group of young athletes see the world through a clear lens. After a particularly hard loss, I called a team meeting in which I sat down with my players and introduced the WHB:

1. Bubble one (what happened): We got our asses kicked. We shot 30 percent and lost our tenth straight game. We turned the ball over too much and had a difficult time breaking the press. We missed eight layups and shot eight of twenty-two from the free-throw line.

2. Bubble two (emotional mind): Our immediate response? *We suck. We don't have any talent. We are no good and never will be. We can't compete with anyone. We are inadequate.*

3. Bubble three (wise and logical minds): What's our overall interpretation of the experience? *The other team was more talented than us. We aren't a good shooting team. They outrebounded us. We hustled our butts off but didn't win the battle of the 50/50 balls. We didn't execute our stuff.*

Do you see the difference between bubbles two and three? The self-talk that comes with the emotional mind is harsh, judgmental, defeatist, and crushing, clearly leading to a strong case of POS-itis if that talk becomes habitual—which it often does. The self-talk spurred by the third bubble, however, is realistic and honest without the punitive disdain for oneself—a much more realistic and grounded view.

Life is hard enough as it is. If you choose to take charge and lead from the heart, there will be times when haters attempt to bring you down; but *you* don't need to be your own worst enemy. If your self-talk isn't helpful, *change it.* I've found the WHB to be a powerful arrow in the quiver of dealing with adversity, but you may have another method that works better for you. However you choose to deal with life's challenges, you must learn to drown out the noise and listen to your conscience—that which you *know* to be right. Then and only then can you lead from the heart, and experience the fulfillment and purpose that comes from being an authentic leader.

CORE VALUES

So what encompasses the ingredients of your platform—what you are about and what you wish to become? Two words: core values.

For me, it's an easy question to answer: I'm about love and character; being a dedicated father; and being resilient, scrappy, and durable. I'm also about family; and about being an activist, a Yellowstone Country Guardian, and a game changer. I stand for providing my daughter with love, goodness, and stability; for Yellowstone, wild places, and wild species; for social justice, equality, biological integrity; and for that which I believe to be right and just.

When someone asks me what I do for a living—a difficult question for a guy with many slashes (father/advocate/speaker, etc.)—I simply answer, "I'm an inspirer of people." I didn't graduate from the University of Montana with a degree in inspiration, of course. And I can't say I stood for many of the things I just shared when I was sixteen years old. It was by the time I was twenty-one that some of these values began to emerge; and by the time I was twenty-five, I had a solid grasp on what I stood for and what I was about. But then, just weeks after my twenty-eighth birthday, my daughter was born and my world changed forever. Now, there is nothing in this world that I stand for with more passion and fire than being a father to my audacious little girl. Case in point:

I've always been one to run my mouth. And as I shared earlier in this chapter, my mouth's filter is very porous—if a filter exists at all. So my mouth has been known to get me in trouble from time to time.

Since I was a boy, I've prided myself on standing up for what I believe to be right. But as we grow, mature, and develop our "muchness" (as the great Joyce Bender, a leader in the disability community, would say), what we are willing to tolerate and what we stand up for changes. I've never been one to tolerate masochistic, antiwomen posturing, for example, but now, as a father, my sensitivity to this kind of talk has reached a climax.

Take a recent day when I was finishing up my workout at the gym. I couldn't help but get edgy and perhaps a bit belligerent in the locker room as three machismo men in their early twenties bantered back and forth, loudly talking a bunch of contrived and played-out sexist nonsense. As the proudest dad west of the Mississippi, my blood was already boiling. But when one of the knuckleheads started saying that girls wearing skimpy clothes, liquored up while walking through nasty neighborhoods, are basically putting targets on their backs, well, things got real testy, real quick. It's safe to say I threw caution to the wind.

Standing in my purple boxer briefs and baller socks (with purple, pink, and lime-colored stripes that Kamiah loves), I went into what my friends like to call "Mamba Mode." I got into the face of the most brazen in the bunch to let him and his cronies know "as the single dad of a beautiful little girl, talk like that makes me want to knock somebody the hell out." (Okay, not my most diplomatic moment nor how I would encourage you to handle contentious interactions, but I think you get the point.) I then gave all three of these intellectual lightweights a little lesson on the realities of life and the struggles of young people—especially young *women*—out in the real world, outside of the Pollyanna bubble of Bozeman, Montana; and I warned them to be *much* more thoughtful before running their ignorant mouths in the future.

So that illustrates another cause I stand for: we cannot accept any culture in which girls and women are objectified by boys and so-called "men." It's long overdue that we men of the world rise up and unite against derogatory, inflammatory, and misogynistic language and attitudes toward our daughters, wives, sisters, mothers, friends.

My favorite commercial in this year's Super Bowl (where my Hawks lost a heartbreaker in dramatic fashion) was an Always advertisement that challenged the old adage "like a girl." The ad attempts to shatter the stereotype of "run like a girl," "throw like a girl," and "fight like a girl" by showing young girls running, throwing, and fighting with strength, grit, and courage—not only refreshingly beautiful but so moving that I made my father rewind it so I could share it with Kamiah. Then I rewatched the commercial teary eyed, observing my six-year-old daughter so focused and mesmerized by the words of young girls—her peers—who were not yet scarred by the "like a girl" phrase.

We are bombarded by so much patriarchal nonsense and rampant misogyny in movies, in music, on TV, and in advertisements that this propaganda has become accepted as a cultural norm in far too many corners of our world. This simple but powerful ad told the real story: to do things "like a girl" is beautiful—*and* audacious. It's far beyond time for us boys and men to become more in tune with our feminine side and to advocate on behalf of that which is just, fair, and right—a world in which women receive equal pay for equal work, are treated with the dignity and respect they *always* deserve, and are never made to feel "less than" for their gender. Women make the world go around. We owe it to them to wage a war on abuse (verbal and physical), sexual assault (such cowardly bullshit), and our image-based society (from topical appeal to one fashioned by character and heart).

●●●●

Whether you are fifteen, twenty-five, or ninety-five, don't fret or expect to have all the answers. Life is a process, and each phase we pass through is akin to a season: some last longer than others while some are quite ephemeral in nature, but each season passes eventually. The foundation is what matters most to your life's journey—what ultimately determines what *you* are about.

As an individual, father, and basketball coach, I always develop a list of core values to serve as the foundation for my life, the life of my daughter, and the lives of my basketball family. Each day, as Kamiah and I drive our car or ride our bikes to her school, she rattles off our eleven core values like it's nothing; it's just part of our morning routine. And each evening, as part of her bedtime routine, we review one of our core values—what it means and how it fits into our daily life. Combine this with our positive-visualization exercise, three books, a five-minute dental-care routine, and three nightly songs that I sing over and over until she fades for the night, and it's safe to say that my little one is wrapped in a cocoon of love, stability, and predictability by the time she drifts off to sleep.

I share this because you, too, can create your very own cocoon of routine and core values. You just need to start building your platform.

Whether you are formally aware of them or not, we all have a set of values that guide us. If this weren't true, we would grab whatever we want from the mini mart, sneak our way into the movie theater, cheat our way through exams—simply live life doing our own thing, without regard for how our actions impact others. But it is in our nature, as descendants of tribal peoples, to care about others in our community, and to care about being accepted and honored in that community. So we behave a certain way, act a certain way, and talk a certain way—to maintain the good health and solidarity of the tribe.

I'm sure you've all heard some version of this saying: "Character is what one does when no one else is looking." Well, what drives that—our conscience? Yes. But I believe it is more than that: it is the core values we've been taught, learned, or adopted, as children and throughout our lives.

I've always believed that the word carries unmatched power; this is why I challenge you to be impeccable with yours—to *say what you mean and mean what you say*. But there is something of even greater significance about the *written* word. (Perhaps this is what has drawn me to a career as a writer.) Though our spoken word ultimately drifts away in the wind, the written word lives on. It's one thing to set a goal, to have a thought, or to dream aloud, but it's another thing entirely to put that vision on paper. Putting your words down on paper represents a formal action toward permanence—like the signing of a marriage certificate once the vows have been verbally exchanged. Then and only then do we begin to *live* that thought, goal, idea, or dream. Because the power of the written word is binding. What better covenant can you make with yourself than to draft your very own set of core values?

Practice Exercises:
CHANGE FOR THE BETTER

I shared in this chapter my belief that we can't change who we are but we sure as hell can change what we are about. While it's nice to know who we are and where we come from, the *real* story—the real *truth*—lies in what we are about. So much of life is out of our control (our DNA, our family, where we come from), but these aren't the things that ultimately matter. What does matter? What we are *about*.

Have you ever heard the saying "those who stand for nothing will fall for anything"? If you were to apply this saying to yourself, what would be your platform(s)? What is it that you stand for? If a handful of words don't immediately come to mind, you've got homework to do.

EXERCISE #1: YOUR CORE VALUES

This exercise is perhaps one of the most powerful I will share with you. So give yourself the patience, time, and space you deserve by setting aside at least thirty minutes in a place where you feel inspired and won't be bothered. And know from the start that this will be an ongoing and evolving process.

1. Sit down in a place of quiet reflection, with a pen and some paper in hand and a willingness to be open and honest with yourself. It may be helpful to do some belly breathing to tame the brain train and set your intention (see the exercise in chapter 1).

2. Contemplate what really matters to you, and write down what comes to mind. It can be anything—micro and macro, conceptual

and realistic—but try to lean toward the bigger picture of your life's story, your legacy. For example, who makes up your inner circle of influence (family, friends, significant other, pets, work colleagues)? Why are they important to you? What about your outer/larger circle of influence—the bigger causes? Are you a member or volunteer of any organizations, and why did you choose these organizations? You may come up with half a dozen things or you may come up with thirty, but most importantly, *start*. (I'm convinced that once you do, you will have a hard time putting this exercise down.) And keep it a stream-of-consciousness effort, as we'll be getting more specific later.

3. Now go to a fresh page and consider what you are about *now,* in the present. In other words, what are the qualities and skills that are unique to you? Are you kind, generous, outspoken? How would the people in your inner circle describe you? How do you see yourself? (List the good *and* not so good.) What do you admire about the people you deem important or influential? Remember to be honest.

4. Turn the page and take a trip into the future to explore what you *wish* you were about. What needs improvement? What part of you would benefit from expansion or further development? What have you been afraid to try? Who are your heroes and why? Keep the voice of judgment out of this; this exercise is all about *action*, and applying judgment only hinders moving forward.

5. It's time to take a step back for a broader view. Go back to the three pages you just worked on; you may even wish to spread them out in front of you, so you can take a look at all of them at once. Do you see any similarities between these three lists— unifying concepts, themes, or people? Start a fourth list of commonalities.

6. Now that you have all of the ingredients for your personal legacy recipe, are you ready to set your current core values? With your fourth list in hand and your editorial eye engaged, see if you can whittle down these concepts to single words like *Compassion*, *Outreach*, *Family*, and so on. And try to keep the list within reason—a minimum of four and a maximum of ten—as you want to be able to remember it easily. Here are Kamiah's top four core values (listed in order of importance): Love, Family, Nature, and Character. And over the course of the last few years, we have added Compassion, Gratitude, Kindness, Integrity, Courage, Respect, and Honesty.

7. You've done it! You've started to build the platform of your legacy. If you really want to make it official, go to a computer to spice up your core values with some baller fonts. Then print out two versions—a pocket-size for your wallet and a larger one for your bathroom mirror—and review your values until you can rattle them off. Make them a part of your daily routine so they become second nature, ingrained in you.

8. Revisit your list of core values regularly. As you saw with Kamiah's list in step 6, these values expand and evolve—and should continue to do so throughout your life. The quest to live authentically is a lifelong endeavor.

"Authenticity, humility, and compassion. These are the characteristics I strive to embody and look for in the people I surround myself with." This is part of a quote I wrote for the first group of high school girls' basketball players I had the opportunity to coach. When I wrote it, I hadn't written down my core values yet, but it was a fantastic place to start. That's all I'm asking with the exercise above—for you to start somewhere and keep plugging away.

One thing that might be helpful is to bring in a partner—someone who can lovingly guide you if you fall off your core-values wagon. With Kamiah and me, when either of us is not representing our core values, we remind each other of what we are about. Awhile back, when I was battling a slight case of road rage, honking at the car in front of me to get moving, Kamiah quickly called me out: "Dadda," she said, "that was not kind. Remember kindness is one of our core values."

There is nothing I love more than being checked by my six-year-old.

EXERCISE #2: THE WHAT HAPPENED BUBBLE

Another way to keep your core values in check is to examine adversity through the What Happened Bubble. (If you need a refresher on this, go back to page 104.) Are you enlisting your core values when you are confronted with challenges? Do you find that you're getting too emotional—too caught up—in the moment? Let's apply a WHB to something in your own life:

1. Find a quiet space where you can reflect uninterrupted. I recommend having a pen and a piece of paper so you can review your progress, though you can also do this exercise mentally. (I'm going to proceed as if you have chosen to write this down.)

2. Think about something that recently challenged you, then write down the facts of what happened in your first bubble—the "What Happened" bubble. (You don't need to make a bubble literally; you can just list the facts in the same way I did earlier in the chapter.)

3. What was your immediate reaction to this challenge—how did it make you feel? List your emotions, and be thorough. (This is your emotional mind coming through.)

4. Now sit back and take a look at the first and second bubbles—

the first and second group of things you listed. Engage the help of your wise and logical minds to interpret (or examine) what *actually* happened and the reasons behind it.

5. Use your answers from the third bubble (the wise and logical minds) to make a plan for the next time you encounter a challenge like this. What would you do differently? What would you do the same?

6. Last but not least, *let it go*. You are a fallible human—*forgive yourself*. Breathe in and out to affirm the present moment, and recite your core values if you have them. Then *move on* with your life's work and your legacy.

CLOSING THOUGHTS

While there is certainly a time and a place to fake it till you make it, authenticity is a potent ingredient in the recipe for living a life that matters. There is only one of *you*, and you only get *one* chance to walk this journey; so you might as well make the most of each day. Harness your potential to make a positive impact on the world around you; be an authentic leader.

When we embrace the path of the authentic leader, we unleash our higher self and tap into the power of being audacious.

We live during a time of unmatched materialism, greed, indulgence, and ego. This is not only wreaking havoc on our planet and other species, it is leading to disconnected communities where few individuals prosper while many more flounder. At one time intact and functional, our ecological and societal fabric is now unraveling at the seams.

But the authentic leader strives to remedy this by living intentionally, purposefully, and in alignment with his or her core values, ultimately spreading much *aloha* spirit—respect, love, kindness, compassion, and goodness. This is his or her *chosen* path, but it isn't an easy one; it takes much heart and courage—the guts to be vulnerable, humble, and real. It's an ongoing battle against fear and shame, and a host of societal "norms" embraced by followers (*not* leaders).

A key component to authentic leadership: *say what you mean and mean what you say.* Though it's tempting to tell people what they *want* to hear, without an "all in" intention to follow up, it is a surefire way to burn bridges—break connections—whether they be with friends, family members, teachers, coworkers, or employers. To be an authentic leader, you must be impeccable with your word, intentional with your choices, and purposeful in your actions. But again, the beautiful thing about this is that these are all choices *you* have the power to make.

Pursue the path less traveled, blaze your own trail, chart your own course, strive and keep striving. Don't stop until you reach your own personal mountaintop, and even then, keep striving. *Never* stop showering the world around you with love and humble grace.

The Be Audacious mission is simple, "inspiring people to pursue their passion, live a life that matters, and change the world." If enough of you choose the path of an authentic leader, I assure you that our world will never be the same.

4

Embrace Criticism

To avoid criticism, say nothing, do nothing, be nothing.
—Robert Gates

When writing the previous chapter, there was a point when I got stuck and worried about how I was going to recapture my flow. Fifteen thousand words later, however, my concern wasn't whether the current pulsed strongly enough but whether I'd be able to dam the waters.

It's ironic that I use the above analogy because I *despise* dams. I love water, and—even more so—I revere *flowing* water. For me, moving water serves as an ideal metaphor for writing and for life: when my writing flow is really banging, it's like a river at the peak of spring runoff, when the nighttime temperatures rise well above freezing and send a surge of snowmelt—unbridled and barreling, downstream. For anyone who has run an undammed river like the mighty Yellowstone at the height of spring runoff, the *mana* (Hawaiian for "power") is unmatched. There is simply something about moving water that awakens the senses. Perhaps it is the fact that our bodies are nearly 70 percent water and our planet is approximately two-thirds H_2O. More likely, it is the humbling nature and unrestrained power of the raging torrent. Whatever the reason, moving water represents life at its fullest.

Oceans, rivers, streams, and creeks teem with vivacity and pulse in a life-affirming rhythm capable of calming a restless spirit and quieting a racing mind. Thousands of words are dedicated to my love and reverence for water in my memoir, *Grizzlies On My Mind*; like author Norman Maclean, I am haunted by it. No other element has made a greater imprint on my life story than water—rivers, lakes, oceans. And as someone with this deep, burning love—combined with a porous mouth filter—I have no problem freely expressing my disdain for anything that impedes the free flow of life-giving fluid that makes our planet not only livable but evocative and spirited as well.

So what does this say about the deserts of the world, where a paucity of water exists? Are they soulless and lacking spirit? Anyone who has spent a day, week, or month wandering the enigmatic Red Rock Country and slot canyons of southern Utah knows the answer to this. Many of my most soulful adventures have occurred sauntering through the labyrinth canyons of the Desert Southwest, and nowhere have I experienced more spirited two-wheeled joy than bombing down a slickrock trail on my mountain bike. But even here, water—whether it be in abundance (flash floods) or in scarcity—determines whether plant and animal life thrives or perishes.

The lack of water makes the high-desert ecosystem of the South-west fragile and vulnerable. More water would lead to erosive forces that would quickly dissolve the sandstone formations that make Arches National Park and the rest of Red Rock Country one of the most striking and stunning landscapes in the United States. While my Arches National Park geology is somewhat elementary, it's safe to say that its eight to ten inches of annual precipitation creates the perfect recipe for one of nature's most impressive natural processes—erosion—and results in a thriving landscape that resembles God's art gallery.

If you are still with me here in chapter 4, you are well acquainted with my propensity to share metaphors. Living an authentic life is at the very root of what it looks like to be audacious. And to thrive while living an authentic life, we must find our niche—the habitat where we will flourish and prosper. Whether it is in the desert, on the coast, or in the mountains, it is essential that we find our flow. How and where will we blossom?

FLOWING WATERS, OPEN ROADS

It is so easy to settle and remain idle—to simply accept others' interpretation of how we should be and what we should do. But this is not the path to a meaningful, impactful, and passionate life. And this certainly isn't the path to inspiring a legacy and living a life that matters.

Far too often, we let the fear of other people's perceptions dam our waters of creativity, our flow, and our rhythm. I know this because I've often fallen victim to the engineers and dam builders (haters and poo-pooers) whose very existence seems to depend upon obstructing and taming the pulsing waters of vision and ingenuity.

When I was younger, I simply assumed these people knew something that I did not when I shared my dream of becoming a ranger in Yellowstone National Park. I still adopted a lifestyle of nonconformity, of course, but not without help. I chose to embrace the potent "slash model" I learned about in Marci Alboher's brilliant book *One Person / Multiple Careers: A New Model for Work/Life Success*. And thankfully, with the backing of two free-spirited parents, I learned to question authority at a young age, unwilling to blindly believe what I was told simply because the information came from someone who held seniority or rank. Respect for our elders is a must—in this I'm unwavering. But the idea that you need to accept what *adults*, superiors, and others in authoritative roles have to say simply because they say it is ludicrous.

If I listened to the common belief of society, I would probably be working a nine-to-five, driving a new Subaru Outback, putting money into retirement, dressing like an "adult," and exploring nature through golf. Instead, I'm doing *my* thing—I'm living the slash model. I'm working as a writer / motivational and environmental speaker / high school basketball coach / wildlife tour guide and Yellowstone guru / single dadda; investing in my professional future; dressing like Justin Timberlake while driving a baller Toyota Tundra with 200,000 miles on it, or weaving in and out of traffic on my cyclocross bike. Had I listened to all of the noise from 90 percent of the adults I spoke with while in college—had I succumbed to our social standards—I would have never left Seattle to journey to Montana and become a park ranger and fly-fishing guide in Yellowstone National Park. I would have never gone against all odds to start a non-profit and then *leave* it (when I was on the verge of joining the ranks of another well-established and deeply ingrained nonprofit organization) to launch the Be Audacious movement. And I sure as hell wouldn't have written a number-one, best-selling memoir or been venturing to my Bozeman office—Sola Café—each day for my morning writing sesh with *this* book.

Would I have more financial security if I took the traditional path? Perhaps. But I made the choice, many moons ago, that I was going to live audaciously and do things my way by pursuing a life that resonates with my spirit, passions, goals, dreams, and hopes—currency that feeds the soul before the wallet.

Right, wrong, or indifferent, I've resisted the urge to placate others by following the traditional model. Do you know how many times folks have told me that it's *irresponsible* and *reckless* to pursue the path I've chosen? Too many times to count. And I'm not going to lie: living the way that I do has created sketchy moments where I haven't always known how I'm going to pay the next series of bills or keep nutritious food in my daughter's belly. But in the end, life is all about the pluses and minuses equation, and the BA Balance I talked about in chapter 1.

People often compliment me for following my heart, stating how they wished they had the courage to do the same. The funny thing is, I get the impression these people think I'm like Nike and "Just Do It"—as if I'm predisposed to going off the beaten path. But the difference between people who throw off the shackles and those who don't isn't some genetic code or synapse in our DNA that keeps us from caring what others think; it's simply developing the willingness to face uncertainty while having the guts to take risks—to embrace a showdown with the fear of the unknown.

Hell, I would argue that the placid nature of stagnant waters that many conformists and traditionalists inhabit represents a stale, static, and sluggish existence that would surely dull the senses and ultimately quell the desire most have to rebel against the status quo. To live authentically, we must identify the barriers that block our flow in the same way that concrete walls of a dam alter the cycle and biodiversity of a river. In order to thrive and succeed, we must tear down these metaphorical dams and simply learn from flowing water.

No matter the obstacles standing in your way, you must find your way around the boulders and keep things moving forward. When others (especially old-schoolers) are threatened by your move to break away and pursue your own path, remember the words of Terry Cole-Whittaker: "What you think of me is none of my business." If you want to live authentically, embrace this mentality, because there will always be detractors when you break the traditional mold.

Ultimately, it's a matter of choice. If following the old-school, traditional path suits you, by all means walk that trail, as you have to be true to what's in your heart. For some, this may be the audacious path to happiness and prosperity. And it is a far easier route than navigating off-trail through downfall. But for the adventurous spirit who explores the boundaries of the path less traveled, I predict that you'll uncover a more meaningful and momentous mastery of your *own* authentic self. "Be audacious" is the mantra for breaking free of the main field of racers around you— the *peloton*—in search of the open road and your own circuitous route.

Take a call I received recently from one of the most audacious people I know:

I've known Scotty B for over a decade. We first connected during my second stint in a walking boot cast, while rangering in Yellowstone, and we've since become like brothers. He has been one of those unwavering, bedrock friends who represent a steady source of support and stability. Last summer, I officiated his wedding in an ancient grove of redwoods in Northern California, along the coast, amongst towering trees the likes of which I'd never witnessed. It was an honor to be there for my friend— a friend who, throughout my divorce and journey into single fatherhood, and in my recent brush with eternity, has checked in on me multiple times each week. May we all be so lucky or blessed (best left to interpretation) by one such friend of his quality in our lifetime.

I've never met anyone like Scotty B. He is truly his own man, walking to the beat of his own drum. He bumps 2Pac and indie, Bay Area rap one day while rocking out to the knarliest metal he can get his hands on the next.

After growing up in Southern California's seemingly waterless Mojave Desert, Scotty B journeyed north to the fertile valleys, verdant mountains, and coastal waters of Humboldt County. Then, one bold and adventurous summer, while attending Humboldt University, he ventured east to the heart of the Rockies, to work as a ranger naturalist in Yellowstone National Park. We first connected on a fortuitous drive from Mammoth Hot Springs to the Norris Geyser Basin, after hearing that Steamboat Geyser (the world's tallest geyser) was erupting for the first time in nearly two years. Scotty and I found ourselves sitting in the backseat of a government vehicle together.

You know how some people just seem like long-lost friends and kindred spirits from the get-go? Well, our relationship was something like that. For the rest of the summer, we were audacious as hell at the visitor center desk and off hours, hiking trails, chasing trout, riding mountain bikes, camping—having all kinds of adventures as we explored our newfound friendship.

I knew I had formed a lifelong connection with Scott; but in the years following his Yellowstone summer, something seemed awry. Scotty didn't appear to be the same bold, unrestrained, uninhibited guy that lit Yellowstone afire for three glorious months. After graduating from college, obsessed over paying off his student loans, he took a job for a major car rental company. Now there is nothing wrong with working a job like this— nothing at all—but Scotty B majored in environmental science and was the last guy I could ever see working for a big corporation in such a nonenvironmental field. What was supposed to be months of service turned into years; and during this time, Scott seemed to turn off many of the qualities that made Scotty B Black *Scotty B Black*.

Scott felt dejected, depressed, and discouraged. And to dampen that pain, he partied, drank, and simply blocked out the part of him that wanted so much more. Society made Scott feel like he *had* to pay off his debt at all costs. When I would challenge him over the phone, telling him to break free, his answer was always the same: "Once I get my student loans paid off, I will start looking for a job and lifestyle that is more fitting for what I want."

Here is the problem, my friends: this mind-set is self-fulfilling entrapment. Let's say it was going to take Scott three years to meet his goal— three years of working a job that, to him, was akin to selling his soul. By the time he paid off his student loans, he would likely have a car payment, credit-card debt, and perhaps even a home mortgage. Either way, he's left with debt; wouldn't it have been better to feed his spirit for three years instead? This idea that we will *wait* to follow our heart (and therefore live authentically) until the time is *right* is a surefire way to box ourselves in. Perhaps it is extreme to compare working at a major rental car company to being in prison, but when we succumb to the pressures and expectations of our culture's norms, we quickly become prisoners to a life of conformity. And think even bigger: if debt is the measure of whether or not we are free, then we are always trapped—for even those who are independently wealthy (less than 1 percent) are in debt to Gaia, Mother Earth, and all her life-sustaining gifts.

There comes at least one point in every person's life when he or she either caves in to the false safety of the wrong path, surrendering to a life unbefitting of authenticity, or that person comes out swinging, in defense of that which he or she wishes to become. Being the bold, bighearted fighter, Scotty B chose the latter—his authentic self. Knowing he wanted much more out of life, including a job that allowed him to return to the environmental field, Scott decided to go all in by applying for every and any job that would speak to his core values and passion.

Within months of making the decision to leave the car rental company, he landed an interview at the California Academy of Sciences. I've come to believe that something *pivotal* happens when we go from *thinking* about something to actually *doing* it. When we fully commit and make the audacious decision to go all in, karma kicks into high gear and providence aligns in subtle yet profound ways. This was the case for Scotty B.

Soon after his first interview, Scotty was walking the floor of one of the most impressive natural-history centers in the world, sharing his passion for the environment and the remarkable biodiversity of our planet. Was Scotty in the right place at the right time? There is something to be said about this cliché, as showing up and being present is a vital factor in many of our most important endeavors—but I'm not one who believes in chance. Yes, Scotty had bills to pay; but as talented, intelligent, and passionate as he is, there was absolutely no reason why he should have been working a job that deflated his spirit and made him question himself on a daily basis. I want to reiterate here that there is nothing *wrong* with taking a more traditional path, or working for a corporation like a major car rental company (as some will thrive in this setting); it simply wasn't right for Scotty B. And once he made the decision to be audacious in his pursuit of living his dream life, the game changed.

For the next five years, Scotty was a rock star at the academy, leading tours for Hollywood celebs, congressmen and women, high-profile CEOs, and everyday visitors. While he continued to lead tours as only Scotty could, he climbed the ladder until he found himself overseeing an annual budget of over one million dollars, supervising an entire staff of high-quality naturalists. He was living his dream.

But dreams change.

IN THE FACE OF DOGMA

Following a four-day vacation to visit Kamiah and me in Bozeman, I received a text from Scotty B that would rock my world in the most positive way imaginable. He and his wife were considering quitting their jobs and relocating to Bozeman. I was both shocked and stoked. This would be *all time* (surfer slang for "epic").

While he cherished his time at the academy (as I had my time rocking the green and gray as a Yellowstone National Park ranger), Scotty was ready for change. And he and his wife, Lauren, were willing to be audacious by making the biggest, boldest, and bravest decision of their life, throwing caution to the wind and drowning out the voices of those around them who thought they were crazy for doing something so unpredictable and scary. Willing to stare the beast of uncertainty in the face, they made the decision to chart their own course and write their own brave story.

For the last several months, Scotty and I have spoken on an almost daily basis. He was there for *me* when Kamiah's mom and I made the audacious decision to sell our house on our home turf in Livingston, Montana, where we were very comfortable, to embark on an uncertain journey to one of the most remote archipelagos on our planet—Hawaii.

Now it is my turn.

Each day, I'm blown away by the magnitude of his excitement and the speed with which they are pushing forward. So it was with understanding and compassion that I gladly stepped away from my writing flow to provide counseling and a friendly ear when he texted to ask if we could talk.

"Mamba, I'm tripping a little bit today."

I could hear the angst in his voice.

"What's up, Scotty B?"

"I'm getting some cold feet today, bro. I mean, this is *crazy*. I'm throwing away my job at the academy and applying for jobs at Target and Costco. All these apps I'm filling out are talking about a career with them. I'm not seeing a career with any of these big-box stores."

Cool, calm, and collected, I knew I had this one.

"Scotty B, it's all good, brother. Take a deep breath. You got this, my man."

I went on.

"Here's the deal: You are being too absolute and definitive. Pluses and minuses, yeah? There is no doubt that the negative of making this audacious move is the fact that you are leaving a solid gig in your field of choice, and you are probably going to need to take a Corporate-style gig for a little bit until you get things squared away. But that just is what it is. You are making a major life change, and you are choosing lifestyle—living in Montana—over your career right now. And that is totally cool, Scotty B."

Still a bit flustered, Scotty continued, "I know, bro. I definitely want to make this move. I'm just questioning myself a little because I don't want to go back to that headspace of working at the car rental company. And I start to wonder if all the peeps telling me that this is crazy are right."

"You just have to reject that right now, Scotty. That is simply 'worry mind' doing what worry mind does. You are doing something super bold by making this big move, no doubt about it. And not everything about it is going to be good. Pros and cons. Pluses and minuses. But you are a different guy now than you were when you worked in car rentals. You've killed it as a manager at one of the most prestigious scientific institutions in the world. You've got your swag, your passion, your charisma, and your resume. Any gig you take right now is just a placeholder for you to get out here and pursue your dream of living more simply and in wild country."

I could sense that Scotty was really vibing with what I was saying, so I continued.

"All the people who are hating on your big shift are just unwilling to face uncertainty in their own lives, and it freaks them out that you have the balls to go toe to toe with it. Uncertainty is one of the most challenging emotions we can ever face, so most avoid it at all costs. But regardless of how much we try to avoid uncertainty, it's always there—so we might as well face it head-on. That's what you guys are doing. You are making this choice, and there is so much power in that. This is very different from being a slave to your bills by hustling rental cars. And as far as the 'career' stuff goes at the big-box stores, you know the drill. Fake it till you make it."

I felt as if I could hear him nodding over the phone.

"Thanks, Mike, this all helps a lot. I want this so bad. I'm just a little scared and want to believe we are making the right decision."

"It's all good, Scotty B. You know I've always got your back. And I feel you. Remember how sketched out I was about the big move across the Pacific to Hawaii? That was *crazy*. What you have to remember about any of these stopgap jobs—jobs that will allow you to make this move—is to simply go at it one day at a time. You have to get like Socrates in *The Way of the Peaceful Warrior*. He was this brilliant philosopher who worked at a service station, pumping gas in Berkeley. What he did for a living and where he worked wasn't a measure of his value or contribution to society. He killed it. You just have to be intentional each day, put a smile on your face, and do what you can to have a positive impact on the customers and your peers during the time you are there—until we find you a gig that's more fitting for your passion, energy, and talent. Simple, yeah?"

With a Scotty B chuckle, he responded, "For sure, bro. That's the word—*intentional*. Ever since you told Lauren and me to 'be intentional' the day you officiated our wedding, that's become my mantra. You're right, Mamba. I've got this."

Knowing he was in a good place, but also feeling indebted to him for all of the days he talked me down during times of heartache and despair, I wanted to share more.

I told him the story of Elwood.

For years, I had been eating at a local burrito shop. I grew up on the same burritos on the Eastside—across the water from Seattle—and continued the tradition when I moved to Yellowstone. While the Bozeman burrito bandits changed often, there was always one constant behind the counter, where the builders did their thing: Elwood.

I always loved interacting with Elwood because he just had this vibe that was uniquely E. Where other employees curved the bill on their hat,

Elwood always wore it flat, tilted up, and a little to the side. He spoke like a *haole* (what local Hawaiians call a white boy) surfer and always remained upbeat, positive, and inquisitive. Every time I came in to grab a burrito, he'd ask me about my work as a motivational speaker, sincerely interested in what I had going on.

One day, not long after we had founded BA and launched the website, Elwood asked me about the bright green Livestrong-style bracelet I was rocking on my right wrist. When I told him about the BA movement, he immediately said, "Dude, I totally want to represent."

I took the bracelet off my right wrist and tossed it to this man that I had come to respect and appreciate.

Truth be told, I figured Elwood was just another skater/surfer turned ski bum, and that he was working at a burrito shop in his early 40s after missing out on getting his degree—because the draw to powder and waves had pulled too strong. But one day when it was slow, Elwood came over to my table, and with his big smile and remarkably friendly spirit, sat down and began to "talk story" (another beloved Hawaiian phrase—this time for chatting).

Rarely one to talk about himself, on this particular day, Elwood let me into his world. After twenty minutes of listening to him, I knew I was in the presence of some kind of guru.

Turns out Elwood not only had a college degree, he had earned a master's in history. His father was a well-respected professor at Cal State Fullerton who had encouraged him to follow in his footsteps. After hearing that I had plans of launching a Be Audacious clothing line, Elwood expressed interest in helping me out. I learned that he had started and run his own Montana-made skate brand for five years, the logo of which he wore inked into his right calf. Elwood also started and operated a nonprofit, and was instrumental in raising the money for the new skate park being built in Bozeman.

The guy was nothing short of amazing. I actually found myself intimidated at one point, so rich was his vocabulary and intellect. He had mad game.

I absolutely love Elwood's story because I have never met a more authentic dude who demonstrates what it looks like to live authentically. As I learned more about his philanthropic and entrepreneurial endeavors, I recognized that Elwood also represented authentic leadership in action. He didn't give a shit about what others thought of his path and didn't let his work define him. Instead, he used the burrito shop as a platform to shower the world around him with much *aloha* while giving himself the time, headspace, and energy to pursue the passions that mattered most to him—passions that didn't necessarily pay the bills.

Elwood is a living example of the tremendous power that comes with living authentically: sure of himself, comfortable in his own skin, warm and welcoming to others, making a positive difference in the world—walking his talk. It is so easy for us to get caught up in what others think, making our decisions from a place of emotion rather than a place of wisdom. But not Elwood.

To live authentically, we must not let the dogma of what others think drown out our own inner voice.

How often do we base our decisions on whether they will be socially acceptable? I vividly remember a text I received this spring from one of my basketball players who was in a bad place mentally because his peers at the high school were clowning his girlfriend. What I shared with him was pretty simple, but I like to believe it was pretty powerful too:

"What others think and say is irrelevant. All that matters is what's in your heart and in the hearts of those you love—what you believe is what matters. Ask yourself if you really care what people say? If you love someone or something—a girl, family, friend, sport, or hobby—by all means love them/it. I would argue that outside of your mom and tightest circle (and sometimes not even then), it isn't really relevant what others think about who you are or who you love. That's *your* business. Stand up for what is right and for the people you love, but don't fight what others think. That's a losing battle. Speak your opinion and what's in your heart. If people don't support you, what you are passionate about, and who you love, and if they don't have compassion for your struggles, they aren't worth the salt in your tears. And they sure as hell aren't worth the indignation in your belly."

THE 30 PERCENT RULE

The fact of the matter is this: the world is full of haters. I've said from the get-go that I'm not going to paint a rosy picture for prosperity's sake; I'm going to tell it like it is. Our world is plentiful with haters, and it is what it is.

Taking it a step further, my go-to life coach, Dr. John Wimberly, teaches what he calls the 30 Percent Rule: if 30 percent of the people aren't hating on you, you probably aren't pushing things or doing something very meaningful. It doesn't matter whether you're big time like LeBron, Jennifer Lawrence, or Beyoncé, or whether you are doing your thing on a smaller level as a local nonprofit guru, community activist, teacher, or coach; when you push the envelope, challenge social norms, or find success doing it *your* way, detractors will follow.

I've dealt with this most of my life because I've always walked to the beat of my own drum. I can remember having a serious chip on my shoulder back in high school because of how many detractors I had. When we would travel to other schools for basketball games, I would receive chants like "Leach is garbage, Leach is garbage," and to be perfectly honest, I loved it. I had this goal of turning heads when I walked into another school's gym; and if people didn't know who I was at the start of the night, I made damn sure that they did by the end. This was the competitor in me who wanted to reach the big time.

But when many of my detractors came from my own school, this didn't sit very well with me. It pissed me off and made my chip that much bigger. How did I cope with this adversity? My game was flashy and my style even flashier—white boy with the knee-high socks, baggy shorts, tightly faded hair, and a mouth that never stopped running. And I always responded with the same edgy, punchy, cocky front: "I don't give a fuck."

While I thrived in the hostile confines of other schools' gyms, doing everything I could to keep the bantering loud and energized, I now realize that my "I don't give a fuck" mantra, though true to some degree, mostly represented the wall I had built up to try and plug the holes in my vase of self-worth. This was my attempt to fake it till I made it. I had put in the time on the hardwood, I had the skill set, I yearned to be "The Man."

In later years, post basketball, I began to understand how false many of my concepts of self-worth really were—none more potent than the idea of being The Man. And don't get me wrong; I love Aloe Blacc and think that his jam "The Man" is the cut—but only when put in the proper context. The idea of being The Man as a single father; as the lone volunteer or visionary of a project; as a crusader for a cause; as a friend, sibling, or son—well, that makes some sense. And I hope it goes without saying that "The Man" metaphor crosses over equally for the girls and women of the world. Whether it be a parent, athlete, entrepreneur, artist, CEO, teacher, doctor—women have proven they are capable of anything they put their energy toward.

If taking pride in knocking it out of the park inspires you to give all you have to benefit others—in my case, my daughter—well, by all means, start bumping Aloe Blacc's cut and take pride in what you're about. Stand up for someone being bullied or speak out against bigoted and hateful language—whatever feeds that fire within. But beyond that, I think this concept of being The Man is played out, a remnant of the traditional/old-school leadership model.

I love the 30 Percent Rule because I think it is a strong barometer for where we are on the authentic leader scale. If 70 percent of the people are hating on you, for instance, you better take a look in the mirror and challenge your current path, because something ain't right. Likewise, if you only have a few detractors and are hovering at 10 percent, it's time to ratchet things up a few notches. If I could have my high school time back, I would go about things differently. I now recognize that my cockiness was a compensation for this innate fear that I somehow wasn't good enough, yet I was also afraid of being the worst thing imaginable: a pretender.

The beautiful thing about the authentic leader barometer is that it helps you to make the necessary changes. Far too often, we get stuck being who we believe we are, which tends to be a mirror of how we believe others see us. It's important that we uncover who we *really* are and then head in the direction of that which we want to *become*.

I remember a girl that I dated off and on in high school who was beautiful, fit, and the model cheerleader. Though she was attractive in every way, she developed a reputation for being ditsy. Having spent a little time with her, however, it was clear that she was far from the *classic* cheerleader that TV and movies portray; she was actually very intelligent. But this didn't fit how others saw her, so she let them pigeonhole her and simply played the part.

One of the things I took great pride in through my high school days was my ability to stay the course and do things my way. I rarely waivered in my convictions and didn't fit the mold of your classic jock (cockiness aside). I hardly experimented with alcohol either, only partying on occasion with my peers, and I still don't drink to this day as a matter of choice (and perhaps as a defiant "to hell with the social norm of our culture!"). Like so many of you, I can now look back and see that people didn't get me. They saw me as arrogant, elitist, and lacking school spirit because I did my own thing. But the truth is, *I* didn't really like myself, so how could they? (It was tough with that Montana-sized chip on my shoulder.) I just knew that I wasn't going to be what I was *supposed* to be. So, I have remained steadfast in my desire to be my authentic self, but that self is now governed by my core values and life's mission rather than the crowd.

SWAGGER VERSUS PEER PRESSURE

This is where swagger comes into play.

I believe that swagger matters in our pursuit of living an authentic life. While things get easier to navigate in college and the years thereafter, no matter what arena we find ourselves in, peer pressure abounds in our culture. From glamorous TV ads to conflicting definitions of what makes a family, expectations are *everywhere*. Swagger is your filter to the noise.

What, you might ask, does swagger look like? Swagger takes on many different shapes and forms, but it shouldn't look like arrogance or cockiness. Swagger is a term often used in the athletic arena, a place where confidence and a belief in one's ability can represent a game changer—the difference between success and failure—and this is where swagger often gets a bad rap. Far too many athletes, in their insecurity, misconstrue their arrogance as swagger. There is a big difference between LeBron James's approachable, loving, philanthropic, and free-spirited swagger and Johnny Manziel's pre-rehab arrogant, destructive, and defiant escapades.

Regardless of what the dictionary says, the swagger I'm encouraging you to embrace is authentic and palpable—a state of mind. It's the rhythm with which we walk and talk—our flow—and it is as unique as our DNA or fingerprint. It's the confidence that we can push ourselves mentally, physically, or spiritually when facing the demons of uncertainty, knowing that we aren't measured by the outcome (win or lose) but by our actions instead.

When did confidence become a bad thing? In reality, confidence is a beautiful thing—for it isn't a choice we make but the result of repeated effort and excellence. Swag is the aura that surrounds us when we walk into a room. Some come by it naturally and some don't, but I'm unwavering in my belief that we *all* can cultivate it. Just remember to keep your BA Balance: walk with a swagger as you shower the world with humble grace. Ultimately, swagger comes from a place of knowing that we are authentically pursuing a life that matters.

Take the fly-fishing guide culture that I've worked in for much of the last decade. There are a handful of guides and outfitters that I know well and respect deeply, but I find the vast majority of the fishing culture disturbing. In a setting that I believe should be filled with reverence, character, authenticity, and gratitude for the wild encounters we pursue while floating rugged rivers under a banner of majestic mountains, the reality is quite the opposite.

On a recent float with my father and one of my former basketball players who participated in my nonprofit's River Guardian Fly Fishing

School, we journeyed to the hallowed waters of the Upper Madison River. It's one of the most scenic rivers in the country, in the heart of the magnificent Madison Valley. They call it the "fifty-mile riffle," as its water pulses over miles of river rocks deposited by a gigantic glacier millions of years ago.

While I love this section of water lined by bountiful willows as it courses through a rich fir and spruce forest, with hardened cliffs of lava rock towering above, the scene *on* the river has kept me away for three calendar years.

You might expect the heavy boat traffic to have detracted from the overall experience of our half-day adventure, but in reality, what rubbed all of us the wrong way was the arrogant *attitude* on the river and at the boat ramp. The fly-fishing guide culture here in Montana is a classic antonym of authentic leadership. Paling in comparison to the agro saltwater fly-fishing guide culture of the Florida Keys, where being a dick is not only par for the course but clearly an accepted norm, Montana has its own thing going on. Though applying that statement to everyone in this business is, of course, an overstatement, I'm going to plead with you to stay the course with my message: it really doesn't matter which "river" you're navigating; whether you are in high school, college, or older, you will—we *all* will—at some point, and probably on multiple occasions, face our own "fly-fishing guide culture."

Humility is a key to authentic leadership. So when I see arrogance in any of our numerous outdoor cultures here in the Northern Rockies (fly fishing, road biking, rock climbing, river running, backcountry skiing), I'm immediately put off by the lack of authenticity. Exploring our wild world is a privilege and should be treated as such—with respect and reverence rather than the disconnect and possessiveness that runs rampant in many circles of the outdoor community. During my time working the waters of Yellowstone Country, few cultures have rubbed me raw like the guide culture here in Montana.

Unlike the old-school guides, who ventured out with clients in pursuit of a fun, memorable, and meaningful day on the river in a beat-up drift boat, the *new* guide culture resembles a fraternity where everyone looks alike. I could write a novella about my frustration with the local guide world, but it really comes down to the irreverent, copycat, chameleon culture of guides who are too cool for school. Are there still top-shelf guides who are doing things the right way—the authentic way? Without a doubt. But I'm afraid they are now the exception, not the norm.

I've never fit into the guide culture as a self-proclaimed "fish head" (anglers with nothing but fish on their brain). From my first full season, I became disenchanted by the fratlike nature of a culture that poo-pooed less desirable native fish species; failed to place quality over quantity, obsessing over fish count (numbers of fish boated during a day); and served up little on the plate of conversation beyond powder (skiing), hunting, hockey, or fishing. I chose to do things *my* way, remaining authentic to myself while resisting any temptation to fit the mold. This didn't help me gain more trips or acclaim as The Man in the guide culture, but it did give me much satisfaction to know I provided a positive, soulful, and spirited experience to my clients (while sharing my reverence for the mountain whitefish, demanding respect for Señor Blanco, a native species deemed less desirable by the guide world).

Was this easy day after day? No, it never is. That's why people follow—to avoid the difficult questions that arise when we uncover our authentic self. But for me, there is no other way. With the exception of a handful of great angler friends and industry leaders with whom I have become close, I always feel like something of an outsider in the fly-fishing guide world at large. Would I gain more guide friends and perhaps even line my pockets for the long and arduous Montana winter if I chose to go drink beer at a local tavern and speak the "Oh, it's just a whitey" (mountain whitefish) jargon? Without a doubt. But first and foremost, I have to stay true to my objective: to live authentically and to lead from the heart.

So how do we avoid caving in to the peer pressure of cultural norms? How do we stay on our chosen bearing while remaining true to who we are?

You already know the answer: *swagger.*

SWAGGER VERSUS ARROGANCE

Swagger gives us that little chip on our shoulder and empowers us to endure the onslaught of criticism that will inevitably come when we follow our own path and chart our own course. And there is nothing wrong with having a little chip on your shoulder. Being a little "chippy" simply demonstrates that you've faced adversity and remain unflappable in the path you've chosen. It's only when your chip becomes too big that you need to revisit your authentic leadership meter (the 30 Percent Rule). And you will undoubtedly know when that time comes because your authenticity measure of haters will swell—perhaps even *soar*—into the fiftieth percentile or higher, where you are more disliked and criticized than respected. Then you can *choose* to take it down a notch and learn for the next time, continuing your evolution and refinement as an authentic leader.

Malala Yousafzai. President Obama. Kris Carr. Macklemore. What do all of these people have in common? First, they all have achieved tremendous success. Second, they all have major swagger. Third, they all have battled their way to the top—with an audacious chip on their shoulder. Lastly, all of these people have done things *their* way.

Perhaps you don't have the desire to become a civil rights leader; the president of the United States; a best-selling author and wellness advocate; or a pop star spitting lyrics about adversity, LGBTQ rights, and struggle, but it sure as hell doesn't hurt to look at those who have defied all odds, reaching the summit of success in seemingly impossible ways and in improbable genres.

I wouldn't be surprised if, right now, you're going, "Swagger? Not me!" After all, we live in an egocentric world that places far too much attention on the hero worship of athletes and celebrities while ignoring the essential nature of self-improvement and a focus on community—on empathy. While we often praise modesty and condemn ego, *false* modesty runs rampant. Nobody wants to be seen as having a big ego, so it makes sense that people have shied away from swagger. But just as there is a difference between traditional leadership and authentic leadership, there is a difference between the individual who only seeks to gain personal wealth and accolades, and the individual who strives to use their talent to strengthen the vivacity of their community.

Remember, you can walk with swagger and still shower the world with humble grace. I'm talking about *humble swagger, authentic swagger*— what I like to call "swaggage." I love these terms, as I've seen them work with young adults, inspiring a more contemporary and audacious kind of confidence. But many never try the swagger hat on for size. Swagger is lacking in most of the population, young and old—yet I'm convinced that it's difficult to accomplish anything big without it.

While modesty is a positive attribute, if it's inauthentic, it's as unbecoming as arrogance. I've spent time around people who are damn good at what they do—and they know it—but they refuse to acknowledge it, choosing to let others boost them up with praise instead. If you know you have game, *own it*. Take pride in it. Develop your own authentic swagger and humble grace, but by all means, remain authentic and true to yourself—to what you are all about.

Developing swagger helps us to weather the storm of critics and haters who will condemn us for being audacious and original—and even for being successful. But swagger doesn't come overnight, and its formula varies for each of us. The one universal ingredient that I believe is key to the swagger recipe: developing the *chip*.

In order to deal with and embrace the 30 Percent Rule, you must have that edge—that chip on your shoulder. This doesn't mean being an ass; it simply means encouraging that little something extra that helps you to grind your way up the mountain. It's the platform for your inner voice, which reminds you what you are striving to become each and every day.

Being audacious is not something you turn on and off. After you own it, it's something you are or you aren't; it's a choice you make daily. And there is no better time than this moment, right here and right now, to make the commitment to start your legacy—to begin living a life that matters.

BELONGING AND A THICK SKIN

As you learned in chapter 3, I was tested for a learning disability when I was in first grade and the tests came back negative—no learning disability. But after struggling through school for over a decade and literally finding it impossible to learn math, my parents had me retested at the age of seventeen. Turns out I didn't just have a significant learning disability, my reading comprehension was that of a third grader. And by then, I had all kinds of self-doubt baggage to go along with it. Even in my final year of college, after I had spent eight semesters on the dean's list and was one semester away from graduating with high honors, I still struggled to believe that I belonged.

Belonging is a powerful, complex concept. Since the beginning, we have been a tribal people, depending upon one another for our survival, which has led us to *need* others in both minor and major ways. We need to feel we are a part of something and feel valued for our contributions. Whether this is within our family, our friendships, our intimate relationships, our team, our school, or our workplace, it's essential that we feel this connection—this belonging—so that our contribution to the greater good is sustainable and impactful.

For me, it was almost as if *no* amount of success in the world of academia could quash the wounds that had developed during my years in elementary, middle, and high school classrooms—my sense of inadequacy and resulting lack of belonging. Ironically, these feelings were at their strongest in my final semester at the University of Montana. I say "ironically" because my confidence in the classroom had never been higher— I had even enrolled in an upper-division wildlife biology course. I was on a mission to maintain a 3.9 GPA through graduation, walking side by side with my peers as the distinguished gold tassels of high honors dangled from my shoulders. This would surely represent some sort of redemption, right? The lack of belonging that had ravaged my spirit and quelled my desire to do the necessary work would surely leave me at last; I would finally be a "capable" student. And with a job awaiting me at Yellowstone National

Park upon graduation, I anticipated a long and fruitful career with the Park Service. Things were definitely looking up.

As an environmental studies major, my program was light on science and heavy on social awareness and activism. Even on the cusp of graduation, my struggle with math and science remained a constant trigger for self-deprecation and Piece of Shit-itis. Unwilling to embrace the fact that I simply didn't shine in these academic arenas, I had decided to enroll in that upper-level class I mentioned—one that focused on the natural phenomena of migration. There were only eight students in the class who were all seeking biology related degrees, many of whom were graduate students. So I was the low man on the totem pole from the get-go. Thankfully, what I lacked in statistical analysis I made up for in passion for the subject.

Talk about audacious journeys! I've long been enamored by the majestic and enigmatic nature of migration. Take the Pacific salmon migration, which represents one of the most extreme and truly epic migrations in the animal kingdom: after journeying upwards of 2,500 miles from their freshwater birthplace and spending four to seven years at sea, the members of this anadromous species (migrating into freshwater rivers from the sea to spawn) utilize their natal homing ability to perform the remarkable. Tapping into the Earth's magnetic field and their home river's chemical cues, these salmon find their way back to their natal stream, where their powerful sense of smell absorbs pheromones that literally *remind* the aquatic gurus where they come from.

One of my favorite members of our aerial community here in Montana is the Swainson's hawk, with whom I spend many an evening as I observe their masterful and joyful dancing in the thermals of wind—soaring above our backyard in search of an unsuspecting ground squirrel. Every time I hear their sharp screech or witness them dive-bombing into a meadow, I find myself marveling at their seven-thousand-mile migration from the Northern Rockies to the wilds of Argentina.

My fascination with the topic led me to read our textbook, cover to cover, feverishly studying every handout in an attempt to digest each topic—as if I were a malnourished pronghorn frantically gobbling up every ounce of available nutrition in hopes of making it through the winter.

And then the first test came around.

I studied my butt off, and went into the exam feeling confident and prepared; but for the first time in my college life, I scored a D. I knew I was in trouble. Not only did my learning disability make it improbable to improve (it had always been most acute in math and science), I simply didn't have the background to comprehend the extensive graphs and statistical analysis it took to succeed in this class.

I had two options: (1) stay in the class and risk failing it, losing my high honors and dean's list status, and—worst-case scenario—possibly not graduate; or (2) withdraw from the class.

Then I reminded myself that life isn't that black and white. And figuring I had nothing to lose, I opted to take the more audacious path of scheduling a meeting with my professor.

Sitting in his office two days later, I explained my conundrum and told him of my desire to remain in the class. After a few moments of quiet reflection, he asked me my thoughts on how I could finish the course. I had come prepared, having met with my advisor and the chair of the environmental studies department, who had always shown great empathy for my struggles: I pitched the idea of writing an essay in lieu of a final exam. Intrigued by the idea—but clearly not on board just yet—this PhD bio professor took me aback when he broke the mold of his classes' stylistically rigid approach by pitching his own idea: he wanted me to write a popular-science article on the topic of migration and get it published.

At first, I was thrilled. My confidence in my writing was solid after my first peer-reviewed essay in my nature-writing course. But by the time I got back to my single-wide trailer on the Bitterroot River, the gravity hit me in the gut. It was one thing to write an essay that received props in my writing program, but *this* was taking things to the next level. Publication—*me*? That's crazy. I knew enough about the writing world to understand how challenging it was to get published. But this was my only shot to stay in a course that I loved, so I'd have to push myself out of my comfort zone and do something audacious to wrap up my college experience.

For the next two months, I hammered away at the keyboard of my laptop, watching out the window of my trailer as the snow flurries flew and winged migrants from the south provided inspiring fodder for my project. After numerous edits, I turned it in the week before finals. A week later, I received an e-mail from my professor, beckoning me to his office.

Serious as any biology professor, he simply handed me a manila envelope and told me to open it. As I slid out the contents, I immediately saw a massive "A" scribbled across the front of my paper. I shook my head with a stoked smile as his extended hand met mine with a friendly clasp.

"This article is very good, Michael. You can really write. I want to see you get this in *National Geographic*."

I simply shook my head in disbelief. A brilliant PhD, wildlife biologist telling me that my article was the shit.

It would be a Hail Mary to get my piece in *Nat Geo*, but I knew the perfect home for it: *Wyoming Wildlife*.

Celebrated as the top-shelf publication for fish-and-game agencies across the West (largely due to its legendary and award-winning editor, Chris Madson), I always relished reading the stories filling the pages of each issue. But breaking into the literary community and helter-skelter world of publication is a steep uphill climb—one has to pull all of the strings they have to make the dream a reality. So I reached out to an old professor friend and mentor who had been writing for *Wyoming Wildlife* for nearly a decade and asked if he'd be willing to make the introduction.

Not long after getting my article into Mr. Madson's hands, he came back with a big thumbs up, expressing his desire to publish my piece. I was through the roof. Twenty-five years old, just graduated, and dreaming of making a career as a writer, I had received my first contract—and it was a good one. One of the things that excited me most was knowing my article wouldn't need substantial editing, as the process of preparing it for my professor had been intense and arduous.

Or so I thought.

When I received the onslaught of edits from Chris, I sat there staring at them for a good fifteen minutes. Just staring at the red ink. *What the . . . ?*

How the hell was this possible? Who was I to challenge a legendary editor? But come on, man. This piece was tight.

As intuitive as he was skilled at editing, Chris could hear the disappointment—and perhaps a bit of dejection—in my voice. The powerful words he shared with me at that moment have stuck with me for nearly a decade:

"Michael, one must develop the skin of a rhino to write for public consumption."

I share this story because I think the same can be said for those living an authentic life, and certainly for those who choose the path of authentic, from-the-heart leadership. If you are going to put yourself out there—which I seriously hope you will—you, too, need to develop the skin of a rhino. But like so many of the concepts I've shared up to this point, this one is easy to say and very hard to do.

As a high school basketball coach in rural Montana, I sure as hell needed to develop thick skin. And I can tell you, from the heart, that I was in desperate need of a thickening of my epidermis during my first four years as a head varsity coach.

Here I was, giving my kids everything I had, coaching from the heart and showering them with discipline, compassion, and love. They loved playing for me. We had forged bonds that I will take to the grave (or in my case, to the Lamar Valley in Yellowstone National Park, where I hope friends and family will drag my body so I can be recycled back into the food chain when my spirit journeys elsewhere). Yet some in the community hated me. It wasn't an easy pill to swallow; and for a long time, I simply couldn't wrap my head around it. But there came a time where I recognized that doing things my way—which I wasn't about to change—was going to inspire some to love and others to hate. It is what it is. And I was able to let it go.

The more we are able to fill the holes in our vase of self-worth and retain the water that nurtures our essence, the thicker and more resilient our epidermis becomes. During hard times, I've always found comfort in reading stories, watching movies, or listening to motivational speakers as they share their journey of overcoming hardship. There is something about overcoming adversity, facing the gauntlet square in the face, and coming out the other side that enhances our authenticity and certainly our resiliency. Perhaps there is a connection there. (I've become convinced there is.) Take a look at the most authentic people you know, and I would wager that they are also some of the most resilient and thick-skinned.

YOUR PERSONAL MOUNTAINTOP

One of the poets who has provided me with much fight during the more challenging times—times when giving in to the mainstream path seems an inescapable option—is Somalian rapper K'naan. There is an undeniable authenticity to his style and flow. He knows what it's like to struggle and fight for survival. In a genre that far too often spews misogynistic nonsense, K'naan's meaningful lyrics are refreshingly poignant.

K'naan once said, "To reach your goal authentically is probably, in the end, going to mean much more to you than having reached it in a false way." K'naan is one of the most authentic artists in the hip-hop world and he doesn't appear to let the opinion of others detract from his craft, style, and message; it's not what others think that derails us and takes us off the authentic path; our insecurities of not being good enough drive that train. Alternately, when pursuing a life of nonconformity, the more successful people become, the less they are impacted by the noise around them. But why the hell should we wait until we've become successful to learn to ignore the noise around us? Far too often, people give up before they reach their desired outcome—or worse, they're too fearful to even start.

Imagine for a moment that you're embarking upon an epic five-day climb of a remote and little-explored mountain. During the first two days of your climb, you trek forty miles a day through rolling hills, mosquito-invested forests, and sagebrush flats beneath a scorching sun and with a sixty-pound pack on your back. By the time you reach base camp, you are already exhausted, and the naysaying words of your friends and family begin to occupy your headspace: *Your summit attempt is out of reach—not within your physical ability.* You lie awake all night with the negative thoughts racing through your mind. And when you emerge from your restless sleep on day three, hours before the sun has risen, the weather has dramatically shifted. It's cold and wet, your muscles are tight, and an achy pain seeps deep into your bones. This is the big day—the summit attempt. Eighteen hours, twenty miles, and six thousand vertical feet await.

Midway through your day, you realize that you haven't eaten or had anything to drink for over four hours, so intense was your meditative trance and hiking rhythm. But now you are on the verge of bonking (cycling jargon for hitting the wall), you still have four hours of climbing ahead, and you are questioning your sanity for undertaking such an arduous and uncharted climb.

Now imagine the detractors and haters who discouraged you from attempting something so bold and daring randomly standing along your route, harassing and heckling you as you try to find that place in the deepest recesses of your soul that will help you to keep going. Beaten down, tired, dehydrated, and malnourished, it would be easy to cave in, give up, let go of the dream, and venture back to the "real" world.

Head down and tail between your legs, you look one of the cynics in the face, shrug your shoulders, nod your head, and give in. That's a wrap. To hell with what your authentic self wants or yearns to pursue. The pessimists were clearly right. It's time to give up on your aspirations of breaking the mold and accept the conventional life of conformity they demand of you.

This sort of thing happens every day. The authentic self is beaten out of us by people who tell us we aren't being "realistic enough," "responsible enough," or (my favorite of them all) "practical enough." So we quit. We accept the cultural norm and fall in line.

Let's go back to the climb for a moment. You were so close to fulfilling the dream of summiting one of the most remote mountains in the Northern Hemisphere. What would have happened if you had put on the blinders and kept going? What would it take to uncover the courage to say "Fuck it!" in the face of the critics, munch on a Clif Bar, down some water, and just keep grinding away? The key resides in embracing, accepting, and honoring our authentic self while keeping our personal toolbox handy (remember chapter 2?). When we do this, our insecurities of not being good enough begin to fade.

The inability to weather the onslaught of whispers and doubters destroys more adventures and summit attempts than any factor. But adopting the *I'm not going to let the opinion of others drown out my authentic voice* philosophy enhances the likelihood of becoming successful a hundredfold, uncovering our power to live an authentic life.

The ancient Chinese philosopher Lao Tzu put it best: "Care about people's approval and you will be their prisoner."

If you haven't seen the movie *Shawshank Redemption*, you better get on Netflix to check it out. It's a classic. Near the end of this epic film, Morgan Freeman's character is preparing to be released from prison—something he has dreamt of his entire life, as he was imprisoned as a young man. But as his release date nears, he begins to question his desire to live as a free man. In prison, he doesn't have to think for himself: his clothes, days, and meals are planned for him, and he has a job he's comfortable with—a purpose he's learned to accept. Freedom scares the living hell out of him.

I'm afraid the same can be said for many of us living inside the concrete walls and barbwire fences of our cultural penitentiary. There may be no armed guards fixing rifle scopes on us whenever we attempt to break out, but the opinion and approval of others represent the metaphorical firing squad in our mind. We've let the fear of not being good enough in the eyes of others dictate our freedom and therefore our imprisonment.

When beautiful spirits such as the South African leader and hero Nelson Mandela are willing to face the gauntlet (ultimately spending twenty-seven years in prison in his fight for racial equality against the South African apartheid government), who are we to take the easy route by caving in to the judgments and opinions of others? Imprisoned, Nelson Mandela was more free than the vast majority of people I see pursuing the "American Dream." Until we are willing to challenge the cultural dogma that makes us feel the only "responsible" route is to secure a nine-to-five job after receiving a degree from a "worthy" institution—becoming willing participants in an upscale version of indentured servitude and virtual prisoners to our debt-riddled system—we are anything but *free*.

This is what excites me the most about our current generation of young adults: there is a growing dissent amongst the ranks. Young people want something *more* meaningful, *more* inspiring, and *more* in tune with what they are all about. How many times have you seen "responsible" adults in submission, unwilling to question the status quo and accepting the way their life has played out? I see it every day, wherever I go. This idea that you get to "be a kid" and take risks *only* in your teens and early twenties is bullshit.

Life is hard. Life is short. Life is precious. So why waste this limited time being confined by the approval of others? Why not throw off the shackles of our societal dogma and embrace a path of nonconformity, choosing to live authentically and from the heart—a freedom that never ends? As Mr. Freeman so gracefully stated near the end of the film, "Some birds aren't meant to be caged. Their feathers are just too bright."

If a traditional nine-to-five suits you, so be it. There is absolutely *nothing* wrong with that path if that is what speaks to you. In fact, it would even be admirable if you worked a job that you aren't particularly passionate about to provide for your family; this is another way of living from the heart. But this book is for those of you whose feathers are just too bright to be caged—whether that cage is the status quo or *any* path that doesn't feed your soul. This book is for the free spirits yearning to take risks in pursuit of finding their true self while en route to living a meaningful life—one that contributes to the world around them and stays true to what lies in their heart.

ONE TRIBE: LOCAL AND GLOBAL

My mom is fond—actually, *proud*—of saying that she spent much of my youth cleaning up after my mouth. As I've shared, my mouth's filter is very porous, but I'm not ashamed of this; I consider it a big part of being my authentic self. While it's not always comfortable and sometimes creates restless nights, I've never shied away from expressing myself on the issues that matter most to me. Some would go as far as calling me an instigator, which always makes me smile.

One of the things I'm very passionate about—especially living where I do, in a state that isn't rich in ethnic diversity—is breaking through the racial barriers that frequently exist in ethnocentric rural places. When I coached in Gardiner, Montana, another very small community, I was both dismayed and horrified to learn of the racial tensions that exist between the rural white towns and the rez teams (the reservation communities throughout the state). While attending the state tournament the year before I took over as the head varsity basketball coach, I was disgusted and disturbed by the discriminatory nature of what I observed. The demarcation that I witnessed between the Caucasian and Native American communities was hard for me to wrap my head around.

Here I was, a graduate from a large high school in a Seattle suburb that represented a melting pot of cultural diversity, and I was just finishing up my first season as an assistant coach in a small Montana community; my first state tournament experience was a culture shock simply because I had witnessed virtually *no* ethnic diversity during that first season. So I was beyond stoked to see one of the best rez teams in the region competing there. While my deep and spiritual connection to an Assiniboine–Gros Ventre man (whose people hailed from the same reservation as the Hays-Lodge Pole team that was taking the state by storm) had something to do with my bias toward the only rez team in the tourney that year, the truth is, no matter which rez team was playing that weekend, they would have had my support. And with the best hoopster I had seen since breaking into the Montana high school basketball scene—a six-foot-four standout named A. J. Longsoldier—I couldn't understand why the entire gym hadn't jumped on the Hays-Lodge Pole bandwagon to cheer for the Thunderbirds.

While we've all heard about the hardship of life in the ghettos and inner cities across the country, few people truly understand the rugged nature of life on most Indian reservations in the United States. In far too many ways, the first people have become a forgotten people by our government and our society as a whole. Attend a high school basketball game at the state tourney with a rez team on the floor and you will surely recognize that Indian culture is alive, vibrant, and thriving. And anyone in attendance at the tournament *that* weekend won't forget the name A. J. Longsoldier or the legend he became, nor will they forget the inspired play of the Thunderbirds. Yet this didn't stop the majority of the rural, white communities from rooting *against* the only Indian team in the tournament.

I was not among them. Though rumors were swirling about the potential of my becoming the next head boys' basketball coach at Gardiner High, it wasn't enough to keep me from remaining true to my authentic self. Any naysaying, anti-Indian community members were welcome to criticize my outward demeanor. In the meantime, I rooted loudly and proudly for the Thunderbirds.

Two years later, after leading the mighty Bruins of Gardiner through the gauntlet that was our district tournament for the second straight year, the celebration of hoisting the consolation championship trophy quickly dulled when whispers of who we would meet in the first round at divisionals began to spread. As we were leaving the gym after the announcement that we would be battling the Arlee Warriors from the Flathead Indian Reservation, I heard racial garbage being spewed by a few community members. When it came to the adults, over whom I had no control, I could do little but express my disgust and disapproval—but on the bus, it would be a different story. When a racial comment was uttered by one of our players, well, that was it. That one comment represented a game-changer moment.

When we live and lead from the heart, unafraid of the repercussions of what others think, we put ourselves in a position to effect positive change in our community and the world around us. The minute I heard the derogatory comment about Indian people, I instructed the bus driver to pull over at the next rest stop. Unloading the bus on a cold February evening, I began a tirade amidst the blowing wind and flying snow as the team huddled together for warmth. I shared stories of my brother Darrell (the Assiniboine-Gros Ventre elder who had taken me under his wing), and told them of my adopted *Diné* (Navajo) family and five beautiful sisters who hail from the Zuni-Edgewater clan. Making clear my frustration and disgust at the comment, I also made it clear that I didn't care who had made it. No such words were *ever* to be spoken again:

"If I hear another racial comment toward Indian people, you are off this team. And if you're off this team, you're off this bus. And if you're off this bus, that means you are going to be freezing your ass off, waiting for your mom and dad along the side of this highway."

I wasn't through.

"Now that we are clear on this, whoever made that ignorant comment about Native people has just gotten all of you into practice thirty minutes early the entire week for a Native American Appreciation Week."

Pluses and minuses, yeah? The minus was that one of our kids said something ignorant. The plus was what unfolded, which was far more powerful than a stupid comment made about a people these boys knew nothing about.

One of the things that makes living an authentic life so powerful is the opportunity we have to turn negatives into positives by living boldly, unafraid of how others perceive us and unwavering in that which we believe to be right. That entire week of practice, the boys arrived early, and we talked about the twenty-six tribes associated with Yellowstone National Park (the twenty-six tribes that called Yellowstone home before it was a national park). We spoke about the injustice, the trials and tribulations, and the tension that exists between the rural white communities and the reservation communities. Throughout practice, I blared powwow music over the PA system in hopes of sharing the powerful rhythm of the life-affirming drumming and singing while preparing my team for a raucous crowd and intense environment.

En route to our showdown with Arlee, we stopped at a spot that had become sacred to our team—Missouri Headwaters State Park. Being a strong believer in the power of place, I had stopped the bus at Headwaters on our way to districts and divisionals the previous year, as well as on our way to the district tourney the week before. I always used the analogy of the Lewis and Clark Expedition and the uncertainty that awaited these explorers as they ventured west over the Continental Divide in search of adventure and success, drawing parallels to our own journey over the Divide and our hopes of living to play another day. We had watched a full lunar eclipse at this spot; shared hugs, tears, hopes, and dreams. We had meditated, prayed, and shared mesmerizing motivational speeches along these sacred waters.

But this journey to Headwaters would be different. Instead of speaking about Lewis and Clark, I spoke about the Blackfoot, the Shoshoni, the Flathead, the Assiniboine, the Crow, and the Bannock. And after honoring the tribes that have called this landscape home for hundreds of generations, I busted out a bundle of sweetgrass and sagebrush (sacred medicine to many of the Plains Indian tribes), a large seashell that Darrell had given me, a raptor feather, and a lighter. Lighting the sweetgrass and sage, all but one of the sixteen boys lined up and awaited their turn to be smudged. Smudging is a ceremony of many Indian tribes—a way of cleansing and shielding one's body, especially before entering a long journey or battle. In this way, I was teaching my boys about a culture for which they had little understanding and far too many misconceptions.

That night, in a thriller none of us will ever forget, in a hostile and rowdy gym pulsing with energy and the hopes of two vastly different communities, we *beat* the Arlee Warriors. Missing a game-winning shot at the buzzer, the Warriors were heartbroken. But everyone won *something* in that first game—something that started with a shift in perspective and a newfound respect.

●●●●

What unfolded throughout the course of that electric weekend could be a book in and of itself. While I knew I was going to be criticized for my actions—especially my smudging of a group of rural kids hailing from a Christian community—I threw caution to the wind. And the results were overwhelming.

The next day, as we were preparing to battle the number-one team in the state—the Twin Bridges Falcons—for the fourth straight semifinal, parents and grandparents of Arlee players came up to me and expressed their gratitude for how I had interacted with their son or grandchild after the game the night before. I had hugged every player, speaking to him with respect, and I held the faces of those who were crying. That night, as we battled the Falcons, the Arlee crowd cheered for us as if we were their own. And the next morning, as we played a district rival of Arlee, they were in our corner once more.

During both games, in the huddle, before we would break from our pregame and halftime pep talks, I held the tethered sweetgrass above the heads of my team as they circled around. We all put our hands together in unification. Then, breaking the huddle, we shouted, "One, two, three: *Love!* Four, five six: *Family!* Seven, eight, nine: *On a Mission!* This led one of the Arlee elders to ask me what I knew about sweetgrass. When I shared my understanding that it represents powerful medicine to his people, he shook his head, dismayed.

"No wonder your big boy played so well and you beat us."

Doing what's right, living authentically, leading from the heart without concern for what others think—this way of carrying ourselves had earned the respect of an entire tribe of people. And before we played Arlee for the consolation championship (they had won each loser-out game to keep their fight alive) and a chance at the state tournament, the elder I had spoken with beckoned me to come to where he was sitting. He had clearly shared our conversation with the others around him; and there, in front of my coaching staff and team, I received an honor I will always cherish. Dressed as if they were preparing for a ceremony—with braids, bright-colored shirts (turquoise, salmon, and blue), eagle feathers, and ornate jewelry—they said a prayer. (My assistant still tells the story to anyone willing to listen—so powerful was what he observed that day.) In closing the prayer, symbolically wafting their hands through the air, the small group of elders smudged me before tipoff.

The Arlee Warriors ended our season and the high school careers of a special group of seniors that night. This time, the tears flowed from the eyes of *our* boys, not the Warriors. Whooping war chants echoed throughout the gym.

After walking through the line, shaking hands with the Arlee players and coaching staff, my team began the long walk back to the locker room. As I hugged and spoke with each Arlee player again, just as I had three nights earlier (but under far different circumstances), I heard the Arlee crowd erupt in applause. It took me a moment to recognize what they were cheering for: *my boys.*

For those who don't understand the depth of the sinewy tension that exists between communities like Gardiner and those of the reservation, it would be hard to comprehend the magnitude of this turn of events. Following their defeat three nights earlier, the Arlee fans were hostile toward our boys. But after learning of our *intention* to honor and respect a beautiful people long oppressed because of the color of their skin and misunderstood traditions, their interpretation of us had changed.

Still, my heart was heavy as I gave my last hug to the Arlee players and their head coach at center court. Knowing the flood of emotions that was going to cascade when I walked into my team's locker room, my eyes welled with tears.

I slowly sauntered across the gym floor.

The crowd behind the Arlee bench began to rise, cheering, chanting, and clapping in unison. I had honored their boys—treating them with love, dignity, and respect—and now they were giving me "chicken skin" (Hawaiian for goose bumps). Our team may have lost on the scoreboard, but the cultural bridges we spanned represent a win that will last longer than any trophy. It was an honor and an experience none of us will forget.

●●●●

Earlier this spring, I shared what I like to call a "Power Moment" with my daughter.

We've followed Shoni Schimmel, a University of Louisville basketball player who hails from the Umatilla Reservation in Oregon, for much of the last two seasons. *Off the Rez*, a feature-length documentary, chronicles Shoni's audacious story from the life of a girl on the rez to a college superstar. While her entire career was celebrated, on this night, during a seemingly meaningless exhibition of three-point shooting prowess, I shared one of those powerful and memorable moments with my daughter.

On this night, in front of a packed crowd, Shoni pulled off one of the most audacious feats I've witnessed in a long, long time. First, she went on a tear by shooting the lights out, winning the college three-point competition against the best lady sharpshooters in the country. But then, the girl with the cleanest of strokes took on the men's three-point champ; and with a shooting display for the history books, she knocked down shot after shot, and came out victorious. I was moved to tears as I watched this event unfold with Kamiah, awestruck and smiling by my side.

Though it's just a game, Shoni's courageous feat represented a win for girls all over the world. And thirteen hours later, over breakfast, with the most glorious of smiles, my six-year-old was still talking about the girl they call "Shoni."

This was just the beginning of Shoni's powerful story. She was not only drafted to play in the WNBA, but as a rookie, she made the All-Star game. In a shootout, she helped guide her East All-Stars to a 125–124 victory, netting twenty-nine points and earning herself the distinct honors of All-Star Game MVP. Imagine the storms that Schimmel weathered to go from reservation life to being a WNBA star.

While I try to avoid the overused declaration "there's nothing you can't do" (because this simply isn't reality, as we all have limitations of some sort), I do believe that there are few things we can't accomplish when we combine passion, love, and resiliency. Without resiliency, Shoni never accomplishes her dream.

Most of life is pretty damn complicated, but one thing is simple: be true to yourself and those that you love. You can only control the controllables—that's it. We must learn to let the rest of it go. Let it flow down the river of life. Life's too short to worry about what people say, and nothing big will ever occur when we avoid criticism. Get out, smell the roses, and enjoy the sunshine.

What others think of us is not what's relevant; it's remaining authentic in all of our endeavors that matters most. When we learn to lead from the heart, unafraid of those who will criticize our path of choice, we tap into the power of living an authentic life personally, in our local community, and as global citizens. This is the path to a life of richness, fulfillment, and truth—the path to your legacy.

ARMOR AND TRAINING

As one of my great teachers often says when sharing his wisdom regarding how to journey through life with as much grace as possible—especially in the face of hardship and challenge: "This is easy to say and hard to do." It's easy to pontificate on the importance of living an authentic life while professing the need to let go of criticism; but putting this into action is hard to do. If it were easy, there would be no need for this book and everyone would be audacious. Anytime we journey into uncharted waters, or face the fear of what others will think of our choices and actions, *we need armor.*

Think of it as a melee for your freedom—a modern-day war of attrition. We have to wear down the doubters and haters—or better yet, be unwilling to let them wear *us* down. Undoubtedly, they will continue fighting, insistent upon following the traditional and safe path as they criticize your uninhibited desire to pursue your own authentic journey. When so much in our society strives to imprison us in a life of conformity, we must be courageous, scrappy, and resilient to stay true to our authentic self. *This is the most important battle you will ever fight.* Win this skirmish and you win the war. While this goes against the passive nature of our cultural norms, there is a time and place to get *belig* (short for "belligerent").

My boy Scotty B Black always says "The Mamba [his nickname for me] is getting into *belig* mode" when I'm standing up and fighting for something I believe in. What could be more important than fighting for your authentic self—for what you hold near and dear to your heart, and believe to be true? There is a time to passively sit back and watch from afar, and there is a time to be the instigator. But when we are venturing into hostile territory, where gunfire and bombs in the form of criticism are known to fly without mercy, we must be prepared with our bulletproof vest.

Going back to the climbing metaphor I used earlier, where the detractors heckled us during the crux of the climb, when we were so close to reaching our own personal mountaintop, it is important to recognize the power of *choice*. As adults, you are now in control of your own destiny; nobody else is going to walk this journey for you. *You* get to decide when you'll keep pushing and when—*if*—you'll cave. In order for you to defeat those who protest your authentic self, you must train your mind to endure the onslaught. Just as you wouldn't embark upon a marathon without first training your body, you must train your mind to withstand the grueling gauntlet of conformity in your quest to uncover your authentic self.

This training is far more challenging and cerebral than training for a marathon, however, so you have to develop a quiver of arrows capable of guiding you through a multitude of situations. You need skills, tools, and mantras to enhance your ability to endure criticism and, in the process, thicken your epidermis.

When you are no longer in a state of avoiding criticism, you are going to have unannounced bombs tossed your way; that is part of living an authentic life. Some are going to support your mission while others are going to feel threatened. When people are placing doubts in your mind, it is easy for self-talk to become destructive. I can't emphasize enough the importance of positive self-talk in our quest to live authentically and lead from the heart.

It's so easy for us to get into a pattern of critical and destructive self-talk—I know because I've been there. There was a time when my self-talk was beyond critical: I didn't beat myself up, I *crucified* myself with destructive chatter. I had one of the worst cases of Piece of Shit-itis (POS-itis) imaginable. While I projected to the world my "don't give a shit" attitude, in reality, my skin was paper-thin. I knew in my heart that I could never be content with living a traditional life and simply falling in line, but I struggled mightily with the criticism. This was, in large part, because of the physical changes that were completely out of my control. My identity was as an athlete—I found self-worth in what I could do physically—and when my body began to fail me, my self-talk spun out of control. POS-itis hit a fever pitch.

Remember that powerful mantra from Dr. Wimberly: *Acceptance is allowing reality to be as it is without requiring it to be different.* As I said at the start of this section, *easy to say but hard to do*, yeah? It was only when I learned that I was my own worst enemy that things began to change.

Beating ourselves up keeps us stuck in a place of inaction. If your self-talk isn't helpful, change it.

But how do I do this?

When the pathways and patterns in our brain are wired in a way that reiterates what others think, it's difficult to find the audacity to leave the relative comfort of the well-traveled trail even when we know it leads to a place of heartache and shame. But that's what we have to do. To unearth our authentic self and become unflappable in the face of condemnation, we must travel our new route day after day until the trail is smooth and navigation is no longer an issue. Once we can put away the compass and simply follow the trail we have blazed, the opinions of others fade like leaves scattering in the wind

First and foremost, I want you to always recognize that personal growth and introspection is both tender and holy ground. Be kind to yourself as you break free from the pack (the *peloton*). If you've ever watched the Tour de France—perhaps the most impressive physical feat of endurance there is—you will come to love those who break free from the *peloton* in what always appears to be an act of defiance. While the long breakaway rarely works, as the strength of the *peloton* more often than not reels in the disobedient riders seeking personal glory, the rebellious effort always earns the respect of peers and spectators; and most importantly, it allows the daring riders to sleep in peace that night, knowing they did things *their* way.

Every time a rider breaks free of the main pack, there is a "to hell with it" look on his face and punch to his pedal strokes. The beauty of the Tour is that they not only award the stage winner of each day, but they honor the rider who has been deemed the most aggressive in each stage. I find this beautiful—inspiring. And while those of us who break away from the pack in pursuit of nurturing our own authentic self don't receive an award from our peers for doing so, the metaphorical Most Aggressive Rider award goes to those of us with the panache and gusto to throw off the shackles.

But just like the riders whose confidence in their fitness fuels their gutsy decision to break away and go at it alone—which is a far more difficult ride than it is for those who sit back idly and enjoy drafting amongst the swarm of riders, reducing effort and getting them to the finish line safe and sound—we need to train our minds to endure the relentless force of those who wish to reel us in.

Practice Exercise:
THE THREE Rs

To combat the naysayers, we must be ruthless with our mental training. One of my favorite training tools comes from the world of cognitive behavioral therapy. They call it the "Three Rs," and it has served me well in my own audacious journey of self-discovery and nonconformity. *Recognize, reject, and reinterpret*—seems easy enough, yeah?

Just like a professional bike racer, it takes much time, dedication, and repetition to master the skill of the Three Rs, but once mastered, their power is transformational.

For much of the last decade, the best and most successful cyclists have utilized an illegal strategy called blood doping to enhance their oxygen levels and, therefore, their performance. Think of the Three Rs as a natural, safe, potent, and *legal* doping for the soul.

So how does it work?

Find somewhere quiet to sit and put your contemplative hat on. Drum up something that triggers self-doubt and negative self-talk, and begin exploring how you can reinterpret and create a new meaning by utilizing the Three Rs:

1. *Recognize:* When a negative thought about your authentic self and chosen path arises (which most often comes in the form of noisy dogma from the outside), you simply *recognize* the thought for what it is: a thought. Through my journey of personal growth and self-acceptance, I've finally wrapped my head around the fact that a thought doesn't equal truth. There is only meaning in the thought if we give it power.

Let me give you an example: I used to really struggle with my chosen path as a writer and motivational speaker, as the world of an author and speaker can be feast or famine. Especially in the beginning, before I secured my first book contract, the outside pressure and cultural norms of our society said that I should be in a traditional nine-to-five, earning an "acceptable" salary with benefits. While this wasn't a path that my authentic self wanted to pursue, my POS-itis ran rampant with thoughts of inadequacy. I was spending far too much time in the emotional mind. (Remember the What Happened Bubble in chapter 3?) The problem for many of us: when we spend too much time in the emotional mind, it's easy to succumb to the pressures of the world around us. For the Three Rs to be effective, we need to learn to tap into the power of the wise mind.

2. **Reject:** Next, you *reject* the thought. This is where it is essential for you to be intentional. Just like any other endeavor, there is no power if you don't believe. If you walk into the gym every day with the mission of losing weight and becoming fit, you are spinning your wheels if your self-talk says, *This is a waste of time.* Only when you are intentional about your workout, focused on the task at hand, can you create meaningful and lasting change.

Let's say that your thought is that you are a bum for not having your own place, as you are still living with your parents post graduation. We tend to use strong, harsh, and punitive language when we are dealing with ourselves—much more so than when we are helping others. ("Helping" is a key word here.) Why is it that we help others when they are struggling but we beat ourselves up when the roles are reversed? Perhaps our fear of self-acceptance is a more powerful force than we first imagined. Regardless, we are going to reject the nonsense that you are a "bum" for remaining under the roof of your folks.

3. **Reinterpret:** Now the power begins. Once we've recognized and rejected our thought, it's time for *reinterpretation*. While the first

two steps are important, it's our ability to reinterpret the meaning that represents the game changer. This is where we must get into what the brilliant Dr. John Wimberly would call "wise mind."

There are a multitude of factors that contribute to your current status. If yours happens to be that you are without a *good* job and/or you're living with your parents, chances are it's not because you are a bum lying around playing Xbox for no *good reason*. I emphasize "good reason" because there may very well be a valid reason you are at home playing the latest version of *NBA 2K*. Let's say you are battling an illness or recovering from an injury—well, your options may be limited. And it is important for you to recognize this in your reinterpretation.

Again, I revisit the What Happened Bubble in chapter 3: it's not about what happens but your *interpretation* of what happens that matters.

Let's look at two different interpretations of why you are living with your parents as a twenty-three-year-old college graduate. The first will be from emotional mind: *I'm a piece of shit. What a fucking loser. I have a college degree, I'm twenty-three years old, and I'm still living with my parents. I'll never get a good job, and I'm sure as hell never going to meet my future partner living like a chump.* Sound familiar? Unless you are a narcissist (one with a grandiose view of themselves), you've likely experienced something along these lines.

Let's say you just scored a C on a test: *God, I'm stupid. Natalie hardly studied and got an A while I studied my ass off and got a C. WTF. I'm never going to amount to shit. If I can't ace chemistry, how am I ever going to get into the college of my dreams? I'm so screwed.*

Do you see the vicious cycle?

Let's take a look at these two examples from a wise-mind perspective: *Okay, I'm not happy about living in my parents' basement as a twenty-three-year-old graduate; this certainly wasn't how I pictured things in my postcollege life. But I'm doing my best. I'm applying for jobs and putting myself out there even though I'm not getting interviews yet. I'm going to be proactive about this and have a few people look at my resume to see if I can tighten that up. Beyond that, whether or not I receive the call is out of my control. This isn't what I wanted, but living under my parents' roof sure as hell doesn't define me. I'm going to make the most of this time until things turn around.* Now it's essential to recognize that no matter how challenging the job market is, you control your own destiny and things aren't going to turn around by osmosis. You must be proactive to change your circumstances. You've got to develop a plan, a roadmap, and then you've got to get out there and beat the pavement, networking, volunteering, taking classes at the local community college (if available), and going to presentations, workshops, and seminars with your business card in hand until you land that first gig.

Another wise-mind interpretation: *Wow. I can't believe I just got a C on this test! Natalie got an A, and damn, that stings. I thought I studied my ass off, but perhaps it's not all about the time spent studying but the way in which I study. I'm going to have to study more effectively and efficiently for the next exam. But regardless of how efficiently I study, chemistry is a hard class and not a great fit for my learning style. All I can do is my best.*

Do you see the difference? Though the two examples didn't change, the interpretation *did*. Getting into the wise mind was the difference maker. The emotional mind is distorted and delusional, while the wise mind is rational and realistic.

As my mentor Dr. Wimberly used to tell me, "Three-R the shit out of things, Michael."

The next time the pressures of your peers or our cultural expectations are weighing you down, and the doubts about your authentic self and path cause you to venture down the wrong route in your mind, tap into the power of the Three Rs. Remember that *this*, just like any other skill, will take practice, steadfastness, and massive amounts of repetition. And there is no better time to start the exercise than *right now*.

CLOSING THOUGHTS

We can't spend our life trying to be liked by everyone else. It's not only impractical, it's irrational.

The purpose of this book extends far beyond the boundaries of self-improvement; it is my purpose and hope that it will also imbed in your hearts and minds the importance of community and legacy work. Remember the 30 Percent Rule: if you are without people who disapprove of your style, your tact, your passion, and your mission, you probably aren't being very edgy. And that is fine if you want to get by and get through life unnoticed. But this much is certain: you are going to have a very hard time nurturing positive change in the world by going at it unnoticed.

I'm convinced that we must find our own authentic edginess—our unique "chippiness"—to be effective leaders in the twenty-first century. I can tell you from my personal experience so far that this isn't easy, but it sure feels good to say, "To hell with it! What you see is what you get."

There are few things more refreshing than coming across someone who is authentic, isn't afraid of criticism, and is passionate about a cause. The mission of this book is to inspire people to pursue their passion, live a life that matters, and change the world. And rest assured: the world *needs* changing. There is still far too much ignorance, intolerance, bigotry, and hate poisoning the minds of our youth and adults alike. Whether it's a vitriolic rant against animals like grizzly bears, bison, and wolves that elicit deep-seated emotions across the West; homophobic slurs spewed toward the gay and lesbian community; or racist remarks about people of color, we can no longer accept or tolerate this in the modern world. Enough is enough.

Remember the words of Robert Gates—"To avoid criticism, say nothing, be nothing, do nothing"—and then accept *my* challenge: *Say something, be something, and do something.* Continue to uncover your authentic self, and don't let the perception of others blow you around like trash in the wind. Stand up and speak out for that which you believe to be right. Read; study; seek out mentors; learn about the world around you and about the threats to our wild planet; and become a voice for the voiceless. Authentic leadership in action is what inspiring a legacy is all about.

PART III

UNCOVERING PURPOSEFUL

PASSION

5

Harness Your Potential

The most powerful weapon on Earth
is the human soul on fire.
—Marshal Ferdinand Foch

I'm convinced that the principal difference makers in most successful endeavors are gritty determination; perseverance in the face of overwhelming obstacles; guts (throwing caution to the wind); and deep, burning passion that inspires an unwillingness to settle. And in this recipe of success, passion is *the* ingredient that holds everything else together. Passion is what separates the pretenders from the contenders. Passion represents the fire within. If you genuinely have a love for something—a passion for something—and can develop the audacity to pursue that passion, you can become an effective leader in whatever arena you choose on your personal journey of legacy work.

When we combine passion with the authentic-leadership model, we have uncovered a potent recipe for positively impacting the world around us. Think about it for a minute: which teachers, professors, peers, bosses, and coaches have inspired you the most and, in the process, had the biggest impact on you? More often than not, it's those who displayed passion for their subject matter, sport, or platform. (This is part of the heart piece in chapter 1's BA Balance wheel.) There is nothing worse than sitting in a classroom or conference lecture with a teacher who has lost his zeal. Conversely, when we walk into a room lit afire by a person passionate about what they do, we can't help but gravitate toward their energy. The subject matter isn't relevant; for when we are in the presence of passion, we can't help but be inspired. Passion creates a gravitational pull that attracts people from all walks of life. Passion is the catalyst.

Now, those of you who know me or have heard me speak know that passion is a cornerstone of what I'm all about—but this wasn't always the case. Passion doesn't develop overnight, and it isn't something you can force. *You can't pretend passion.* Passion is, by its very nature, *authentic.* It is something to *unearth.* Think of it as a long-lost treasure—an archaeological dig with massive implications. The map to its location isn't clear, but you know it exists; and your purpose is to discover it. And though the journey may be arduous and unpredictable, once this passion is discovered, the world—*your* world—will never be the same.

There have been times in my life, periods of transition and transformation, where I've felt dejected as I've struggled to find my place in the world. And the universal factor that has always been present during these times of idle confusion has been a lack of connection—*a lack of passion.* We feel most alive when we are doing something that we are passionate about. And while it isn't rational for us to believe that we will always walk through life with a passion burning as hot as white gas, the pursuit of purposeful passion represents the audacious path to a more meaningful existence.

One of the fears often expressed by the young adults that I have the opportunity to speak to and work with is that they haven't yet found their passion. Not to worry; your passions (plural) will come. But just like anything worthwhile or meaningful, you've got to put in the time and approach life in a certain way—an *intentional* way—if you are to uncover and harness your passion, and achieve your fullest potential.

Before we delve too deep into the passion equation, I want to emphasize a very important concept: in your quest to unearth what you are passionate about, don't limit yourself by believing you have to find that *one* great passion. We live in a big, wild, and abundant world; and I encourage you to embrace multiple passions.

If we are to live a life that matters, inspire a legacy, *and* relish the ride, it's essential that we discover and nurture passion in our lives. What makes you want to get out of bed in the morning? What makes you tick? These are the questions you need to ask yourself. Don't fret if you don't have the answer—but *do* begin asking. Because *this* is the time of your becoming—the foundation has been laid, and now you get to build the structure of your house and legacy, choosing what you are all about.

It's true that being a gritty, scrappy, and resilient dude has played a major role in any success I've achieved in life, but ultimately, I have to credit passion with where I am today. One of the great mysteries and joys of life is our search for the perfect match—the right combinations of sweet and spice, the partner who helps us to feel complete. I'm not sure that I know of a more meaningful recipe or more potent union than that of passion and love. Though I've always been fond of the saying "love makes the world go around," I think it's safe to say that these two intangibles of intangibles represent a most-powerful symbiotic relationship.

If you've picked up this book and are still with me this far along, I'm confident you aren't someone who is content walking through life without making an impact. There is no doubt in my mind that you are someone hoping to harness your full potential. While I don't pretend to have all the answers, I am certain of this: *unlocking the power of purposeful passion is paramount.*

What do all great leaders, teachers, coaches, entrepreneurs, and community activists have in common? *Passion.* This Pollyanna nonsense proclaiming that the most successful leaders are those who are unwavering in their confidence and sense of purpose is garbage. Confidence isn't something you have, it's something you *acquire* over time, through the result of positive outcomes. Learning to accept the ebb and flow of confidence and purpose is a big part of our life journey; that is the power of vulnerability and authenticity. We simply aren't going to feel confident and purposeful all the time. So don't sweat the older adults who are riding you about what you are going to do with your life. That's *your* business. And you need to become familiar with what you are passionate about before you can even begin exploring what you want to do with your life.

Whatever you do, unless it is a stopgap (part of the plan and a means to an end), don't settle for a future you aren't passionate about. The traditional concept that you have to graduate from college, get a job (regardless of whether or not that job resonates with your soul), and simply live to enjoy your weekends is played out. There is certainly a time and place to do what you have to do to survive and to make the dream a reality, but we must not settle for a life without passion. As always, if the traditional path of a nine-to-five gig followed by weekends of fantasy football and dirty dashes is what you dream of, well, dream on. But I have faith that *this* time and *this* generation will not only change this paradigm but enlighten the passage in the process.

CHANGE HAPPENS

The one constant in this life is change. No matter how much you want things to stay the way they are, many changes will be out of your control. Therefore, the more we learn to embrace change, the less heartache and despair we will experience when facing uncertainty.

At some point in our lives, we are all going to have to remake ourselves. We can't be captain of the football team, homecoming queen, valedictorian, PG1 (starting point guard), or the big man on campus forever. "To every thing there is a season." Some seasons last longer than others, but the season, phase, time will always pass and the next adventure will always begin. The challenge is to not hold on to or get stuck in the past, as the power of *now* is a substantial component of the *being intentional* equation.

You've all heard it before. How many times has your dad gone on and on about his glory days on the football field; or what about your grandma talking story of the *good old days?* It's fun to look back, reflect, and rehash our Golden Era; and perhaps we all suffer from a slight case of revisionist history from time to time. But there is a big difference between those who fondly reflect on special times and those who live in the past, afraid to embrace the uncertainty of the future. If you find yourself wanting to say "get over it" or "move on" when hearing these reveries, you're likely dealing with someone who's stuck in an old loop.

One of my favorite bands of all time is the Dixie Chicks. Talk about audacious. The lead singer, Natalie Maines, doesn't hold back, always speaking her mind with a bold, "I don't give a fuck" attitude that I can't help but love. And the audacity with which she sings and her bandmates (the dynamic sisters) perform is a lesson in the power of purposeful passion (PPP). Their music awakens the senses and reminds us that we get to *choose* what we're passionate about. In one of my favorite Dixie Chicks songs, Natalie flows about taking "The Long Way Around," doing things her way by striking out on her own to pursue music while all of her friends from high school married their high school boyfriends, bought houses close to home, and called it a day.

Now don't get me wrong—there is nothing wrong with landing in your hometown, nor is there anything wrong with being close to your parents. My parents are two of my best friends, and I couldn't be more grateful that they have followed my daughter and me to bountiful Bozeman, Montana. But when we stay home out of the fear of pursuing our passion, unwilling to remake ourselves and accepting the status quo instead? Well, that's far from audacious.

As you journey through life, you will learn to appreciate those with the guts and panache to remake themselves—those doing something bold in their pursuit of a life lived with passion. You will also shake your head in dismay at people you know from "back in the day" who haven't changed since high school, so afraid are they of accepting transformation.

Change is hard. Uncertainty is scary. But there is no doubt that the lives of those who are living with passion are those willing to navigate through the gauntlet of conformity and criticism, eager to embrace the potential that awaits on the other side.

THE REMAKE

The remake is always intimidating. If we are striving to live a life that matters, however, unwilling to accept mediocrity and a life of conformity, we will all have to remake ourselves at some point—and most likely, *more than once*. This presents one of the greatest challenges of one's personal journey; and in my thirty-plus years of walking this Earth, I've already been thrown into the fire of metamorphosis on multiple occasions. Sometimes change is chosen and sometimes forced, but no matter the reason, it's only when we learn to welcome the change that we begin to unlock our potential.

After putting all of my eggs in the hoops basket for my entire youth and teenage years, the passion that fueled my three hundred jump shots and pushups a day was stomped out with a car accident that triggered an autoimmune disorder—all against my will. What next? I didn't have the answers. And because I had been so focused, so passionate about that one thing, I sank into a place of utter despair. I knew that life without passion was like a river without trout—lifeless and without spirit.

But the thing about passion that many people can't wrap their head around is that it's not something that can be forced. *It's no different from love*: the first encounter may be subtle or it may hit you like a ton of bricks, but once discovered, it must be fostered, nurtured, and developed. Personal growth is holy, tender ground; and fostering passion is like tending to a fickle and sensitive plant. The mission? It's not to create one bomber crop that yields a bountiful payoff while ravaging the organisms that add biodiversity and nutrients to the soil. Instead, our mission needs to be akin to permaculture—sustainable and self-sufficient.

If our passion burns out and depletes the habitat that is our spirit, we are on an unsustainable path. Thus, I'm going to introduce a new concept—one created by one of the edgiest and most passionate dudes I know (Scotty B Black). He came up with it one brilliant summer day in Bozeman following my morning writing sesh. I read him the above paragraph over lunch, and his response? *Permapassion*.

PURPOSE AND PERMAPASSION

Just like nurturing a plant in the style of permaculture, permapassion is tricky. But if we can foster the development of a sustainable and self-sufficient passion, the harvest has potential for unlimited prosperity.

After my diagnosis with ankylosing spondylitis, I hung up the basketball kicks, left the Seattle area, and returned to the place of my birth—Coeur d'Alene, Idaho—where I enrolled at North Idaho College. For the first time in my life, I wasn't a standout athlete receiving the extra attention and academic leniency athletes often receive. The first semester was hell; and I contemplated dropping out each and every day, totally unsure about whether I could pull it off. But I persevered and endured, finishing up the first semester and, ultimately, my first full year on the dean's list—with a 4.0.

This was empowering beyond my wildest imagination. For the first time in my life, I felt cerebral. What was the difference maker? I had developed a new love and passion, and this one had nothing to do with what I could or couldn't do physically. This new fire burning from within was for the environment and conservation. After a few weeks in my first environmental science class, I was hooked. School remained a struggle for the remainder of my college years, but I managed to graduate NIC with my AS and then the University of Montana with my BA—and both times on the dean's list, something I never thought possible.

The game changer was my newfound passion. This dream of becoming a voice for the voiceless (wildlife, wild landscapes, wild rivers) consumed me throughout my entire college experience—one of the many powerful things about passion. It inspired a sense of purpose. And purpose represents the *It* Factor when it comes to unveiling a meaningful existence.

Without a sense of purpose, it is easy to feel like we are blowing in the winds of perception, spending far too much time consumed with what others think. But when passion is ignited and we uncover how to pursue that passion in a purposeful, sustaining way (permapassion), we unleash our highest potential. The power of purposeful passion therefore represents the most potent of recipes for inspiring a legacy and living a life that matters.

Ask yourself what you're passionate about. Even if you don't know the answer already, you still need to start asking the question. Our fear of failure can keep us from addressing these difficult questions, but we can never discover the answers to life's puzzles until we find the audacity to start digging. So make it a habit. In class, at work, on your team: ask the question *(What am I passionate about?)*. Don't worry about what others are going to think about the answer or the fact that you don't know it; simply start asking the questions that lead to answers—the passions—you don't yet know.

If someone had told me when I was twenty-one that my life's work and passion would be inspiring people to nurture a commitment to our wildest places and animals, I would have thought he or she was crazy. If someone had told me seven years ago that the most important thing in my world would become a beautiful, bold, and audacious little girl, I wouldn't have been able to wrap my head around it.

Journey through life with an open heart and mind because you never know what is going to motivate you five, ten, fifteen years from now. Remain open to the endless possibilities in order to experience the most intense passion imaginable.

In your twenties, you aren't going to have all the answers; that simply isn't how it works. Hell, I'm thirty-five years old, and I'm certain I don't know everything. I'm always searching, stretching, and striving in hopes of uncovering the most meaningful existence I can muster, tapping into my fullest potential. That is the quest. *Where do I want to be in five years?*

That's a question I ask myself all the time. And when I answer the question, I begin the chase.

I've often said that when we stop striving, spreading our wings, growing, and transforming, it's time to turn the lights out. Now, I'm not advocating checking out on the world, but we don't want to be spongy, soaking up oxygen and putting out nothing but CO_2—and warming the planet to boot. If that's all we're doing, then it's time to (figuratively) turn out the lights, ask the difficult questions, and reemerge into the world when we are ready to shed light on what matters—what we are passionate about.

If we are on the path to legacy, we will continue growing, transforming, and evolving—permapassion at its best. And while we don't have to know all of the answers in regard to what our future looks like (that would rob us of the mystery and beauty of our personal journey), it is essential for us to know *who* we are, *what* we're about, and who we *hope* to become. Though answers to these questions may change, our foundation—our core values and the essence of who we are—should remain solid. Yes, we may have to do a little rehab work from time to time, to patch up the rough spots that have been plagued by invasive roots or simply weathered over time; but when we lay down the stable bedrock of who we are and what we're about, we can get through fairly unscathed.

Unless you are a believer in reincarnation (and even then, *this* journey in your present body is a one-timer), we only get one time to walk this Earth. This life we are given is the most precious gift of all. And because we only get one time to explore this journey, we ultimately have to reveal what we want our journey to be about. This can—and *should*—change over time as you continue to evolve into your own personhood, but you can't plan everything. Life's going to throw you curveballs, so you better learn to hit the off-speed pitch.

Like it or not, we are all going to face formidable times and challenges, periods of adversity, and sometimes, some really heavy shit. Some folks will be dealt more than others, fair or not; it simply is what it is. But the more I've lived, explored, and connected with people from all over the world, the more I've come to recognize that the strongest and most humble leaders—those living the most meaningful and authentic lives—are the ones who have struggled and overcome hardship.

While I've come a long way toward accepting the current state of my legs (remember, *accepting* is very different from *liking*), I still struggle with the fact that I spent fourteen of twenty-eight months (from 2012 to 2014) on crutches or in a walking boot cast with an Achilles tendon that has been my literal and metaphorical Achilles heel. As someone who exercises six to seven days a week, I've always gone hard. My physical activity is akin to medicine—my antidepressant and my way of connecting on a spiritual level to the landscape that fuels my spirit. When I'm bombing down the slopes of Bridger Bowl or out of the saddle as I climb Beartooth Pass on my road bike, or when I'm paddle surfing my way down the Yellowstone River or riding a wave on the south shore of Kauai, the release of dopamine and brain-enhancing endorphins has always represented my drug of choice. But for most of the last two and a half years, this hasn't been an option—a debilitating, heart-wrenching, and uncontrollable reality. So, I've been forced to battle the demons in other ways, determined to turn a negative into a positive.

Though I've always known that I have a need for these built-in chemicals (which we release naturally when increasing our heart rate), it wasn't until I read Jaimal Yogis's masterful book *The Fear Project* that I truly understood how they work. Studies indicate that dopamine and other endorphins that flood the brain during exercise can promote a positive state of well-being (happiness and pleasure), both mentally and physically.[1]

Remember the ODAAT mantra from chapter 2—*one day at a time*? This critical concept grounds us during times when we are feeling anything but grounded. Even passion is a double-edged sword (pluses and minuses): while it fuels our drive to pursue what we love, the loss of a passion can be equally devastating.

When I'm struggling most with the inability to pursue my physical passions, I often think of a legendary figure in the state of Montana's adventure world. He was a stud—the best skier on the mountain and the boldest river runner in the rapids—and is a dear friend of my parents. I was among the generation of outdoorsmen who idolized him, and I remember the call when we received the tragic news that he had been paralyzed in a skiing accident. Can you even begin to imagine the magnitude of this sudden transformation for a young man who seemed to have the world by the balls?

Though I haven't walked in his shoes, I know the power of the ODAAT mantra as I've trudged through my own big losses. How else could one navigate through the journey from able-bodied athlete to quadriplegic? The transformation was filled with overwhelming challenges—the likes of which most can't even fathom—yet the man who emerged is one for whom I have even *more* respect and admiration than I did before the tragedy. His passion for photography led him to New York, where his edgy style and photos appeared in the likes of *Vogue*, *Glamour*, and *Cosmo*. He also developed his writing skills, and today, his passionate prose inspires me each time I'm blessed enough to read his powerful, purposeful words.

That is the power of purposeful passion. From the depths of despair to a life of meaning, richness, and love, permapassion sheds light on that which is good in our world while inspiring us to trust the value of our contribution to the greater good.

Remember, no situation you ever find yourself in is hopeless. And hope and passion go hand in hand. How can you have one without the other? Hope is essential—the glue that binds passion and purpose together.

We must foster hope every chance we get. To dream is to hope, to hope is to strive, to strive is to live. No matter how dismal, daunting, or desperate things seem, there is always hope; and where there is hope, there is potential. Sometimes that's all we need—the hope that our passion and dream is possible. Much like a powerful love that can endure all things, with passion in our heart and fire in our belly, no summit is out of reach and no period of darkness is insurmountable.

When we learn to live life with love and passion—in a way that is purposeful and intentional—we unleash our metaphorical waters and become uninhibited to pursue our chosen course. We shower the world with humble grace.

This is the path of authenticity. This is the path of inspiring a legacy.

LEGACY WORK

I want to diverge for a moment to revisit the concept of legacy work. What exactly does this mean? Despite its fairly new label, the concept has been around for a long, long time.

A lot of people are content to simply walk through the motions of life, punching the clock, earning a paycheck, and calling it a day. I can't emphasize enough that *there is absolutely nothing wrong with this*; if you are putting food on the table and a roof overhead, this is admirable. But I find that this generation of young people wants something *more*—they are setting a higher bar. Adopting the concept of legacy work is a strong barometer for what they want their short walk on this planet to be about. And I'm a firm believer that legacy work and passion form a synergistic relationship.

As you are exploring your passion(s), I want you to ask yourself a few very important questions. For starters: *How does my passion positively impact society and the world around me?* To narrow it down even further: *How does my passion positively impact my community?*

I'm sure many of you have heard the phrase "think globally, act locally." Though simple in notion, this expression has long been a calling card for those in the environmental community. I've always been fond of stealing the words of the great Muhammad Ali, the original king of trash talk. After knocking out the heavyweight champion of the world, Joe Frazier, he triumphantly danced around the ring, arms stretched overhead, shouting, "I shook up the world! I shook up the world!"

No matter what your passion, make it your mission to be impactful *in your way* by staying true to where you are and what you're about. As a basketball coach, I tell my boys before a big game, "Tonight, we shake up the world of high school basketball in Montana." As an environmental activist, I always strive to "shake up the world" through positive global change—but that's a tall order for one person alone. So, I've come to realize the power of my immediate community in the "think globally, act locally" aphorism.

When we think too big, we can miss the mark. So, I love to apply the concept of the onion approach to legacy work too. Just as an onion grows layer by layer from the inside out, start from the inside (you) and work your way out to the layers of community around you. In this way, you positively impact the world without getting too far ahead of yourself. You embrace the powerful potential of the ripple effect. As Mother Teresa said, "I alone cannot change the world, but I can cast a stone across the waters to create many ripples."

This question of how your passion positively impacts the world around you is critical. There is nothing wrong with being passionate about exercise, outdoor pursuits, music, or any number of activities. My passion for paddle surfing, skiing, hiking, climbing, fly fishing, river running, and mountain and road biking has filled my life with much joy, connecting me on an intimate level with some of the most spectacular landscapes and scenery on Earth. But this is where multiple passions become important. If your passion doesn't positively impact the lives of others in your community, there is a good chance that your passion falls into what I like to call the "fun hog" category. Again, there is nothing wrong with being a fun hog from time to time, but when this passion overtakes us and keeps us from pursuing meaningful and impactful work, we are venturing into chancy legacy waters.

What do you want your legacy to be? If you want to be remembered as the boldest, bravest, and edgiest brosephus on the mountain, then shred powder 130 days a year. But if you are yearning for a more meaningful and impactful legacy as someone who contributed to your community, shared your passion, and positively impacted the lives of others, then it's important to embrace the concept of multiple passions.

Multiple Passions and the Slash Model

Unknowingly, my multiple passions led me to pursue a life in accordance with what author Marci Alboher calls the "slash model." (You may remember my mention of this in the previous chapter.) In her groundbreaking book *One Person / Multiple Careers*, Alboher introduced me to a concept that I had already adopted without knowing or labeling it as a "lifestyle." When people would ask me what I do, my response was always, "How much time do you have?"

The measure of "success" in our society typically places special emphasis on what we do. Especially as you reach the twenty-five to forty age group, you will find that this is the first question people often ask you. As someone who has worked as a ranger naturalist, a fly-fishing and wildlife guide, a freelance writer, a high school basketball coach, and a founder of a nonprofit (where I wore the hats of executive director / programming coordinator / chief fund-raising coordinator), I always struggled with answering the "What do you do?" question.

The timing was perfect when I stumbled upon Marci's book, as I was feeling insecure from the intense pressure to take a *real* job with a *real* paycheck and *real* benefits. Money was tight and I was working damn hard, with many irons in numerous different fires. It was quite the juggling act—too much so at times—but I knew the singular gig and nine-to-five life just didn't fit what I was about. Though difficult, I felt I had to keep plowing ahead with the passions that represented my fuel—my authenticity.

Knowing who we are and what we are about is a big part of leading a fruitful, impactful, and meaningful life. Far too often, we let peer pressure lead us astray from the path we know in our hearts we should be traveling. I've always known I would go crazy in a traditional nine-to-five job. My friends and family laughed (and then discouraged me) whenever I contemplated applying for or taking such a job; some things fit and some things don't. And when we learn to accept this about ourselves, we can focus our efforts, fostering our passion in a way that not only fills our cup but contributes to our community at the same time.

This is where the slash model comes into play for me. As someone who embraces multiple passions (and is perhaps just a tad bit ADD), the idea of doing one thing and one thing only for my work makes me want to scream. There are certainly many positives to taking a traditional job (more security, a steady and predictable paycheck, a 401K, better credit standing when it's time to purchase a car or house, status in the community), but it's safe to say that none of these reasons have been enough for me to ignore my inner voice. The life of a slasher can indeed be unpredictable, with periods of feast or famine, but the "security" of a traditional job is a façade when considering the delicate balance of market trends, office politics, limited thinking (discrimination), and other uncontrollable variables. My retirement package is built on the testimonials I receive from young people expressing how my message has positively impacted their lives.

Our legacy is a choice we get to make. We don't have to fit some cookie-cutter mold of what it looks like to be successful—unless we allow the world to squeeze us into that mold. So, I encourage each and every one of you to pursue multiple passions, as "impractical" as that may sound. I'm convinced that being practical is grossly overrated anyway and best left for the conformist, not the audacious.

In her best seller, Marci Alboher shares story after story of people who have challenged the status quo of our societal standards, pursuing their passion while positively impacting the world around them. And like Alboher's book, *Be Audacious* offers up a perspective that may not be for everyone. This book is for those who wish to embrace the Be Audacious mantra in hopes of living a bold, adventurous, unrestrained life in the chase of uncovering a life that matters. But let me clarify this again: I am by *no* means implying nor do I believe that those who choose a less bold, daring, or unpredictable existence aren't living a life that matters. I can think of few jobs more meaningful and beautiful than being a stay-at-home parent; and I have deep admiration for those who grind it out every day to support their family. If you are content taking a corporate gig, sticking with it for thirty years, and calling it a day, then more power to you. Just know that we live in a big world with an abundance of different things to be passionate about; and based on my personal experience and my work with young people across the country, I question the necessity to restrict ourselves, fall in line, and accept a lifestyle simply because it has been beaten into us as a cultural norm.

To hell with the cultural norms! If you are discontent with the thought of going straight into a career after graduation, then be audacious, pursue your passions, and embrace the slash model: one person / multiple careers. That is most definitely counterculture; and I, for one, have to say that I *love* representing a counterculture style.

The journey to your desired destination isn't going to be easy no matter what you do, so why not keep climbing and seeking, thinking of the traditional lifestyle as your safety net rather than your only route? Why not take a chance and go for that audacious leap into unchartered territory? Even if you miss the mark, you'll be better equipped for the next endeavor (pluses and minuses). What do you have to lose?

Life Success Breeds Work Success

Alboher has opened Pandora's box with her notion that the slash model is a new model for work/life success. I can't imagine Corporate America is overjoyed at the thought of a generation of young people unwilling to enter a workforce equating to Wall Street servitude. But I'm convinced that we have already entered this vast new terrain, and it may be too late to turn back. After all, what is work success without life success? And why can't the two blend together?

Life is short and can end in the blink of an eye. Never before has my understanding of this been more clear than after my brush with eternity a few Christmases ago, so why spend forty-plus hours a week doing something that we aren't passionate about? Why not find a way to do it *our* way?

Just remember: passion isn't something to be forced. It's just like love—it's either there or it's not. While I would encourage all of you to seek out multiple passions, you have to let them come organically, when the timing and conditions are right. And even then, you may resonate most with one particular pursuit. I know many people who are living audaciously and pursuing their passion in a singular way. One of my mentors, Steve Hoffman, is one such individual.

Steve is a raptor guru—he's absolutely *nuts* about birds. Ever since he saw thousands of migrating raptors at Hawk Mountain as a college student in Pennsylvania, his passion has been birds, raptors, and conservation. After graduating with an undergraduate degree in biology, he received his master's in wildlife ecology from Utah State University and immediately jumped into the field of raptor conservation, working for numerous agencies as he traipsed around the Desert Southwest in search of nesting hawks, hoping to protect their migratory pathways and nesting habitat.

As I said earlier, love and passion go hand in hand; I don't think there can be passion for something without love. But love can be fickle too; sometimes it hits us like a hurricane while other times, it grows slowly. There was nothing subtle about Steve's passion/love for raptors, however. All it took was that one encounter—the grand view of thousands of winged migrants soaring above the ridges of the Appalachian Mountain chain—and he was completely hooked. The entire trajectory of his life changed, so great was his passion for these birds of prey.

With passion and a vision to match, he eventually struck out on his own, leaving the security of the government agencies to found his own nonprofit, HawkWatch International. For five years, Steve worked his tail off, continuing to do contract work with local state agencies to pay the bills while he laid down the foundation of his nonprofit. It wasn't until his sixth year that he was able to go all in with HawkWatch, finally paying himself a modest salary. But this wasn't about money; this was about living a life of purposeful passion. Steve had uncovered the power of passion, and it had consumed him in every way.

Never before have I met anyone more passionate about one thing than Steve is for raptors. His contagious love for the winged community has enabled him to raise millions of dollars for raptor conservation in his thirty-plus years working in the field—a field that fills his soul and makes his spirit soar. In fact, having been a director for multiple bird-related nonprofits, his unbridled passion for conservation often threatens those who've never experienced a love as vibrant and burning as his.

When I first met Steve, he was between jobs in his chosen field—a result of haters who just couldn't hang with the intensity and magnitude of Steve's fire. For a nine-month period, this man who had spent his entire adult life working in bird conservation found himself selling trucks at a dealership here in Bozeman. Unwilling to accept this as his path, he knew this was a stopgap—a means to an end—until he could land another gig in his chosen field. But admirably, Steve showed up every day to a job I know must have haunted him; and with a smile on his face and a jubilant personality, he showered each customer with love, attention, and respect, killing it with sales. And whenever he found a window to preach raptor conservation, he jumped at the opportunity to share his true passion.

While many say things happen for a reason, I'm a believer that it's more about making the most out of any circumstance, doing all that we can to shed light on the positives. That said, had I not been in the market for a new truck when I met Steve, I'm not sure that I would ever have connected with one of the mentors I cherish most in this world. I was working a bear jam in Yellowstone National Park that day, and he was leading a bird-watching tour for a group of naturalists from South Africa on one of his days off.

Six months after our chance encounter, I purchased a truck from him. Twelve months later, he was advising me as I left the Park Service and founded my own nonprofit. Nine years later, our friendship has flourished like alpine wildflowers in late July.

Steve and I share two very important commonalities: we are both survivors and inspired lovers of our natural world. I sat with Steve for four hours every Wednesday for five weeks as he endured chemotherapy; and he stood by me through my health saga, divorce, and the dissolution of my nonprofit. And because of Steve's unmatched passion for raptors and his uncanny ability to share it in the most palpable ways, I am now a lover of the aerial community too. Each August, we journey into the high country on the plateau of the Gravelly Range (in southwestern Montana) and spend forty-eight hours with eyes locked to binoculars and spotting scopes, seeking sightings of our beloved raptors.

Steve is a testament to the power of purposeful passion in the truest sense. His passion fills his life with meaning, love, and goodness while impacting the lives and landscapes of those around him. Whether singular or multiple, when we uncover our passion and learn to share it, we tap into our ability to leave our mark. *Think globally, act locally.* Sharing our passion is a local act that has the potential to change the world.

Life's too short for us to waste time doing what others think we should. Follow your heart, pursue your passion, chase your dreams—that is what Steve has done ever since that fateful autumn day on Hawk Mountain. Like him, when we have passion in our hearts, we can uncover the hope to keep pursuing the climb to our personal summit, no matter how harsh the critics.

FIRE PLUS VISION

When we live passionately and love deeply, we ignite the fire that fuels the soul. But it is equally essential for us to develop and foster our *vision* for what we hope to accomplish with this passion. As a high school basketball coach, for example, I start each season by sharing with my team a mission and vision statement for what we will be about—the foundation for how we will conduct ourselves on and off the hardwood—no matter what the season sends our way.

So much of life is out of our control. We don't get to choose the body, mind, or circumstances we are given; we are what we are. Our mission is to work with what we have and make the most of it. As an avid road biker and fan of cycling, I can't help but think of the eccentric Jens Voigt. He entered the professional cycling scene in 1997. For seventeen years, I watched the six-foot-three, 168-pound German develop his legacy; no other rider rode with more style, gusto, or panache. Always willing to take on the *peloton* and never afraid of going at it alone, this man split apart more road races than any rider I've ever witnessed.

I watched Jens compete in his final race last year, just weeks before his forty-third birthday. It was a sight to behold. There he was in the USA Pro Challenge, an epic seven-day tour of Colorado, racing against riders half his age, and his propensity to attack led to long breakaways, one of which almost culminated in glory.

With a thousand meters left, he was still in the lead. It was only in the final 800 meters that the *peloton* finally swallowed him up. My heart ached as a group of twenty-plus riders overtook him, but ever the optimist, Jens just nodded his head and proceeded to the finish line. Along the way, he sat up in his saddle and extended his left arm to give high fives to the spectators. Loved for his positive attitude, in what should have been heart-breaking—his last chance at victory—Jens summed it up best when he acknowledged that he wasn't built to be a sprinter or a climber; he was just an ordinary rider who was passionate about cycling. But this passion, combined with his total disregard for cultural expectations, has inspired a legacy in the *peloton*. Jens made the most of what he had and let his passion serve as fuel in his tank. Never afraid to turn himself inside out for a chance at victory, he was a renegade, a pioneer, an audacious German who emptied his tank for the sport he loves.

But one doesn't reach the pinnacle of the professional cycling world without first developing a vision. *This is critical.* Passion without vision has no direction. Purposeful passion requires a road map—or at least an idea of what we hope to achieve. Once we know the endgame of what we wish to accomplish, we can work backward, creating a time line or sketch of how and when we are going to reach the summit.

In my life as a guru of slash, I had the dream of writing a book of essays chronicling my love and passion for Yellowstone Country. It was a long, arduous, inspiring, and sometimes daunting adventure to write my memoir, find a publisher, go through the editing process, and then—finally—see it in print. Even after it reached number one on the local best-seller list here in Bozeman, I'm not sure I fully understood the nature of this accomplishment. Perhaps it was in part because I worked on this project for such an extended period of time. I always saw writing *Grizzlies On My*

Mind as an equivalent to earning a graduate degree: while it may not have cost me as much in tuition, the time and commitment was no less demanding. But there was no hard deadline for my first book; it was something I wrote over the course of five years. When I inked a deal for *this* book, however, the deadline presented a very different beast. Though I had been talking up a Be Audacious book for over three years, I had never sat down to actually do the challenging work of putting pen to paper (or in my case, fingers to keys).

It's one thing to talk about the things we hope to accomplish and are passionate about, but it's another thing entirely to be audacious enough to actually *embark* upon a bold adventure into uncharted territory when uncertainty overwhelms our senses.

I was stoked about writing this book, and my cup runneth over with gratitude when I finally signed the contract with Graphic Arts Books after months of pitching the project—but the deadline was more than a bit intimidating. They wanted the manuscript by the first of November, giving me six months to put it all together. I rebelled against the idea of mapping out a schedule with a series of weekly deadlines, as I had always preferred to work more organically. In the past, when I had deadlines for magazine articles, I always waited until the final seventy-two hours before sitting down to actually hammer out the content. My articles were akin to a long two-day climb: there wasn't a lot of prep work or endurance involved, just a need to focus on the task at hand. But that simply wasn't going to cut it this time around; writing this book was akin to a massive expedition. I couldn't just throw gear in my pack and wing it.

So I busted out a calendar and sheet of paper. Starting with the end date, I worked backwards, calculating that I had three weeks per chapter. Accounting for speaking engagements, book-signing events, and mini summer vacations with my daughter, I realized that two weeks per chapter was much more realistic. And there it was. Time to crank. For the first time in my life, I scheduled morning writing sessions: Monday–Friday, from 8:30 AM to noon. I knew where I wanted to go (first round of the manuscript done by November 1), and I had developed my vision (daily writing sessions). Then it was all about digging deep and being relentless in my commitment to make it happen.

Passion is a beautiful motivator. Without my passion to positively impact the lives of others (especially young people) by inspiring more heart, more love, and more commitment to equality and to our wild world, I wouldn't have found the motivation to sit down every morning to write. But I also needed to develop my vision—a road map or at least a rough sketch—of where I wanted to go before I could uncover the full power of *purposeful* passion.

THE TIME FOR PURPOSEFUL ACTION

It's great when a kid flies around a basketball court with passion and a desire to contribute to the team, but I'll take a kid who is moving around the court with *purpose* any day of the week over one who is in constant motion. I often tell the teens I coach that there is a *big* difference between hustle and hustle with purpose. There's a young man I coached who wanted to be that guy—the one who outhustled everyone else and was admired for it—but his hustle lacked direction. In fact, his hustle hurt the team more than it helped. Lord knows I want my boys to get after it, but our effort must be channeled in a way that is conducive to our goal.

No matter how youthful we are, energy is finite; therefore, it behooves us to not only be purposeful in our actions but intentional—to unleash the power of purposeful passion. But there is a balance to this combo too, especially in cases when our passion or sense of justice takes over, superseding the best of intentions.

Take a recent incident that occurred when my high school basketball team and I ventured west to the small cowboy town of Dillon, Montana. While the surrounding rivers and national forests make Dillon a great launching point for wilderness-based adventure, I've never been that fond of the town itself. There's nothing in particular that I haven't liked; it's your typical rural western community, with the exception that it is home to Western (University of Montana Western). I've just sensed that Dillon might be a bit of a redneck town, so I've avoided it. Having played high school ball in the Seattle area, I come from a vastly different hoops arena—perhaps why I found myself making judgments when our Dillon opponents hit the floor.

On this, our third game of the day, I could see from the get-go that the Dillon players were athletic, talented, and cocky. Yet on this day, their arrogance outmatched their skill set. (It was going to be a chippy game.) They had been thumping every team they'd played throughout the tournament; and as we tipped off, it was apparent they thought our game was going to be more of the same.

On numerous occasions throughout the game, I had words with officials, the other coach, the other players, and even parents. The scene was out of control and sportsmanship was lacking. But after the game, when our sole African-American player informed me of a racial slur uttered by one of the Dillon players, my anger boiled over.

When confronted with difficult situations, we have two options: (1) remain idle and accept what is or (2) fight to change it. Remember, *acceptance is allowing reality to be as it is without requiring it to be different*; and circumstances dictate which option we're going to take. Being passionate about my boys and equality, it was clear to me that this was a fight worth waging. After exchanging words with a few of the Dillon parents, I made it clear to the parents of my players that we were getting out of Dodge without spending a dollar, as I didn't want to support what I perceived to be a community that brewed with racism and bigotry.

Now, in hindsight, I can see that I let my emotions overwhelm logic, as a few hick kids and classless fans shouldn't paint an entire town as racist—reality is never that simple. Dillon is a beautiful place and full of good people, as I had learned on assignment for one of my first articles after graduating from the University of Montana. But right, wrong, or indifferent, our high school athletes, fans, and parents are a reflection of the community; and my sweeping assessment of Dillon, based upon our experience during that basketball game, was not positive in the least.

Outraged the entire drive back to Bozeman, I contacted our athletic director, Mamba venom seeping through the phone. With him being one of the most celebrated and respected ADs in the state, I wanted to get his opinion before I started contacting local papers, school officials, and the Western coaches who were hosting the tournament. I knew his experience would help me go about things in a pragmatic way, as I have a tendency to run high on emotion, oftentimes losing sight of my wise mind. To my surprise, my AD grew up in Dillon and has deep roots and ties within the community. He asked me to let him handle it.

The next morning, when we arrived at the tournament, a representative from the university met with our player who had received the racial slurs, assuring him and me that they had spoken with the Dillon coaching staff. While I can't say I was entirely appeased by our conversation (I would have liked to have seen the student kicked out of the tournament), it was clear that our frustration wasn't going to change the bigoted way people think overnight. But I was passionate about bringing to light the ignorance that pervaded the gym on that day. I wanted my boys to see the importance of standing up for what is right.

Change only occurs when we are unwilling to accept a played-out and dangerous cultural standard, and then begin taking action against it. While our Dillon experience was small time in the scheme of things, it speaks to what happens when we are purposeful in our passion. Our team shed light on the ignorant words spoken by an opposing player—words clearly accepted as a cultural standard by some—and it was a step in the right direction. Eventually, if enough of us shed light on the darkness of bigotry, misogyny, racism, and hate, we *will* stamp them out on a global scale.

●●●●

Not in my lifetime can I remember a more passionate outpouring of protest than the Egyptian Revolution that began on January 25, 2011. Consisting of demonstrations, riots, marches, strikes, and civil disobedience, millions of protesters from differing economic and religious backgrounds joined together to overthrow President Hosni Mubarak.

There is strong evidence to suggest that social media played a significant role in igniting the flame of the rebellion to oust Mubarak. After seeing a disturbing picture online of the bloodied and disfigured face of Khaled Mohamed Said, a twenty-eight-year-old man who had been beaten to death by Egyptian police, Wael Ghonim knew he had to do something to shed light on this atrocity. With outrage burning in his belly, this humble, soft-spoken, self-appointed introvert (and marketing director at Google) launched a Facebook page—"We Are All Khaled Said"—to bring attention to the rampant abuse of power taking place in his homeland.

Passionate about the place of his birth and the immense struggles facing an entire nation of people, where corruption, torture, poverty, and unemployment had become epidemic, Ghonim played a major role in inspiring the revolution. I can't think of a greater legacy than a passionate plea to end oppression. Armed only with words written from his heart, Ghonim ignited a nationwide fire.

Passion is contagious. Sometimes all it takes is one believer to make history.

The Egyptian Revolution of 2011 stands as a testament to the potent recipe of passion combined with a refined message: with it, we can indeed change the world. Passion without focus peters out, but directed passion— with a clear meaning, message, and purpose—has limitless potential. Regardless of the scope, scale, or subject matter, Ghonim's purposeful actions are an example to all of what is possible when we make the choice to be audacious in defense of something we know to be just and right.

When we tap into the power of purposeful passion (PPP), we honor the very root of who we are and breathe life into the source of our becoming.

THE WATERS OF PERSONAL GROWTH

Ever since I was a child, I've been haunted by waters. And my love affair with flowing rivers has only strengthened over time—perhaps because water occupies approximately 70 percent of both our planet and our bodies; water metaphors seem so apropos when writing or speaking about personal growth.

Think of purposeful passion as the headwaters of a free-flowing river pouring from the high mountains of wild country. As the snow melts, hurried waters begin a tumultuous descent down the mountain to the valley floor. Once there, the river begins its long, circuitous, and meandering route to the ocean. The water that falls on the west side of the Continental Divide (the spine of the continent) ends up in the Pacific, while the water on the east side of the divide winds its way to the Gulf of Mexico, the Atlantic. The journey is long, with many obstructions deterring the water's passage; but eventually, most of the river works its way to the sea.

Each river has its own beginning and terminus. Some run fast while others run slow; some meander while others shoot straight; some end in the ocean while others finish their journey in lakes; some are celebrated and glamorous while others are subtle and without fanfare. In their own way, each river, stream, creek, and babbling brook is glorious; they each tell a story. And through the changing seasons, they continue to flow with purpose toward their destination, breathing life and biodiversity into the world they've shaped. What a beautiful metaphor for our own lives.

The river of life flows before us all. We may not know the final destination, but passion can serve as our gravity, keeping us in the main channel and moving downstream, around the river's bend, knowing we are on the path we are meant to travel. The key to any endeavor is no different from the flow of a river: no matter the obstacles standing in our way, we must navigate around the boulders and keep things moving forward. In this way, our passion can flourish like a budding cottonwood sending succulent scents of glorious fragrance on the winds. Much like these fragrant buds, when our passion is in full bloom, the world around us changes from a drab, dull, distilled environment to a landscape pulsing with life.

May you foster your passion at every bend in the river and uncover purpose to pursue whatever lights your spirit afire. For this is the path to personal growth—the force that feeds your legacy while keeping your vessel afloat.

A WORD OF CAUTION: RECOVER AND RECHARGE

When our passion leads us to give of ourselves we are on the path of legacy work. Philanthropic work (whether aimed at helping people, pets, land, wildlife, water) is noble, needed, and to be commended, but this work is draining. In order to be effective at it, we need to recharge—especially those audacious souls who adopt the PPP mantra. *Recovery is essential.* Just as you wouldn't go into the gym and spend an hour getting yoked with a massive chest-and-back workout without allowing forty-eight hours of rest and recovery before getting after it again, we must be conscious of the fact that we can run ourselves into the ground.

During my most frantic days, when I passionately wore the hats of fly-fishing guide, wildlife guide, nonprofit director, wedding officiant, basketball coach, motivational speaker, and environmental education contractor, often working sixty to eighty hours a week for months at a time, I would rarely go seventy-two hours without someone I respect telling me I was going to burn out. But I couldn't wrap my head around what they were trying to tell me, let alone heed their warnings. They called me Ironman Mike and Superman Mike for going hard and pushing myself beyond what others perceived to be my limits. Even after ten-hour guide days, I would return home, have dinner with my daughter, and then jump on my road bike as the light of another day began to wane. Grinding my way up a massive climb four or five nights a week, pushing my lungs and legs to failure in my own personal time trial—this is my drug *du jour*. The feeling that my legs are going to pop and my lungs are going to burst is something I love.

Besides, how could I possibly burn out when I was so passionate about my work? Yes, it was a grind, but these people just didn't get it.

Or so I thought. Until I burned out.

As if all of the literature on the Web and books on the topic aren't enough to give credence to the fact that burnout is real, I can tell you from firsthand experience that it's not only real, *it's brutal.* No matter how expensive, well built, and bomber a truck or vehicle is, if you run it into the ground, revving up the engine, pulling big loads, failing to keep up with its maintenance, eventually (and far sooner than it should, I might add), the engine will crash. We are no different. Adequate sleep represents our recovery period. Proper nutrition signifies our oil change. Exercise keeps our joints and muscles (pistons and spark plugs) lubed and firing. Vacations and mini vacations represent our opportunity to recharge, detox, and reconnect.

Think of extended vacations and those of the mini variety as a transmission flush, spiritual enemas—a cleansing of sorts. I've become a firm believer that both extended and short sabbaticals from purposeful work are as important as the work itself. No matter your youthful exuberance, spirit, or endurance, don't just go, go, go—even when our society praises you for it. I loved that people called me Superman Mike for driving myself into the ground; it fueled my drive to go harder and longer, even though my body was screaming at me to slow down. Ever since I was young, if people told me I couldn't do something, it was a sure way to get me to make the attempt. The more dire the warning, the more I rebelled and pushed back.

Even now, as a grown-ass man, I'm still hardheaded and stubborn as hell when it comes to doing things my way. Take the Ice Bucket Challenge rage that went viral on Facebook last year. Though my empathy for those who are diagnosed with ALS (a crippling disease of epic proportions) overflows, I simply couldn't wrap my head around dumping a five-gallon bucket of water over my dome at a time when the state of California and its thirty-eight million residents are facing one of the most extreme droughts in the last one hundred years. And what about the children all across the globe, in places like sub-Saharan Africa, who walk miles each day in hopes of receiving a cupful of drinkable water? Jason Ruiz, who writes for the *Long Beach Post*, estimates that over six million gallons of fresh water were wasted during this fund-raising effort.[2] Though the trendy campaign raised millions of dollars for ALS (brilliant), I can't help but believe 95 percent of its participants are going to forget about the struggles of those living with ALS about as quickly as this popular project fades.

Dumping water over your head doesn't make you a champion of the

30,000 Americans who live with ALS, but conserving water or donating to an organization like The Water Project does make you an advocate for the estimated 358 million people in Africa who don't have access to safe water.[3] Come on now, we can do better than that, yeah?

So I get it when young people shrug their shoulders and put on blinders when an "adult" warns them that they're pushing too hard for something they love. These people don't know a damn thing about you, right? As a prideful, passionate, and purposeful young man, I had resigned myself to pushing until the wheels came off, truly believing that the wheels would just keep rolling. But I learned the hard way that I was wrong.

Some adults are definitely haters and are perhaps threatened when they see a young person with the guts to pursue their dream; but I think most have good intentions when they share such dire predictions. The problem is typically *not* their concern but the way in which they present it. So, I'm going to ask you to pause, take a deep breath, and *consider* my counsel. As someone who desperately wants to see more empathetic, loving, wild-natured, passionate, audacious, and courageous souls willing to put their hearts on the line to change our world for the better, please *do* contemplate for a moment the importance of self-care, minis, and extended vacations in your efforts to keep your passion alive, well, and prospering.

Though I pushed too hard during my summers of madness (there *is* such a thing as going too hard despite what our manic culture likes to endorse), I uncovered enough wisdom to take two weeks off every year at the end of October and beginning of November, following five frantic months of guiding and environmental programming. Within days of ending my nonprofit's Yellowstone Leadership Challenge, I would board a plane with my family for a tropical escapade. Immersed for ten to fourteen days in the Polynesian culture and Pacific Ocean, I would wake early before my daughter and my then wife, throw my board in the rental van, turn on my favorite island radio station (a hybrid between 90s hip-hop and reggae), and journey to my favorite break. For two hours each morning (and every evening too), I rhythmically bobbed with the swell of the ocean, in between catching waves that hijacked my winter reveries.

The Pacific is filled with *mana* (Hawaiian for "power") and has the restorative quality unique to moving water. After spinning my wheels for months at a time, stressed to the max, exhausted and exhilarated by my work, my racing mind finally quieted once I was immersed in the ocean. It's a place that has become my refuge—a source of rejuvenation.

Taking time for yourself is fundamental if you hope to live a life that matters. Though each person's recovery methods will be personal in nature, these sojourns are universal in that they are critical to the sustainability of our passion. But personal growth and success for the sake of the individual is played out, my friends. There are currently 7.2 billion people on our planet, and we are expected to reach 9.2 billion by 2050.[4] It's time to change the personal growth and leadership paradigm to focus on the big picture—the community. The power of purposeful passion lies in its capacity to contribute to the greater good by positively impacting the lives, landscapes, and biota around us. But none of that is possible without self-care.

Remember the onion: start at the center with yourself and then work through your layers of influence to witness the power of the ripple effect. Sustainability is a key component to permapassion and to the building of your legacy too.

Practice Exercise:

EXPLORING YOUR PASSION(S)

Let me remind you that you need not trip if you have no clue what you are passionate about at this time. Passion isn't something that can be forced; it's either there or it's not. But you will know when it takes hold. And when it does, it may be subtle or it may hit you like a hurricane. You just have to be patient and receptive to it, providing the fertile soil in your mind for it to take root, grow, and ultimately prosper.

In this exercise, I'm going to ask you to take forty-five minutes to an hour to examine your passion(s) in three separate journaling sessions (or you can choose to do in one session as your time allows). If you don't already have a journal, pick one up. It doesn't have to be fancy, leather bound, and expensive—paper is paper, yeah? (But make sure it's recycled paper!) Our focus is the tremendous power in putting words on a page.

Session #1: *I Am Passionate About . . .*

1. Find a quiet space where you can brainstorm uninterrupted. And if your busy mind is the one distracting you, consider using chapter 1's breathing exercise to calm it down.

2. Start with this basic question: what are you passionate about? If you don't have an immediate answer, write down things that intrigue you, quicken your pulse, and attract your attention.

3. Now ask yourself what you would like to become passionate about. Is there a special cause or a local need that moves you? Is there a global issue that's been on your radar? Write down whatever pops into your mind. Let it go and let it flow.

Session #2: *I Admire . . .*

1. Now I want you to make a list of five people you truly admire—parents, kindred spirits, mentors, personal heroes, historic figures; whomever you look up to. (Leave three or four lines between each name.)

2. Beneath the first name, write a short sentence about why you are inspired by this individual.

3. On the next line, try to describe this person with one word or a short phrase.

4. Last but not least (and in single words, if possible), write down what you believe this person is passionate about. (Chances are you will list more than one thing, as many of the most inspiring people have multiple passions.)

5. Repeat steps 2 through 4 for each of the remaining people on your list.

6. If you are wondering about the purpose of this exercise, please proceed to the story below.

Passion Breeds Passion

What does someone else's passion have to do with fostering my own?

I'll answer your question with another question: when was the last time you had those butterflies in the belly that start up when you come across someone who captures your attention and commandeers your mind—that feeling ignited by potential love?

For me, this happened over Labor Day weekend last year. The wife of Yellowstone's chief ranger invited Kamiah and me to spend the night at their bed and breakfast on the shores of the upper 'Stone (the stretch of Yellowstone River that I've become more intimate with than any other place in this world). As we sat down to dinner, a friend of hers walked in the door and immediately grabbed my attention. Amanda was absolutely stunning, with long flowing hair and an angelic grace. But beauty is beauty. Ultimately, it doesn't really mean shit if, underneath that exterior, there isn't soul, character, and spirit to match. While I was intrigued, I simply opted to hang with my daughter and do our own thing.

But later on, when we ventured into the kitchen and a conversation about surfing, another moment caught my attention. One of our friend's daughters said something about having never been to Hawaii, and my daughter's response was a riot. With a swaggy attitude, she tilted her head, scrunched her face, and said, "What? You've never been to huh-WAH-ee?" Amanda immediately burst into laughter, clearly thinking Kamiah's pronunciation of Hawaii was cute as hell.

Amanda was so attentive and thoughtful, and appeared to be intentional in her actions, movements, and words. She had a presence about her that drew me in. Watching her interact with my daughter over the campfire later that night had my head spinning.

After singing Kamiah her nightly lullabies, I ventured back upstairs to the kitchen, as I had become more than intrigued with this enigmatic mystery woman. As she was doing dishes, I asked, "So, what are you about, Amanda?" Seven hours later, the clock struck 4 AM and we were still talking story.

You're probably still asking yourself, *What the hell does this side story have to do with developing my passion?*

Just as the potential for love inspires us to sit in reverie, envisioning what could be, time spent with passionate people inspires us to explore our own inner passion(s). *Passion breeds passion.* The ability to hope, dream, and envision the future we desire is unique to our human experience—at least as far as I can tell. So, it's natural for me to contemplate what life would be like walking hand in hand with a woman like Amanda, and it's fitting to meditate on one's own passion when inspired by others' passion and authenticity.

Being in the presence of such an electric, alluring, and spirited woman lit my world afire for seventy-two hours as I was left with nothing but Amanda on the brain. The connection that powered a most potent evening could ultimately drift downstream on the currents of the Yellowstone River, or perhaps that night was just the beginning of something transcendent. Nonetheless, I'm grateful for those seven hours with a woman who is clearly passionate about living life to the fullest and boldly pursuing her dreams.

Think of spending time around passionate people as an all-natural fertilizer of fecundity: the more we're around them, the more we foster, nurture, and enhance the soil that will determine whether our passion dwindles or flourishes.

Session #3: *I Can Make an Impact By . . .*

Now that we've investigated the importance of surrounding yourself with passion in hopes of cultivating the most verdant and nutrient-rich soil possible for growing your own passion, there is one last activity I encourage you to do.

You've explored your own passion and the passions of those who inspire you, so let's take it to the next level. Consider this a guided noodling session—but don't get caught up on the content. Just grab a pen and let the ink leave its mark.

1. Envision how you would like to use your passion to positively impact the people around you—your friends, your family, your partner, your neighbor.

2. Next, I'd like you to expand your scope to envision how your passion could positively impact your community. (Remember the onion approach: working from the inside out.)

3. And finally, take a few moments to journal ways you envision your passion positively impacting society—think big on this one. And don't worry about whether or not your vision seems realistic or practical. To hell with what's realistic and practical! You can't accomplish something historic and monumental without first reducing your vision to its tangible form.

●●●●

The extraordinary doesn't simply happen by drifting out of one's mind in vague shapes and ideas until it magically manifests into a reality. We have to dream the dream; put the vision on paper; and then uncover the audacity, tenacity, and scrappy spirit to pursue that passion with a religious zeal.

This is how we change the world. One layer at a time, one step at a time, one day at a time—steadfast and determined. And it all begins with a vision born of the fire of passion.

CLOSING THOUGHTS

It is an undeniable truth that we gravitate toward those who are passionate; passionate people naturally attract positive people in their life. Our journey is hard—full of obstacles, heartache, and disappointment—so it's essential that we nurture the relationships that bring positivity and a supportive vitality to our world. And when purposeful passion is present in *our* lives, we, too, put ourselves in a position to attract affirmative people who will contribute to our mission in a synergistic way.

We live in a world where settling seems to be the accepted norm, but passion is the game changer—and it's addictive. Once we discover what it's like to live with passion, we are unlikely to settle for anything less. To be audacious is to pursue passion with courage, gusto, and an unwavering commitment to our search for a life that aligns with our hopes and dreams. And along this road to being audacious you will discover the essential nature of permapassion (sustainability and self-sufficiency), recognizing that self-care and recharging are equally important to your mission.

But the mission of this book extends far beyond the importance of finding your own passion and reaching your own personal mountaintop. The mission of the Be Audacious movement is clear: inspire people to pursue their passion, live a life that matters, and change the world—to build one's legacy. Remember to work from the inside out: start with yourself, then proceed to your community and beyond. This includes your career path—*life* success breeds work success. Have multiple passions! Live the slash model. The traditional model will always be there, but keep climbing until you can pedal no more and have to switch gears. Expect that you will have to remake yourself at least once—more likely a few times—in your lifetime, but strive on all the same.

When we harness the power of purposeful passion (PPP), we tap into our higher self, unlock our personal mission, and construct our platform for positively impacting the world around us. *But passion without purpose and vision has no direction.* To keep your fires burning hot, you need all three.

PART IV

DEVELOPING YOUR

VISION

6

Think Big and Dream Even Bigger

The future belongs to those who believe in the
beauty of their dreams.
—Eleanor Roosevelt

One morning last summer, I had breakfast with a filmmaker at one of my favorite local spots on Main Street, here in Bozeman. The air was brisk (which is often the case, even in the month of August), yet we chose to sit outside, basking in the glory days and fading light of the season.

I had worked with Leslie on a number of projects, ranging from National Geographic films to short bear-education pieces that appear throughout the region. He's a character—someone who has done things his way for as long as he can remember—and definitely not cut from the traditional nine-to-five cloth. After a successful film career in his home state of Florida, he had ventured north to Big Sky Country nearly a decade ago and purchased a small place along the Boulder River, which streams off the towering peaks of the Absaroka Mountains. Though he loved the home and life he had made for himself here, I could tell at breakfast there was a restlessness about him.

Midway through our omelets, Leslie told me of his plans to put his Big Timber ranch house up for sale. He had a vision of living out of a Mercedes van in pursuit of more meaningful projects that would reinspire his love of cinema and documentary films.

Leslie is a dreamer, authentic to the bone; and he doesn't give a shit what anyone thinks of him. Every couple years, I receive an urgent message from him about a new idea for a television show he wants to produce. And when a successful filmmaker and producer comes to you, asking you to be a major figure in the form of hosting his latest project, you listen. But I never get my head too wrapped up in this because ideas are one thing; coming up with funding for TV shows represents another beast entirely. But Leslie had called this meeting, expressing its compelling nature, and it didn't take long for me to recognize that he was *on fire* with his latest idea.

Leslie has both triumphed with hit TV shows and stumbled through projects that missed the mark. Eccentric, outspoken, and bold to a fault, he is uniquely *Leslie*. You either love or hate him. (Sometimes you love and hate him at the same time.) Leslie is who he is, and he isn't going to change for anyone. Stubborn? Perhaps. But if there is one thing I respect most about Leslie, it's his childlike enthusiasm for life, love, food, and cinema. No matter how hard things get, he never stops dreaming—a lesson to all of us.

Visionary author Napoleon Hill told us to "Cherish your vision and your dreams, as they are the children of your soul; the blueprints of your ultimate achievements." As a dreamer, romantic, and idealist myself, these words (written by a pioneer of the self-improvement genre) have always resonated deeply, reverberating in my rapid reveries—always serving as a reminder of how tightly we must grasp on to our dreams. I firmly believe the ability to think big and dream even bigger is the major factor that separates audacious individuals—those who inspire a legacy and live a life that matters—from those who settle for mediocrity. Again, this is the beautiful thing about being an adult: you get to make your own choices. And I can think of few choices of greater importance and relevance than the decision to live life as a dream chaser.

Why, then, are so few people pursuing their dreams? Why has accepting mediocrity become a social epidemic in our world?

Whether it be a love, place, adventure, job, or way of life, our dreams and most noble intentions are often stomped out of us at a young age by nurturing, well-meaning adults. We are told to be realistic and reminded that we must be "responsible," as if being responsible means selling our soul and giving up our dreams.

When we listen to this noise and let people tame our wildest aspirations, we are no different from the wild broncs who once lived a life of passion, lust, and splendor on the plains. Once captured, wranglers reined in the very essence of the animal—subduing them, breaking their spirit, and in the process, earmarking them for a life of servitude. The wild stallions had only two choices: fight or give in.

Our lives are not so different. We can give in to a life of conformity or we can fight with everything we've got, embracing our dreams while daring the ordinary people of the world to tame our counterculture approach. The mission of this book and movement is to be audacious, and pursuing our dreams is at the very root of what this looks like.

GET UP AND TRY

One of the things that keep us from *actively* pursuing our dreams is the fear of failure and rejection.

Let's start with relationships. Think about the last time someone captured your attention upon first sight. Guy, girl, straight, or gay, why do people struggle to find the audacity to walk up to a stranger they'd love to meet and spit a little game? The answer is simple: a fear of rejection.

While the fear of rejection certainly exists, I've come to see the expression of my admiration for a perfect stranger—in hopes of making a connection of any kind (not just romantic)—as a way to forgo living with regrets. I strive to live my life without what-ifs. Why spend time dwelling on the past and stressing about the future? What's done is done, so we might as well lay it all out there—because you never know what the results are going to look like unless you enter the race.

I recently had someone tell me, "You are so forward, expressive, and willing to share what's on your mind. I admire your courage." Though this may come easier to some of us than others, it's more about fostering the *choice* we have to be courageous in our interactions with others. There are pluses and minuses to everything. My knack for saying exactly what's on my mind can be a double-edged sword—both potent and painful. Another example: if you've had your heart broken and/or your trust betrayed over and over, I understand why you would have a hard time being vulnerable by expressing what's on your mind and in your heart. But that is the very nature of what it means to be audacious: uninhibited, unrestrained, and courageous in the face of prior or conflicting ideas.

Be audacious—uninhibited, unrestrained, and courageous—that's my mantra and how I choose to live my life. It's the mantra of young people I've worked with who are now out there chasing their dreams and pursuing their passion. I'm convinced if more of us adopted this philosophy, our world would be a more vibrant place. If enough of us stopped playing games and started shooting straight from the hip, our world would pulse with the magnetic vigor of community and legacy. It's time to stop fronting and start living.

If you see someone who you'd like to meet in hopes of exploring your connection, then put on your "Fuck It" hat and let that perfect stranger know what's on your mind. Will you get burned? Sometimes. But in the words of Pink: "You gotta get up and try."

Sometimes we make the shot and sometimes we miss. More often than not, when you don't hear back from someone, it isn't because you are lacking in looks, presence, or a good flow; instead, it is where the other person, the perfect stranger, is in his or her life. Sometimes, there will be a Hannah Del Waterman—a beautiful waitress and dynamic woman that I first crossed paths with at our local pub and knew I had to meet. So, I summoned the guts to write a note on my receipt and left it on the table with my number and a message: "I'm going to take you to breakfast."

After running through a quick Mock Talk (I'm a *huge* believer in the Mock Talk), I went over to the table she was working and interrupted her delivery on the night's specials.

"I left you a little note on the table. I look forward to connecting for breakfast."

Though Hannah and I didn't pan out, I did score a memorable breakfast with a fiery woman who has subsequently become a friend.

Applying for our dream school or job, entering a race, or submitting our manuscript or demo is just like asking someone on a date: it's a risk that doesn't always pan out the way you hoped. But making the shot is *not* what ultimately matters; it's wanting the ball and having the guts to *take* the shot that counts.

The next time you are contemplating doing something bold, I want you to ask yourself, *What's the worst that can happen?* Most of the time, it's our pride holding us back when we don't put ourselves out there. I know this because I've battled the demons of pride for many seasons. One thing I've learned through my readings, studies, and contemplations is that, while useful in battle—where pride in country or team can inspire confidence in one's ability to outlast his or her adversaries—pride doesn't serve us in matters of the heart.

Don't let the fear of failure rob you from pursuing your dreams. Fear of failure is nothing more than unmanaged pride. Ezra Taft Benson said, "Pride is concerned with who is right. Humility is concerned with *what* is right." To be audacious is to be concerned with what is just and verdant, in your own life and in the world around you.

FALL IN LOVE WITH "IMPRACTICAL"

Now that we've faced the fear of rejection and the pride demons, let's take a look at my favorite argument against following one's heart and chasing one's dreams: "It's not practical." Just writing these words brings a smile to my face. To hell with what's practical! We only get one chance to walk this Earth. Listen to your heart, chase your dreams, pursue your passions, love deeply, achieve the extraordinary—this is the path of authenticity and legacy.

If you have a dream and a vision for how to make that dream a reality, don't let "practical" matters deter you from pursuing it. Being practical is grossly overrated and best left to the conformists, not the audacious. I'm convinced that there is no killer of dreams more venomous than that of the practical mind. If I had listened to 99 percent of the people with whom I spoke about my dream and vision of leaving the National Park Service to start a nonprofit organization, I would have missed out on one of the most beautiful, meaningful, and powerful experiences of my life. Had I never started Yellowstone Country Guardians, I wouldn't have inked a contract with a book publisher for my first manuscript, ultimately opening the door to write this book.

To be audacious is to think outside the box. Forget the feasibility studies—they call it a "dream" for a reason.

How many times has someone told you that your *love* isn't practical? Well, let me break it down for you in the most real way I know: Love isn't always easy, convenient, or practical; it's often hard, scary, and heartbreaking. But love is the magic that keeps the world spinning. When given the choice, *choose love*. When given the opportunity, *fight for love*. To love is to dream, my friends.

How practical do you think people thought it was when Mahatma Gandhi embarked upon his defiant 1930 march to the sea in protest of the British monopoly on salt, ultimately becoming a leader in the Indian Independence movement? Not very, but this brave act was the most significant challenge to the British who occupied Indian land, ultimately kick-starting the movement that led to India gaining back its freedom.

How practical do you think people thought it was on a glorious day in 1963 when a young Baptist pastor from Montgomery, Alabama, spoke at our nation's capital of a dream that blacks and whites would go to school together, live together, play together, and love together? Martin Luther King Jr. called for an end to racism, intolerance, and hate. He was a brave and audacious leader of the African-American Civil Rights Movement—a man who defied all practical reasoning in hopes of creating a more just and equitable world.

How practical do you think people thought Elizabeth Cady Stanton was during the dark ages of the nineteenth century, when her fight as a women's rights activist and abolitionist challenged the white-male societal norm? A visionary well ahead of her time, Stanton's passion for social rights and equality made her a pioneer of the women's suffrage movement who was hell-bent on shedding light on this important issue. Stanton (and her better-known cohort, Susan B. Anthony) inspired a most audacious legacy.

How practical do you think people thought Nelson Mandela was when he came out fighting the very government that had unjustly incarcerated him in prison for twenty-seven years, so great were his hopes of freeing a nation from the ruling National Party? After being imprisoned for challenging the apartheid government that was implemented in 1948, which segregated a nation, making blacks outsiders in their own country, Nelson Mandela's dream of seeing his brothers and sisters free to pursue their life's mission without the oppression of apartheid was so strong that he risked going back to prison. His dream—like Gandhi's, Stanton's, Martin Luther King Jr.'s, and so many others who have inspired a legacy and changed the world—was so strong, and his commitment to seeing it through so great, that he was unwilling to settle by giving in to the practical mind.

I often wonder how many people who had the guts initially to pursue their dream have given up when the ridicule and push of the "practical" became too much to bear. Pursuing your dream, while beautiful, creates a burden. While giving up on your dream is likely to haunt you at some point in your life, the daily grind of pursuing a dream that others consider impractical can become so burdensome that "it makes sense" to abandon the very thing that makes a person want to get out of bed in the morning. When I see people giving up on their dream for matters of practicality, the words of

Thomas Edison always come to mind: "Many of life's failures are people who did not realize how close they were to success when they gave up."

This quote makes me think of my friend, actor Carter Roy. Carter's father, Tom Roy, is a legend here in Montana. I once wrote that I never believed in heroes until I met Tom Roy. Tom is the salt of the earth—full of passion, vigor, and energy to this day. As I write this, Tom is on day two of a five-day, two-hundred-mile bike ride on the winding and climbing back roads of Montana, seventy-two years *young*.

I first met Tom when I enrolled at the University of Montana. Though his master's degree was in the field of social work, he had long been a bold champion of the environment in Montana and served as the director of the environmental studies program that I was about to begin. Though a school's director typically only advises graduate students, Tom has never been one to follow rules. After we connected in his office, he agreed to serve as my advisor. The friendship that we built during my time there thrives today, a decade after my graduation. Also serving as one of my founding board members of Yellowstone Country Guardians, Tom remains a massive source of inspiration and hope as my friend, mentor, and cherished guru of dream chasing.

I can't help but believe that Tom's "fuck it" approach to things, his belief that nothing is impossible, and his eagerness to help any passionate soul pursue his or her dream is a major factor in how Carter became *Carter*. Carter Roy grew up in the Garden City (Missoula, Montana), and after graduating cum laude from Amherst College, he said "to hell with it" and hit the road. As a nomadic globetrotter, he spent a year traveling the world, living out of his backpack and sleeping in a tent. His travels took him across Europe, Africa, and Asia; and his dream of becoming an actor was strengthened and fostered by his experiences and encounters with the wondrous places he visited. Twenty years later, and Carter is still "killin' it" as an actor. (Check out "Killin' It with Paul Crik" on YouTube. It is funny as hell, rich, and full of wisdom.) He's worked beside the likes of Marcia Gay Harden, Jeff Daniels, and Christopher Walken in roles on a multitude of TV shows, and in movies and plays across the country.

When I asked Carter via text a few days back if I could tell his story in this chapter, his response was a classic Roy reply: "Absolutely. I'm thrilled to be part of any message about breaking out of the boxes we find ourselves in and pushing forward on our own path. And I couldn't be happier that Paul Crik has been part of your own experience in staying true and on fire!"

The reason this is a classic Roy response? He wasn't saying, "For sure, that would be great exposure"; it wasn't about Carter at all. Instead, he was thinking about the greater good—the bigger picture of inspiring others to break the mold in the same way his father inspired him. Carter is a promoter of living authentically—of killin' it—even though he has yet to catch his *own* big break; he's still unrelenting in striving toward his desired destination. While his talent is indisputable, most older adults in our society would say, "Come on, Carter. You've done the acting thing and you've had success; but it's not working out the way you'd hoped. It's time to be practical, give up the acting, and get a real job." But Carter trudges on, still taking the time to encourage others to maintain hope and do the same. *That's* someone living a BA life!

AVOID DREAM STEALERS

I love sitting down to talk with Carter about our dreams (his acting and my speaking/writing). Talking story with him is spirit food for the soul.

One thing that is absolutely critical when we are breaking the norm, striking out on our own in pursuit of our dreams: we must find people who believe in our goals and inspire us to keep chasing the proverbial rabbit—people who, like Carter and his dad, cheer us on and inspire us by their own example.

The thing that kills me about the people I like to call "dream stealers" is their loose use of the world "real." Who the hell do people think they are? What kind of person talks to the likes of Carter (a dream chaser) about getting a *real* job? And just what does a real job look like? Is it only a "real job" if it falls into the nine-to-five category? Does there need to be a steady salary, bennies, and a retirement package in order for a job to be *real*? Perhaps this is the time to differentiate between a job and work.

Ask anyone who knows me, and they will say I work my ass off—and yet I haven't had a steady job for nearly a decade. Unless the wheels career completely off the track and it's the only way for me to put food on the table, a roof overhead, and baller clothes on my daughter, I don't plan on ever taking a *job*. A job is something you get paid to do; *work*, on the other hand, is something that you *love* to do. The mission is for us to find a way to make doing the *work* viable. Once you get the slash model in your blood, it's hard to turn back.

Is growing organic food that nurtures healthy bodies and minds not a *real* job? How about writing music that inspires people to pursue love or guides people through the storms of life—is that not a real job? What about stay-at-home moms who send their kids to school with a hug and a belly full of eggs after a solid night of sleep; should they drop this unpaid gig and get a "real job" instead? If so, I don't ever want to hold down a *real* job.

But don't panic if you find yourself in a job you're not passionate about. It doesn't mean you can't—and aren't—being audacious and pursuing the mission of living a life that matters. Remember Elwood from chapter 4? While he certainly added joy to those around him by his cheery nature and laid-back attitude, I don't think he would tell you that he wants his legacy to be the dope burritos he rolled with ease.

The same can be said of my boy Scotty B Black (also from chapter 4). He made the audacious move from the Bay Area to Bozeman—went from a director position at the California Academy of Sciences and living in a swanky little apartment outside of Berkeley to bunking at my house. Right now, he's sleeping on the futon in my daughter's playroom alongside Barbies, Teenage Mutant Ninja Turtle action figures, and stuffed animals. He just landed a job in retail that is far from his dream gig, but it is affording him the opportunity to be in a place he loves—one of the last wild places left in North America. He and his wife, Lauren, are living their Montana dream, and he's not tripping about what others think. For Scotty, the job is a means to an end; and his skills are so strong that there is little doubt he will land somewhere that will allow him to do the work that fuels his spirit. Or perhaps he will find a niche at his new retail gig that will provide the opportunity for him to help me blow up our dream of launching the Be Audacious Foundation.

Open heart and open mind.

Always avoid those who belittle your ambitions and aspirations; dream stealers are robbers of your soul. Just as you wouldn't knowingly expose yourself to someone who carried the Ebola virus, don't willingly expose yourself to someone who infects your hopes and dreams.

Perhaps you are doing something right now that you're not thrilled about, but it's paying the bills so you can pursue your passion on the side (your music, art, activism). Remember: you don't have to go all in from the get-go. And perhaps you will never go all in because you find that your regular job allows you the freedom to do the *work* that matters to you most. If so, that is beautiful. For each of us, how we go about chasing the dream will look different. What is critical is that we never stop chasing, no matter what the dream stealers say.

THE NUTRIENTS TO STAY THE COURSE

One thing as clear as the autumn waters of the Bitterroot River is the importance of building up uncertainty scaffolding in pursuit of our dreams (one of chapter 3's lessons). Just as one must develop a thick skin to write for public consumption, if we plan on following our dream, we must provide the nutrients necessary for a thickening of our epidermis (chapter 4). But what are these nutrients, and how do we go about providing them?

First and foremost—and I can't stress this enough—recognize who the dream stealers are and avoid them like the plague. (If you're still unclear on the importance of this, reread the previous section.)

Secondly, you *must* take control of your own life and learn to be your greatest advocate. Don't get discouraged if you can't get others on your train; there is nothing wrong with riding solo for a while. Unless you make it big in something trendy, you aren't likely to accumulate millions of Twitter followers—but this is trivial anyway. All you really need to get started is that one person who believes in your dream: *you*. If you have more than one, count yourself blessed. Just stay the course, and others will follow.

Thirdly, in order to remain unwavering in the pursuit of our dreams, we must *believe* our dreams are possible. Though this sounds simple enough, it's both challenging and crucially important. Why else would the word "believe" conjure up religious connotations so frequently? When we truly *believe* in something, we are willing to risk the ridicule and retribution that so often comes when others can't wrap their head around our pursuit.

Have you ever been in love with someone your parents or friends didn't care for? What do you do when your loved ones don't support a relationship? This is a time to check in with yourself and get into wise mind (chapter 3 and the What Happened Bubble). When it comes to relationships, it's easy to spend too much time wrapped in the reactionary blanket of the emotional mind. But in matters of the heart especially, it's a good thing to check in with the wise mind from time to time.

Ask yourself: *why don't my folks or friends support this relationship?* Maybe they find your partner to be degrading, abusive, possessive, or controlling. Perhaps they simply don't think he or she is good enough for you. Or is it possible that they just don't get it? Maybe they are asking questions but not listening to your answers, unwilling to give your partner a chance?

Only you can answer these questions through intentional and thoughtful reflection. Still, I find it difficult to believe that most of you would cut the head off a relationship that inspires love in your heart simply because others don't see why you feel the way you do. And why is this—what gives you the courage to move forward when those around you are trashing your vision for a positive partnership with another person? It's the fact that you *believe* in what you feel. You believe what's in your heart.

It doesn't matter whether it's a love you want to pursue, a place you want to live, a school you want to attend, a job you want to get, or a path you wish to travel; when you believe in it with all you have, you harness the power of purposeful passion (PPP) to fully tap into the unlimited potential of whatever you wish to achieve or become. In the words of Walt Disney, "If you can dream it, you can do it." But in between, you have to believe.

Belief

To believe in something is to be unfazed and undeterred when your back is against the wall. If you've never seen the movies *Erin Brockovich* and *Braveheart*, go find them on Netflix, because they're both classics. Each offers so many scenes that demonstrate the power of unshakeable belief, but there is one scene in *Braveheart* that I've used time and time again as a motivational tool during presentations.

In the movie, Mel Gibson plays the audacious character William Wallace, a thirteenth-century Scottish warrior who fights the king of England for his people's independence. As his brothers and countrymen nervously await an epic battle with the English, many—if not most—are contemplating abandoning their dream of ending the tyranny of the British. Sensing their unease, Wallace paces the length of their front lines on horseback, his face painted for battle, and proceeds to give one of the most powerful two-minute speeches I've ever heard. "Run and you will live," he says, "at least a while." Then he goes on to ask them if all of those extra days will be worth sacrificing the only chance they may ever have "to tell our enemies that they may take our lives, but they will *never* take our freedom?"

It's a speech that we dream chasers should listen to periodically. Why, you may ask? Because right here, right now, we are all in a similar battle for our own freedom. The pressures of our society—the cultural norms and expectations that force so many of us to assimilate a life of conformity and forgo the right to chase our dreams—represent *our* fight for freedom. We may not die in battle at the hands of those threatening to steal our breath, but when we give in and give up on our dreams, we die a different kind of death: a piece of our spirit fades like a smoldering campfire. And once doused with water and officially put out, it's a struggle to relight it at all. So once we discover the fire burning inside, even if it's only a spark at first, we must tend to it, stoke it, nurture it, and support it with the mighty fuel of belief.

PLAN FOR YOUR VISION

Each year, at the start of the season, I meet with my basketball team before the first day of practice. We gather in the locker room for what we call our "On a Mission: Setting the Tone" meeting. The objective of this meeting is simple: get each player to believe in the journey that is about to unfold. Everyone must be all in if we are to thrive, achieve our desired outcome, and—just as important—enjoy the journey. There is always a palpable energy and nervous excitement as I walk into the locker room on that night. And by the time our one-hour meeting has come to an end, the team's passion and belief have reached an energetic buzz. Then, to acknowledge the significance of the occasion, we end by gathering in a huddle, hands joined in the air, for a unifying chant: "One, two, three: *Love!* Four, five, six: *Passion!* Seven, eight, nine: *We believe!*" And then we hit the hardwood.

The first step in believing in something worthwhile is to verbalize your vision. There is unmatched power in the word, which is why it is so critical for us to be impeccable with ours, both in our self-talk and in our interactions with others. *(Say what you mean and mean what you say*— chapter 3.) Perhaps before you start sharing your dream, passion, and vision with others, you should take some time to put it in writing. While the spoken word is powerful, the written word lives forever. What could possibly be more meaningful than taking the time to pen out your dream? (Exercise #1 in chapter 3 and chapter 5's journaling exercise can help you with this.)

Putting your vision in writing is not only powerful, it holds you accountable—a critical tool for staying the course. And if you aren't going to hold *yourself* accountable in pursuit of your dream, who will? I believe that all successful people have this in common: each person dreamt the dream and had the courage to vocalize his or her vision. From Beyoncé to Bruno Mars, Jeff Corwin to Jane Goodall, LeBron to Lindsey Vonn—

I would be shocked to learn that any of these people who have reached the pinnacle of their profession didn't start by first writing down their dreams, goals, and vision.

It's not enough to think big; that's just the first step. People who achieve notable success in their field: (1) have a burning passion for their dream; (2) surround themselves with people who support their passion; (3) create a plan; and then (4) call upon their resiliency and dedication, doing everything within their power to make it happen. Passion is the flame that ignites the fire within; but as I shared in the previous chapter, without a vision and a plan, the fire can easily burn itself out.

It is essential that we develop a game plan. As much as we would love an organic approach and simply wing it (I'm the "King of Wing" to one of my closest friends, so I don't deny that there is *some* room for winging it), we can't leave something as important as a dream to chance. This is where goal setting becomes important. Set the bar high—think big and dream even bigger. To hell with what others think! Trust your gut. When we learn to trust our instincts about what is possible, we can begin developing a clear, accurate, and thoughtful plan for reaching our objective.

I like to start with a five-year plan and then work backwards. I often ask myself during times of quiet reflection: *Where do I want to be in five years?* And once I answer that question, I can start creating my game plan.

I do the same when I take over a new basketball program. Where do I want to see this program in five years, and how do I get there? Then I start with the first season, the off-season, and the preseason. Once I've dialed that in, I begin looking toward year two and beyond.

I want to add a bit of caution here, however. Just like a relationship, which is dynamic and fluid (not static), we must remain adaptable when plans go awry or the unexpected occurs. As with passion, planning only gets us so far—the best plans can fail. Ultimately, *any* successful endeavor is based upon our ability to adapt and evolve while learning to make the most of the cards we are dealt. Sometimes, we are going to get some really shitty hands, but that's life—*it is what it is.* Remember, it's not what happens to us that matters; it's how we react to it that's important.

Solitude and Space

There are always going to be those who talk, whisper, and gossip. There are always going to be haters—people who hope you fall flat on your face when you are breaking the mold and taking the path less traveled. So, we must have tunnel vision when pursuing what matters to us; focus is crucial. Put on the blinders and get in the zone. This is where solitude and introspection become so important.

How do we drown out the noise and opinions so we can think clearly, laser in, and focus on the task at hand? We create *space*. So many people today are scared to be alone. We have technology at our fingertips; and with the obsession that is text messaging, Instagram, and other social-media outlets, it takes intentional effort to create the habitat needed for introspection and solitude. But this is where the rubber hits the road— where the vision is created, amended, revised, and inspired. It's during periods of quiet and thoughtful reflection, when we take the time to *really* check in with ourselves, that we are able to tap into what really matters.

In the hustle and bustle of the world, it is easy to lose sight of what truly inspires us, fuels us, makes our heart tick. It's sad to think how many people never allow themselves the space to discover their inner purpose, dreams, or vision because of the fear of being alone. But thoughtful contemplation is a must for anyone yearning to live a life that matters.

Remember to take deep breaths, go for a walk, turn off your cell phone, log off of Facebook (permanently perhaps), and get in touch with yourself. Sit by a river, in a park, or under a tree and think about your dream, your vision—what you hope to accomplish, the places you hope to visit. Trust yourself when you feel like pulling back from the world for a mini vacation in your own headspace (chapter 1). And when you're ready to return, be intentional in your interactions.

If you choose to chart your own course and embrace a life of nonconformity, treat your dreams as you would a crop of tomatoes in your newly planted garden: Make sure to water your garden (surround yourself with uplifting friends and family), but avoid overwatering (too many friends)—you could drown the plants before they have a chance to blossom. Cover the plants on nights when the meteorologist forecasts frost (develop tactics to weather the hard times that threaten your dreams), provide enough shade so the sun doesn't destroy the nutrients in the soil (shelter yourself from the haters), and add the necessary (natural!) fertilizer for the crop to prosper (foster mentors who give you that boost when you most need it).

THE HANDFUL

You might be wondering where I'm going with my latest plant analogy. I'm introducing you to a concept that has suited me well in my journey—a concept that stresses the importance of quality over quantity while giving credence to the significance of solitude and introspection. I call it *The Handful.*

"The Handful" is a term I coined while I was living in Missoula as a college student. By the time I reached the University of Montana, I had already been through a lot with the ankylosing spondylitis diagnosis, which had inspired the need for a personal and spiritual transformation. But even in high school, I had always done things my way. I wasn't a drinker or big partier, and certainly chose to strive for authenticity versus following the crowd. Even at sixteen, I was more interested in hanging out one-on-one with someone than in spending a lot of time with big groups of people, where intimacy and connection is lost.

In college, the social standard seemed to be that everyone I knew had an overflowing abundance of friends. I couldn't really wrap my head around this, as I've long believed that our time is the greatest gift we are given; and when we give our time to another, we are giving them a valuable piece of ourselves. I simply made the choice many moons ago to be particular and picky about whom I spend my time with and where I put my energy. I've said it before, but it doesn't hurt to be reminded that energy *isn't* infinite. Energy is a finite resource, and it behooves us to use ours wisely.

So, what is The Handful, you ask? The Handful is the number of people with whom I truly wish to spend my time. Mine happens to be two Handfuls, as I've been blessed with rich and meaningful friendships; but when we begin pushing beyond this, we risk spreading ourselves too thin, devaluing our time, energy, and relationships with those who truly matter.

When you discover your Handful or make the decision to welcome someone into your circle, you honor that connection, deepening your bond while affording yourself the space to grow. Our nearest and dearest can profoundly impact our journey, growth, and transformation, but at some point, we need to spend time alone, deep in thought; and this is difficult to do if we are so gregarious that we are always surrounded by others. You don't need to overwhelm your life with countless friends. Instead, find your Handful and invest fully in those relationships. Lean on your Handful and let them lean on you. There is only so much room for intimacy and meaningful friendships, especially if you are embarking upon a journey to live a life that matters and change the world. Time truly becomes your most precious resource, so use it wisely.

When forming your Handful (family, friends, significant others), consider who will stand by you when things get rugged and who will flee for the hills. (Oftentimes, you won't know the answer until the storm descends and you see who sticks around to weather it with you.) It's hard enough to go through the heartache that comes with hard times; we don't need those with whom we entrust our gold jumping ship simply because of choppy seas. There are so many detractors out there whenever we embark upon something bold, original, and daring that our Handful becomes essential to keeping us on track.

Your Handful must be a source of goodness, stability, love, and support.

Though others may think your dream is foolish, out of reach, or irresponsible, you can't let them keep you from becoming your truest self and from fulfilling your most noble aspirations. No matter the magnitude of what it is that you wish to take on, it's far better to be proactive than reactive; one can only "rope-a-dope" for so long. At some point, you must take charge of your own ship and head for that unknown horizon.

When we live with intention, we uncover the power of now and the inner compass that allows us to navigate the treacherous waters that represent our fear of failure. We unharness our dreams of who we really are and how we hope to transform. We inspire a legacy and live a life that matters. And *that*, my friend, is what it looks like to be audacious.

THE *ALL IN* MANTRA

You should know by now that I'm a big believer in the power of language, words, flow, and vocal style; and there is something about a mantra or phrase that can ground us during hard times and inspire us when pursuing a life that matters. (Remember chapter 2?) There are many mantras that I use on a daily basis: *It is what it is, Fight for what matters, Always come out swinging in defense of your dreams, Constant dripping hollows out the stone* (by the ancient poet Lucretius), *The difference between ordinary and extraordinary is that little extra* (by former NFL coach Jimmy Johnson), *Think big and dream even bigger, With nothin' but love*. The repetition of a mantra, chant, hymn, poem, or quote serves as a peaceful but powerful reminder that our actions and intentions matter.

I want you to embrace the following mantra: *On a mission: all in!* In a world that is far too often ruthless in squashing dreams, this mantra can serve as a powerful reminder. The first part enlists a sense of urgency, a heads-up that we are indeed on a mission. There is no way we can achieve the extraordinary, throwing off the shackles of our societal norms, if we don't recognize the crucial nature of the task at hand. We must approach our vision with a determined, thoughtful, resilient swagger: *we are on a mission!* What is a mission? *Merriam-Webster* defines a mission as "a specific task with which a person or a group is charged." I can think of few assignments of greater importance than the pursuit of our dreams.

The second part of the mantra is equally important. It's not until we uncover the audacity to go all in that we give credence to our dreams. Going all in validates the significant nature of our journey, requiring the courage to go the distance so that we can experience the fulfillment of a life lived with purpose and conviction. This doesn't mean that you have to quit your day job to pursue your passion full-time, but it does mean you have to adopt an all-in mind-set, philosophy, and vision to make your passion a priority.

Mission and Vision

So what does the all-in mind-set look like? It starts with your mission and vision. Whether I am working as the founder and director of a nonprofit, the head boys' basketball coach in charge of creating a positive culture within an athletic program, or a motivational speaker building a brand with the hopes of changing lives, I always find the simple yet powerful act of sitting down to write a mission and vision statement to be critical. It's a proven formula. Envisioning where you want to be, what you want to achieve, and how you plan to go about things (working backwards from the endgame to the starting point) is your key to success.

Sometimes things don't go as planned and we have to go with the flow. Plans need to be flexible, especially when loved ones are in need. But we must not make a habit of excusing ourselves from the work that matters most, as we can still use even the most unexpected interruptions to continue moving our dream and vision forward. *Open heart and open mind*, right?

One evening that I had vowed to spend writing this book, I found myself journeying over the pass to Livingston instead. Though it's always good to be in the old stomping grounds where I ran my nonprofit organization and opened our first office, this trip to Livingston took on a special importance. I wasn't there to do a reading or signing, or to give a presentation; I was venturing to the country jail to visit a young man who had participated in my nonprofit programs for years. His mom had called to ask if I would come talk to him, as he was in a deep and dark place.

As I walked into the jail, I didn't really know what I was going to say. I trusted that my "King of Wing" would kick in and that I would pull something inspiring out of my hat.

It's funny how rarely things play out the way we expect them to (hence the need to think on our feet while remaining adaptable). Instead of sitting face to face across a table, as I had anticipated, I was led to a room with a telephone latched to the wall and a small twelve-by-twelve-inch screen.

When I sat down in front of the screen, I saw Randall decked out in orange and sitting with a dejected look on his face. For the next forty-five minutes (much the way I did when I visited Naomi at the hospital in Salt Lake City [the story in chapter 2]), I flowed with passion and can hardly remember taking a breath. This is the beauty of love (and I genuinely love the young man who was staring at me through the screen that night with a look of absolute desperation): my passion for his life overflowed as my hopes of inspiring him to keep fighting overwhelmed me.

There was no sugarcoating Randall's situation; it flat-out sucked. My saying that life isn't all roses and applesauce is a gross understatement in relation to the struggles he has endured. Right or wrong, heartache, loss, and trouble seem to follow Randall wherever he goes; and it was clear that twenty-two years of heaviness had taken its toll on the young man. He didn't know whether he wanted to keep battling in the face of such adversity. He had lost all hope.

Without a mission and a vision, it is easy for us to lose track of what really matters and get derailed, careening off course, especially during times of struggle and hardship. After validating the unbearable pain Randall was feeling and sharing stories of my own struggles—my own times of despair—I began asking him questions about his future. What were his hopes, dreams, and aspirations? What were his reasons for why he should dig deep when the demons of despair taunted him with thoughts of giving up?

Though I was told before entering the chat room with him that he had lost *all* hope, I immediately sensed that Randall still hung on—even if only by a thread. He still had dreams of positively impacting the world around him, and that was all I needed to see. Right then and there, we began hammering out his mission and vision statement, giving him something to hold on to when the seas get rough, like in the midst of his current raging hurricane.

Our vision and mission statements can act as a life raft—a buoy to keep us afloat when we begin to doubt the course we are charting. I left Randall feeling—desperately *hoping*—that we had managed to inflate the life raft I had seen him construct years earlier, during his time with Yellowstone Country Guardians.

This book represents my *own* buoy, my life raft. While I had been talking about writing it for years, it wasn't until I was lying in my hospital bed, unsure of whether or not I was going to make it out, that the importance of this project really hit me. As someone who has always chosen to live his life with his heart on his sleeve, I can't say that I was overwhelmed with regrets when contemplating the possibility that my journey was nearing its end; but the two thoughts that slammed into me like winter waves crashing overhead were the dread of leaving my daughter and the fact that I hadn't written this book. I wanted this book to be part of my legacy for my daughter and for the young people with whom I have had the opportunity to work—and who have, in turn, touched my life.

I crafted my vision for *Be Audacious* 25,000 feet above eastern Oregon. Right then and there, on a plane to Portland, I began to flow. In great detail, I painted the picture I envisioned, not only for the Be Audacious series of books but for the Be Audacious clothing line, foundation, and media divisions. I described the building that would house our dreams, the people I would see wearing our swaggy gear, the cities and stadiums where I would speak. I even began to envision meeting the woman of my dreams and the life that we would share.

Lying in that hospital bed over Christmas 2013, I couldn't help but think back to that soggy September morning when I flew from Bozeman to Portland to meet with my publisher, Graphic Arts Books. The agenda was to discuss the release of *Grizzlies On My Mind* and then the interest in doing this book next.

Once I touched down in Portland, I met up with my agent (who affectionately calls me his "401K") for a three-hour strategic planning session before we officially began pitching the Be Audacious book series to Graphic Arts Books. While our preparation for the meeting gave me confidence, as we walked into the Graphic Arts headquarters, sweat began to drip. Doubt is natural when embarking into uncharted waters. I knew this trip could be a game changer, but my vision was clear. I had crafted my mission statement, written it down, and planned in great detail.

Needless to say, my BA meeting went great, and today, as I write these words, I am nearing the completion of another dream.

Though it's daunting to get started, once you begin putting your vision on paper (or on the screen of your laptop), you feel emboldened by that action alone. The written word has so much power—perhaps one of the reasons that song lyrics and love letters have long proven transcendent—and once we harness this power, we begin the process of unleashing the unlimited potential that comes with living our lives on a mission.

Practice Exercise:

YOUR MISSION AND VISION STATEMENTS

I don't want you to panic about or dread the idea of sitting down to craft your very own mission and vision statements—what may sound like an overwhelming process—but it's perfectly natural if you do. It just shows that you recognize the importance of the task at hand. As a coach, I consider the mission and vision statements for our program so important that we don't step onto the hardwood for the first day of practice until we have sat down as a team and read these two statements aloud. Then we revisit our mission and vision statements often, as they serve as our bedrock and foundation. This is the beauty of crafting personal mission and vision statements: they are the road map to and the reminder of the path you wish to travel. That said, try not to get caught up in making your statements perfect, as they will change and evolve over time.

This is an exercise that will likely take more time than other exercises throughout this book, but please don't let that be intimidating. Instead, I encourage you to get creative and have fun—this is all about *you* and what makes you tick! And feel free to break up the steps outlined below, tackling this exercise over the course of a couple days, if necessary.

Session #1: Noodling

1. First, find a place that fuels your creative juices. This could be a local coffee shop, a park, a room in your house, or anywhere else that particularly resonates with you. (Note: you will need your journal and a pen for this one.)

2. Once there, take five deep breaths (remember the belly breathing

exercise from chapter 1?); and then (as I would say to my boys before they step up to the free-throw line) "swish and sweep"— clear your mind of the daily clutter, and focus on the exercise ahead.

3. Now bust out your journal, and start noodling the ideas, key-words, phrases, and thoughts that come to mind when you ask yourself, *What am I about—who am I? What do I want my life's purpose to be? If I were an organization, how would I explain my objective to potential donors in a few lines? What kind of a future do I envision, and what is my role in that future?* Write down anything that comes to mind.

4. If you need more inspiration or direction, go back to the core values exercise (#1) in chapter 3 and/or chapter 5's exercise, "Exploring Your Passion(s)." (I've also provided an example on page 233, but hold off on looking at that until you're ready to move on to the next part of this exercise [session #2 below].)

Session #2: Committing to Paper

1. Now that you've completed the noodling portion of this exercise, it's time to commit your mission and vision to paper. Assemble all the related pieces of paper before you or make copies of the relevant journal pages. The mission and vision statements have a big-picture feel, and being able to literally step back and take a look at your brainstorms will be helpful as you proceed.

2. Start with the mission statement, as it's short and straightfor-ward. Remember to keep it tight, crisp, poignant, and easy to memorize. Be clear and to the point. The mission statement should be one to two strong sentences that reflect what you're about while being simple enough to recite. (An example follows on page 233.)

3. Once you've crafted your mission statement, it's time to up the ante by moving on to the vision statement. (This can be as short as a few sentences or as long as a page.) Here, you want to combine your mission with what you envision accomplishing on your own audacious path (your road map)—it's your chance to be more creative, reflective, and imaginative. You're putting your hopes and dreams on paper, so you should write from the heart. And though you don't have to get too detailed here, make sure your vision feels like something you can see, touch, and perhaps even taste—dream big but keep it real (give it life).

Session #3: Making It Official

1. When you're ready, read both your mission and your vision aloud. (You may wish to give a little time between this session and the last so that you're coming at your statements with fresh eyes.) How do they sound—do they ignite the fire in your belly? Is there anything you would tweak? Get both as close to "done" as possible.

2. Now share your mission and vision statements with someone you trust—someone from your Handful. Though you are ultimately accountable for sticking to your life's plan, having the extra support along the way will help to keep you on track.

3. Print out your final statements and revisit them often, putting the document somewhere visible so the act of merely glancing at it can serve as a regular reminder of the path you've chosen.

Here are my basketball team's mission and vision statements from my time coaching in Gardiner, which you can use as a template as you strive to create your own life raft and buoy.

Gardiner Bruins Boys' Basketball
Mission and Vision Statements

Mission
Gardiner Bruins Boys' Basketball is a character-driven athletic program representing its school and community both on and off the hardwood in its quest to build a powerful force of resilient young men that will one day be the leaders of Park County, Montana, and perhaps a nation.

Vision
I envision a day when . . .

The Gardiner Bruins Boys' Basketball program is a family that boldly represents its school and town. We face challenges both on and off the court with character, integrity, and humility, always demonstrating sportsmanship while serving as the pride and joy of our entire community.

The focus of our program: to contribute to the lives of our athletes and help our boys in their quest to become young men. Through empowering young men on and off the court, we are always in the process of building leaders who live authentically, thus setting the tone for the youth of their school and community.

When we walk into another school's gym, heads turn and people whisper because we are a force to be reckoned with—a program that other schools respect and wish to emulate. We take great pride in wearing the blue and gold. We embody the strength, determination, and courage of the mighty bruin that is our namesake.

We walk onto the floor each day at practice with fire and drive to become more—to become better. With an unprecedented swagger and quiet confidence, we walk into each game knowing that we are prepared and ready for battle.

Our players shine in the classroom and are an example to fellow classmates and student athletes throughout the state. Our players strive to become the pillars of the Gardiner community. We are impeccable with our word, we think big and dream even bigger, and we always do our BEST.

While you want to think big with both the mission and vision statement, they must be believable. One hundred percent believable. If you aren't fully buying into what you're writing, scrap them and start from scratch. And if you aren't feeling it or are getting distracted, table the exercise until you are feeling inspired to write.

A word of warning: don't *wait* to get inspired. One of my favorite quotes by William Butler Yeats reminds us of the need to be proactive. "Don't wait to strike till the iron is hot," he said, "but make it hot by striking." At some point you just have to say "fuck it" and get started. And once you do, make the audacious decision to go all in. While revisions will likely come, I want you to look at your mission and vision statements as a covenant to yourself and your dream.

When we fully commit and make the audacious decision to go all in, karma kicks into high gear and providence aligns in profound ways. While I've long been a proponent of multiple passions and the power of the slash model, I want to leave you with a caveat from the nineteenth-century Hindu monk Swami Vivekananda: "Take up one idea. Make that one idea your life—think of it, dream of it, live on that idea. Let the brain, muscles, nerves, and every part of your body be full of that idea, and just leave every other idea alone. This is the way to success."

On a mission: all in . . .

CLOSING THOUGHTS

Without a crystal ball, we have no way to predict how our dreams will play out when we uncover the audacity to pursue them. Therefore, we must embrace vulnerability. Anytime we lay our hearts on the line and risk exposing ourselves to the elements, the potential for frostbite is alive and real. So we have a choice to make: we can stay in the comfort and warmth of our home (the safe and predictable path) or we can bundle up (develop uncertainty scaffolding) and venture out into the world to search for more meaningful encounters and experiences.

The safe path is to settle. The audacious path is to strive—striving and dreaming go hand in hand. To dream is to hope, to hope is to strive, to strive is to live.

Will there be haters, detractors, and naysayers that tell you your dream is out of reach? Of course there will be—especially if your dream is bold and unconventional. Keep things positive, upbeat; remain optimistic without being naive.

I'm both a romantic and an idealist, but I appreciate the need to develop an edge. While it is always better to have love fueling our drive to make something significant happen in our lives, we have to play the cards we are dealt. Remember, sometimes we are going to be dealt shitty hands. But it's not the hand that matters; it's how we choose to play it. And if your hurt inspires you to do something great and uncover something meaningful, by all means, bottle that up and let it be the fuel to drive you in your pursuit of your dream.

The food we consume is of utmost importance—nutrition that keeps the body moving and the brain functioning. The same is true when it comes to staying on course with your dream. The nutrients in this case are (1) avoiding the dream stealers, (2) taking control of your life by being your own best advocate, and (3) believing your dream is possible. Add in the support of your Handful, and you're ready to roll!

My point? We need different fuel at different times. Passion and belief are the greatest fuels. But if there are times in your life where the detractors add fuel to your fire, then go with it.

Just be sure to leave the time and space for developing your game plan—for solitude to do its work. Unplug, tame the brain train, and find what works for you, whether that's being still or exploring more active forms of thoughtfulness and meditation. Set your mission in motion by building your vision backwards, from finish to start, and seal the deal by putting it all on paper.

One of my best friends from college recently attended a yoga retreat and was asked to describe his closest friend with one word. I was humbled when he told me the word he used to describe me was "pure." While I fail much of the time in my pursuits, I strive toward transparency in my actions and relationships (*get up and try*, yeah?). The key is to remain humble, gracious, grateful, and eager to give others praise and props when the opportunity arises—to make connections. And through it all we must remain authentic. *Say what you mean and mean what you say.* Repeat mantras like this as much as you need; let them serve as a tool to ground you.

Whatever you do, do it with love. Be vulnerable, share your dreams, share your heart, share your passions, and live a life worthy of who you are and who you wish to become. If it matters, fight for it; few wins are truly out of reach. Whether it be a dream, a love, a place, a job, or a game, when we find the audacity to believe, we harness the power of the human spirit and can achieve the unthinkable. That is what greatness looks like. That is what inspiring a legacy and living a life that matters looks like.

Onward and upward. *Think big and dream even bigger. . . .*

7

Weather the Storm, Face Your Fears

Some journeys take you farther from where you come
from but closer to where you belong.
—Ron Franscell

Strolling along the sidewalks of Telluride, Colorado, as a twenty-two-year-old yearning to uncover what would allow me to live a life that matters, I vividly remember walking into a shop called Jagged Edge on the streets of this quintessential mountain oasis. A burning desire for adventure consumed my waking thoughts and nighttime reveries. I was obsessed with pushing the limits and finding my place in the world—on a mission to climb mountains, hike trails, bomb singletrack, and scale rock walls—and there were few places in the Rockies as celebrated for adventure seekers as Telluride. Like many of Colorado's legendary ski meccas, there was a palpable booshiness to the mountain town that seemed to contradict the rugged vastness of its surroundings. I, too, was in a paradoxical place. I felt determined—but lost.

That's when I read these words on the back of a T-shirt in Jagged Edge: "The journey is the destination." I quickly walked up to the register with two T-shirts in hand, the soulful quote gnawing on my brain—what did it mean? *The journey is the destination.* I spent the rest of that summer (and many seasons thereafter) trying to find the answer. This seemingly innocent saying felt as if it were better suited for a religious T-shirt or spiritual practice than that of a backcountry brand. But fourteen years later, this chance encounter with it continues to impact my life.

No matter how much planning we do and how prepared we are, life remains unpredictable, enigmatic—an adventure and spiritual odyssey. And the more audacious we are in our journey, the more adaptable we must learn to become. I've come to celebrate the unknown, for therein lies the potential for the most bountiful catch. It takes guts to venture into uncharted waters with our hearts on the line, which is exactly what we do when we shed the shackles of our societal expectations and take on a life of nonconformity—a counterculture approach to life, love, and adventure.

While goal setting is critical to success, it's important that we learn to embrace and live in the moment. The past is the past; all we really have is the here and now. This can make people uncomfortable, especially in the eye of the storm (adversity), because no one likes the thought of enduring raging winds and torrential downpours with no end in sight. We want to know the storm will pass, but the pain of the moment prevents us from being present in it. So we push the heartache away by escaping with drugs, alcohol, soulless friendships, and shallow relationships. Some distractions are directly destructive, while others are indirectly caustic because of the way they rob us of the most important gift we are given in this life: our time. Time is not something we get back, so why waste a minute of this most precious of resources surrounded by people or actions that don't uplift us—help us to grow, develop, and shine?

Having weathered many storms in my life, I thought I fully grasped this; but it wasn't until my most recent struggles that I truly uncovered the wisdom that surfaces when we learn to sit with the fear, heartache, and loss that often accompany the storm. Consider it a spiritual awakening of sorts. While I know I introduced the concept of resiliency and weathering storms in chapter 2, I can't stress its importance enough: the foundation we've laid with the first six chapters means little without resiliency. So it is essential that we develop the mind-set that allows us to endure the storms life will undoubtedly throw our way—to get to the other side.

No matter what your approach to life (from hard-core realist to Pollyanna bubble), life is hard. It's a labor to turn the negative of heartache into a positive, but the personal growth and added resiliency that result make it worth battling through when things get rough. Make it a point to remind yourself of this frequently: *Okay, this is shit right now. But I'm going to be one badass warrior when I get through this storm.*

While there are those prodigies who appear to be gifted with resiliency from the get-go, most of us will have to work at it. Most people aren't going to be yoked without spending a lot of time busting ass in the gym. And most people aren't going to blow minds by picking up an instrument and skillfully playing it without first putting in the time to learn and hone the craft. Likewise, when it comes to enduring hardship, some people appear to have resiliency built into their DNA while others crumble at the first sight of palm trees bending in the wind.

Just like lifting weights at the gym—which breaks down muscles, encouraging them to grow as they repair and heal—hardship and heartache do the same for our psyche. For each storm we weather, we become stronger—more resilient, durable, and determined. And for many of us, there actually comes a point where we get into "bring it" mode.

Remember the scene from the American classic *Forrest Gump* when Forrest was on the fishing boat with Lieutenant Dan and violent seas were thrashing at their vessel, the skies lit afire with volatility? Having lost his legs at war, Lieutenant Dan experienced a devastating blow that few of us will ever know. But as the seas threatened to tear their boat to shreds, Lieutenant Dan decided he'd had enough. He had already weathered so many metaphorical storms that this gale—the real deal—didn't faze him in the least. Instead of retreating for cover, he taunted the storm—and even God—with crazed cries: "Come and get me!" he screamed. "You'll never sink this boat!"

While I can't say that I've ever screamed to the gods to bring on more pain, I recently experienced a series of "let it go and let it flow" moments as I endured a hurricane *season* of storms, one after the other, that assaulted my health and (as is often the case) my sense of self. Perhaps during the heart of the hurricanes, it would have been a stretch for me to see them as a gift, but that is the power of storm weathering: it's either going to kill you (in my case, literally) or make you more resilient. And we have more choice in the matter than we might think.

RESILIENCY RESERVOIR: PART I

I've never been on board with superstitious beliefs, including the unlucky number thirteen, but most who know me would be quick to say that 2013 proved to be anything but lucky for yours truly. But this is an outsider's perspective. My reality tells a different story.

After reinjuring my Achilles just before Christmas 2012, the first six weeks of 2013 were heavy. For starters, I had to reach out to my boy, Erik Rochner, in San Diego to tell him I was sidelined yet again. He had planned on making a feature-length documentary of my attempt to stand-up paddle surf the length of the longest free-flowing river in the lower forty-eight (my beloved Yellowstone). Needless to say, I was struggling with the tremendous sense of loss that accompanied this injury—especially in light of the fact that we had just moved to Kauai in November (in part to train for this epic adventure). Then, in mid-February, one drizzly Kauai day, my wife broke the news that our ship had sailed away too: our marriage was over. Not one to sit around, I packed one duffel bag for myself and one for my daughter, and less than twenty-four hours later, I boarded a plane in a walking boot cast—on crutches—with fifty pounds on my back; tears in my eyes; and a confused, weepy, five-year-old daughter by my side.

To call this a heavy moment would be like calling the sinking of the *Titanic* unfortunate. Stepping on the plane, leaving our beloved Kauai in such a hurried fashion, and all the while, holding Kamiah, assuring her everything was going to be all right as we journeyed back home to Montana—so much uncertainty represented a game-changer moment. We both knew (despite her young age) that our lives would never be the same.

The next two months, we operated day to day, living out of our bags and my truck as we split time between my parents' place in Lolo, Montana, and a month-to-month rental in Livingston, near the shores of the Yellowstone River. Over the course of eight weeks that spring, we recruited my basketball boys from Gardiner to help us move four times. *Four times.* And through it all, my mission remained simple and yet profoundly purposeful: to provide my little girl with love, goodness, and stability.

Navigating the world of a single dad while attempting to hold down a home in a walking boot cast wasn't exactly "simple," but this singular mission held my focus. Even when an orthopedic specialist told me I needed wrist surgery (due to a bike-related injury twenty months earlier), all I could think about was, *How am I going to make meals, braid Kamiah's hair, and clean the house?* But the pain piercing up my forearm following a noon lap swim had led to a twenty-four-hour period with numbness in my right hand, and I knew it was time to bite the bullet. (Hurricane after hurricane . . .)

It was the last day of May, and I was going in for surgery.

I spent the summer of 2013 in a wrist cast, learning to hold down the fort with one good hand, finally off crutches but walking with a serious hitch in my giddyup. My crash course in solo parenting was far from the glorious Montana summer I had envisioned—one filled with outdoor fun and adventure with my little five-year-old shadow. I was still trying to wrap my head around my ailing body and broken home, let alone the loss of the exercise-released dopamine I depended upon to function. How the hell was I going to stay sane?

The most daunting storms of my life have all coincided with injuries that forced periods of reduced activity. Right, wrong, or indifferent, my mind simply goes into the gutter when I can't get after it. I'd had plenty of practice saying, "I'm the Guru of Go, and when I can't go, I get low." I believed I had no choice but to get depressed during these times. My happiness was so directly linked to exercise and intense outdoor activity that I couldn't see an alternative path. That self-defeating story, which I had told myself so many times, had grown and assumed great power in my life. Without the endorphins that came with exercise, I was convinced— 100 percent certain—that I couldn't be content or complete. This story ran through my mind like a tape loop: it was my accepted reality.

I'm not going to front: the summer of 2013 was a total mindfuck. There I was, a single father going through a nasty divorce and a challenging coparenting situation, and my body—which had provided me with so much of my identity, sense of purpose, and happiness—simply wasn't working. And good-intentioned people who tried to be supportive by saying I was "way too young to be going through something like this" only added fuel to the fire of self-doubt and inadequacy already ravaging my psyche.

Since I'm not the chill, go-with-the-flow Buddha type, I went with my instincts to grit and grind my way through the storm. I just assumed that, until I got healthy, the seas were going to be rough and the skies dark. Then one day, when my inability to braid Kamiah's hair led me over to the neighbor's for help, the light turned on.

Remember that Hawaiian riptide I told you about in chapter 1? Maybe I had been going about storm weathering all wrong. *Perhaps the reason one hurricane had blown in right after the next was because I had yet to learn the lesson these struggles were trying to teach me.*

There is a time to swim against the current in an attempt to escape its danger and pull, and there is a time to simply tread water. So I began to meditate on acceptance: *Acceptance is allowing reality to be as it is without requiring it to be different.*

I asked you from the beginning of this odyssey to join me with an open heart and an open mind because I now know how *intentional* this openness has to be. In the summer of 2013, *I* was the one who was journeying through challenges with a wall built so high (and tagged with black-

and-white absolutisms) that I couldn't begin to see what was occurring on the other side. While I was preaching the importance of adaptability in my work, my *own* thoughts were not only limiting, they were derailing my opportunity to be happy. (*Walk your talk—say what you mean and mean what you say.*) And as it turns out, the seemingly epic struggles of 2013 were exactly what I needed to strengthen my resiliency reservoir for what was to come.

CHANGE YOUR NARRATIVE

I love the word "opportunity" in relation to happiness because it indicates that there is *a choice* to be made—that we are free to act (go for the chance to be happy) or not act. When speaking to members of older generations, you often hear them lament that today's young people feel a sense of entitlement. Perhaps there is some truth to this, perhaps not. But I'm convinced that those who learn to see happiness as an *opportunity* versus a right—unwilling to accept that happiness is directly linked to (and a result of) one's circumstances—are those who experience the most joy.

This is an important concept because we often view happiness as something to experience *when it happens*—but we are missing the boat with this line of thinking. It's when we learn the art of fostering and *creating* happiness that we begin to live fully—in alliance with our higher self. Perhaps this is where that sense of entitlement comes from; happiness isn't automatic, it's work—a choice—like anything else you strive for. And while I've encouraged you to say what you mean and mean what you say, I've also mentioned that there are times in life to fake it till you make it. Seeking happiness provides an opportunity to work on this particular skill set. Something as simple as smiling alters our mood and ability to uncover happiness in the eye of the storm. Numerous studies have even proven the benefits of a smile.[1]

Next time you feel like crawling under a rock and disappearing from the world, try smiling. It's simple, takes little energy, and poses no big risk. Simply try to stay afloat rather than attempting something heroic; it may not be the optimum time to take risks or be daring. Instead, consider these times to *survive*—to hunker down and endure. But even during these times, try forcing a smile. See what it does, not only for you but for the recipient. Do the little things that enhance your sense of well-being: feed a stray cat, bring someone flowers, mow your elder neighbor's lawn, *smile*.

It can be hard to find happiness during times of despair, loss, heartache, and grief. To expect to be happy after losing someone you love is more than a bit unrealistic; but how long you withdraw during those periods of discontent *is* within your control. I've learned firsthand that we have a choice in whether or not we pursue, accept, embrace, and create happiness in our lives. And the first step is to tell yourself a different story.

If you recently lost a loved one and the story you tell yourself over and over sounds like this: *I will never find happiness again; I don't know how I'll ever function without her/him*, then this is probably where you will find yourself. And if you don't change that story, it is perhaps where you will stay. There is a reason why the best-selling book *The Secret* has sold nineteen million copies and been translated into forty-six languages: the power of positive thinking, positive affirmations, and positive visualization is reflected all around us by the law of attraction. While I can't say that I fully embrace every element within the pages of *The Secret*, there is an undeniable power to the simplicity and nature of the book's message.

We must become acutely aware of the nature of the stories we tell ourselves. If our self-talk isn't helpful, then we must accept the choice that we have to change it.

Through the injuries, surgeries, and recoveries, physical pain was not my greatest enemy; it was my self-talk. And it was only when I realized I had the power within me to change my narrative—to tell myself a vastly different story—that I began to find happiness again.

Like building resiliency, it takes time to rewrite the story we tell ourselves. But here's the beautiful thing: with unwavering commitment and diligence, we can change both our story *and* our world without any alterations to our circumstances! It's essential that we learn to be our own greatest champion, not our own worst enemy. Beating ourselves up keeps us stuck in a place of inaction, despair, and frustration. If your self-talk isn't helpful, do the heavy lifting to transform it.

Remember the Charles R. Swindoll quote I shared in chapter 2, "Life is 10 percent what happens to me and 90 percent how I react to it"? When I realized I had a choice in the matter of changing my limiting self-talk, I began working at it the way I had always trained to keep my body fit and strong. While pushing myself physically came naturally for me, the inward work of rewriting the story I had told myself every time I was physically laid up proved Herculean. But I was all in on making the necessary changes. So, one day at a time (ODAAT), I plugged away. I didn't win every battle (far from it), but I made enough progress that I could see I was on my way to winning the war.

RESILIENCY RESERVOIR: PART II

As Yellowstone Country's most glorious season took hold across the region, it appeared I had turned the corner. I'd made it through a maddening summer, and fall was in the air. The wrist was healing nicely, and I was back on my road bike and swimming laps in the pool. Though I wasn't where I wanted to be yet, I was grateful for the opportunity to be back doing some of the activities I loved. There was no doubt that I had a different perspective, which is one of the great gifts that adversity bestows upon us: authentic gratitude permeates our essence when good shit happens again. While my Achilles still flared occasionally, I was on my feet and operating with two hands. I had also met a special woman and was enjoying exploring our connection. My first season as the head boys' basketball coach at Manhattan was about to tip off, and it seemed very clear that the worm had turned.

But something still wasn't right physically. I was super stoked to be back on the sidelines, gearing up for the start of the season, but a piercing pain in my left hip had me questioning whether or not I could pull it off. After struggling through my daughter's birthday party in late October, I decided to get the hip looked at, assuming the pain was simply a result of inflammation associated with my ankylosing spondylitis. Within a week, we had the results: femoroacetabular impingement syndrome with a substantial labrum tear. Shell-shocked, I tried to wrap my head around what this diagnosis meant. When my local doctor told me that surgery would be required and that no one in Montana could do it—that I would want to head down to Salt Lake City and the University of Utah to see "The Man" in the world of the experimental surgery, who could correct this relatively newly discovered syndrome—I shook my head in disbelief.

When it rains it pours, yeah?

Now, I knew in the big scheme of things, this wasn't shit—people are diagnosed with far worse conditions. But I was *just* getting back on my feet after a very rugged year, and the basketball season was three weeks away. The idea of not coaching felt like a massive blow, so I resigned myself to a season of intense pain. Still, I knew I needed to see the specialist to at least begin planning for what was coming down the pipeline.

After sweet-talking the receptionist at the University Orthopaedic Center, I had an appointment with Dr. Stephen Aoki. On November 15, twelve days before the first day of practice, my pops and I took a road trip to his old stompin' grounds for my surgical consult, to learn if I was a candidate for the procedure. And even if I was, the receptionist had already told me that the first date they could actually get me on Dr. Aoki's surgery schedule would be months out.

Following my thirty-minute appointment (during which Dr. Aoki and I hit it off), I sat down with Frankie, his surgical coordinator, to get me on his calendar. Apparently my passion for life had made an impression on Dr. Aoki, as he'd already told Frankie to clear his morning calendar so he could get me on the table Friday. This was Wednesday evening. The idea of doing the surgery on such short notice—when we had only made the trip to see *if* I was a candidate—was more than overwhelming. We were planning on heading back north to Montana following the appointment and had little more than the clothes on our backs. And basketball season was about to begin—how on Earth would I be able to coach days after an extensive hip surgery?

Frankie could see I was struggling with the decision.

"Well, Mr. Be Audacious, it seems like an easy answer to me. Dr. Aoki is treating you like a VIP and pulling strings. 'Go big or go home,' yeah?"

And that was it—*go big or go home*, a big part of the Be Audacious message. The decision was made right then and there: I was sticking around for the Friday-morning surgery.

The next day, I was surprised by how cool, calm, and collected I felt. After a long day of working on my book (*Grizzlies*) and hustling basketball projects from the lobby of our Park City hotel, I journeyed out to the Jacuzzi for a soak under the stars.

Immersed in the water, I marveled at the deep, black sky, lit by billions of balls of exploding gas, and reflected upon where I had been and how far I had come over the course of eleven months. From the banks of the Yellowstone to the tropical waters of Kauai, from the shores of the Bitterroot to the fertile Gallatin Valley—through all of the turmoil and adversity, the one common element and source of stability had been my daughter. Regardless of where I find myself, the starry nights always serve as a reminder that home is wherever my daughter and I are.

There is something potent about overcoming adversity and building our resiliency that gives us confidence—that "been there done that" attitude—when faced with challenging circumstances. Eventually, we become unflappable when things get rugged. I had said my goodnight to Kamiah over the phone and I had communed with the stars—I was ready to let Dr. Aoki do his thing.

Walking into the surgery center the next morning, I was decked out in Utah Utes Nike regalia. A pair of balling Utes sweats and a long-sleeved, quick-dry shooter top were the digs of choice since I thought it would be good mojo to represent the university that was about to fix me up (as well as the university from which both my parents had graduated). And seeing Dr. Aoki walk into my surgical prep room dressed like something out of *GQ* magazine—a palpable sureness and swaggery "I got this" vibe about him—only gave me more confidence.

People often ask me why I get dressed up to write each day. I think it's the same reason I dress up my daughter for school: I send her to school in a way that makes it clear to her teachers that she's ready to learn. For me, dressing well each morning puts my head in a place of success—a "let's do this" place.

We all have our own mojo builders; and for me, witnessing Dr. Aoki saunter into the room dressed like a baller, showering me with authentic charm and support, got me into what I call "airplane mode": No matter how tempestuous the flight, once we're up in the air, it doesn't do us any good to worry about the fate of our plane. You are more likely to get struck by lightning than experience a plane crash. We simply need to trust that the pilot is going to do his or her thing to guide us safely through the turbulent ride.

●●●●

Coming out of the surgery, which involved four different repairs, the pain I felt was like nothing I had ever experienced. But my postsurgical ordeal was just beginning.

Opting to go without a nerve block before the surgery (as I had before the wrist surgery), because I was more willing to accept pain than take the chance of permanent nerve damage, it only took two minutes to realize that *this* surgery was a different beast entirely. Begging now for the nerve block, I got an injection. We had eight hours before the pain would come back with a vengeance, so my father and I made the decision to put me lengthwise in the backseat of the truck and make the push back home to Bozeman.

The drive that followed was (to that date) the most miserable and grueling experience of my life. An allergic reaction to the anesthesia caused me to throw up every fifteen to twenty minutes for the entire eight-hour drive. To call the experience rugged would be akin to calling the Teton Mountains rough—a gross understatement.

The only words spoken between my father and me during the entire drive were short debates in Pocatello, Idaho Falls, and Dillon regarding whether or not we should divert to a hospital. At one point, on one of the most remote highways in the contiguous United States, without a light in sight, the all-consuming nausea and pain were so great that I wondered if I was going to see the next sunrise. But I felt surprisingly calm and kept my fears to myself. I simply remember telling myself, *I'm either going to die or I'm not.*

Every hour or so throughout the seemingly endless drive my dad's phone would ring and Frankie would be on the other end, checking in. I had never seen anything like the care that we received while at the University of Utah and in the days following. Dozing in and out of consciousness, I vividly remember doing math in my head each time we passed through a particular community, calculating how long it would be until we reached our final destination. Sixteen hours after awakening for surgery, and following a most hellish drive that my father and I will never forget, we finally reached Bozeman. (Days after our epic drive, my dad confessed that it had been the worst eight hours of his sixty-two years of life.)

When my dad pulled into his driveway, my mom and girlfriend greeted us—but it was a hurried reunion. Still vomiting and clearly in bad shape, they immediately drove me to the hospital, where I spent the better part of the night on an IV drip to rehydrate—a move I did not dispute. The nature of the ordeal that I had endured on this day left me shameless as I weakly crutched through the doors of the ER.

Perhaps it's simply the nature of growing up in a machismo sports culture, but I had always struggled to seek medical attention when something was out of whack with my body, falsely seeing it as a weakness of some kind. Prior to my hip surgery, I had spoken with a friend and mentor about the Achilles and hip pain that was limiting my mobility. He asked whether or not I thought I could mentally handle coaching from a walking boot cast or crutches. After a long pause and thoughtful analysis of my emotional mind, I said, "Yes, I think so." He then asked whether or not I could mentally cope with coaching from a wheelchair if need be, to which I immediately responded, "Hell no!"

If it came to that I would simply turn in my keys and move on to the next chapter.

I got through that first night and the tough post-surgery period that followed, but days away from the start of the season, the pain and lack of mobility were still far beyond what I'd imagined. It became very clear that the only way to coach was going to be from the confines of a wheelchair, but it was my first year as the head boys' basketball coach at a new school in a rebuilding program. The first year is critical for setting the tone, and I wouldn't be able to demonstrate anything. How would the kids take this? What would the parents think? How would the community and opposing teams look at me? Did I have the mental fortitude to pull it off?

It would be one of the most humbling experiences of my life, even if I did manage to uncover the courage to attempt what I'd previously considered impossible.

After speaking with my team of supporters (family, friends, and coaching staff), I made the audacious decision to go for it. I desperately wanted to coach; and while I would have to be very creative in my approach, I hoped that my passion for life, love, and basketball would make up for my lack of mobility. What I lacked in motion, I would make up for in energy.

It's hard to put into words how much pain I was in that first week. I vividly remember the parent meeting just days before the first practice. It was such a production just to get me into the truck, to the school, and in the wheelchair—let alone to the meeting itself. My hip pain was so intense that I could only get comfortable in a recliner, attached to a Game Ready compression system (a brilliant neoprene contraption that hooked up to a machine pulsing cold ice water to the surgery site). Thirty minutes into the parent meeting, I was hurting like hell. After two of my assistants helped me into the backseat of the truck, I spent the entire drive back to my house wondering how I was going to pull off a one-hour meeting with my boys followed by a two-and-a-half-hour practice in three short days.

For the next several weeks, ODAAT became my mantra. I tried not to think too far ahead, for it was daunting to imagine how I was going to get by day after day. On top of my coaching responsibilities, I still had to get my daughter to school each day—on time—with ten-plus hours of sleep and a belly full of eggs. But endure the pain I did—even when I received far too many "crippled" comments and stares from the bleachers to comprehend. With black-and-orange, candy-striped sticks that my star player decorated before our first game (I refused to call my crutches "crutches"), I crutched to the sideline for the start of a new era of Manhattan Tigers basketball, focusing all my energy on the task at hand, and my love for a beautiful game and a spirited group of young men.

Those first six weeks were a grind. One of my proudest moments during that period was when two coaches from the Montana State University football staff came and observed the entirety of one of our practices. They were recruiting and would later offer a partial scholarship to one of our kids (who looked more like a grown man than a teenager) to play offensive line for the Cats. Only days away from a big game, the focus should have been on preparing for our rivals from across town; but knowing the challenges that our All-State big had experienced on the gridiron (two knee surgeries), I made it clear to our boys that this night would be about showcasing our big man. And showcase him we did. We put on a physical and high-energy practice, with action-packed drills that highlighted his athleticism and mobility. The following day, I received word that he had been offered his scholarship. His dream of being a Bobcat would become a reality.

When I first heard that the head coach of the Cats and one of his assistants were coming to observe practice, my initial thought was defeatist in nature: *What the hell are they going to think seeing a head basketball coach in a wheelchair?* But after the next day's practice, as I stretched out in the backseat of my truck with my volunteer assistant at the wheel, I received two e-mails—one from the head coach and the other from his assistant. They both raved about the pace, tempo, and intensity of the practice. The assistant called it, "One of the best practices I've observed," while the head coach expressed how impressed they were with the overall passion, energy, and intensity. He emphasized that it didn't look like I was letting my condition slow me down much and added something that meant more than anything someone could have said, especially considering who it came from: he could see that I was teaching my players an invaluable life skill about overcoming adversity with character and strength.

Things were looking up; and I was using the sticks more and the wheelchair less. Despite a grueling year of ups and downs, it felt like I was back on a promising (but slow) upswing.

The team had just gotten home from our first road trip, a battle against Jefferson (a community along the banks of the Boulder River), and I was gearing up to celebrate my first Christmas as a single dad with my daughter. We had a little, sparsely decorated spruce tree in the corner of our living room, which she had picked out on a blustery winter day two weeks earlier. It had taken everything I had to simply stay upright on my sticks as my mom held my jacket in an ice-covered parking lot and my dad held the tree for my daughter's inspection. We had all been through a lot, but our trials and tribs clearly seemed to be strengthening our already strong connection—a connection that would be tested beyond our wildest imagination in the days and weeks to come.

BRUSH WITH ETERNITY

It was the day before Christmas Eve, and I had given the boys the next three days off, intending to use the short break from practice to shower my little one with love and holiday spirit.

Upon awaking, I immediately felt pain piercing my back. *You've got to be fucking kidding me* was all that ran through my head—I thought I had pulled something. I had begun lightly lifting weights again four weeks after my surgery, but I had done pull-ups the night before and had obviously overdone it. It was my plan to take Kamiah back to the mall (a festive place with carpeted floors—something you think about on sticks in the midst of a harsh Montana winter) after physical therapy, so we could enjoy the decorations and Christmas cheer. But I had to pull the plug on PT midway through my session, as the pain in my back increased with movement. Plus, it was clear that I was coming down with something, because I was dizzy with exhaustion.

Beating myself up for feeling like shit, I drove home and awaited my little one's return from my parents' place. Minutes after she arrived, I found myself on my hands and knees, struggling for breath. After speaking with my mom and my physical therapist, we decided I should take a painkiller to see if it took the edge off.

The next sixteen hours were intense—I had never experienced such pain. I couldn't take a breath without wincing. By 2 AM, I called my folks: I was in bad shape. But I was determined to see Kamiah awaken to her presents and stocking (which I had painfully crutched around the living room to prepare like a hobbled-up Santa), so I spent the entire night curled into a ball in my recliner, writhing in pain, and with my parents on standby. By the time Kamiah had woken up, both my parents were at the house, urging me to go to the ER. But it wasn't until Kamiah had opened the last of her presents that I agreed to go to the hospital. En route, I began throwing up, the convulsions causing stabbing pains that sent me through the roof.

Once at the hospital, the doctors agreed that I had likely pulled something in my rib but opted to send me in for a CAT scan to rule out anything else. When the doctor returned with the results, he looked as if he had seen a ghost.

"You have bilateral pulmonary embolisms."

I didn't even know what that meant, but his tone made it clear that I was in trouble.

"I'm going to get out of here, right?"

"We need to admit you. You are in serious condition, Michael—these are life threatening. They take people all the time."

"But I'm a single dad," I said. "I've got to get through this."

"We will do everything we can for you."

Fuck. Those words—*we will do everything we can for you*—rang through my mind like deafening alarms from a bell tower. And though I was rattled by the doctor's pronouncement (we would later learn that roughly 30 percent of people die within a couple hours of suffering a PE), my focus was still on spending Christmas with my daughter. My folks assured me that they would bring in Kamiah with toys and movies so we could spend the day together.

The first thing I asked the nurse after they had hooked up my IV and drew blood was when my daughter could come in. It was then that they broke the news that they couldn't allow her in because of her age. Outraged, I began ripping out the IV, insistent upon spending Christmas with my Boo. That was the only time during the raging storm that my dad chewed me out.

"This is very serious, Mike. You don't have a choice. You've got to get through this for Kamiah."

Eyes welling with tears, I simply turned my head, staring at the white wall as the nurse reattached the tape keeping the tubes secured to my arm. As I visibly shook at the thought of missing Christmas Eve with my daughter, my mom promised I would see her.

I'm not sure how much time went by, but I'll always remember the moment when I looked out the window of my first-floor hospital room and saw my mom and Kamiah trudging through the shin-deep snow. Bundled up in a hat, down parka, and gloves, Kamiah was holding the doll that Santa had brought her.

"Hey, Daddy," I heard through the window. Though drained, I perked up instantly. We talked for a few minutes, and then she took off her right glove and pressed her hand against the window. Tears immediately began to stream from my eyes. Unable to climb out of bed, I reached out as far as I could, stretching my hand toward hers. It was a moment of unmatched power and beauty that I will forever cherish.

●●●●

The next seven days are still a blur to me.

Hours after admitting me to the hospital, another series of tests uncovered a massive and unstable clot running from my ankle to my stomach. An extensive, deep-vein thrombosis was the diagnosis, and it was immediately decided that I needed to undergo surgery. Unsure of what to do, my parents were warned that this clot would kill me if they didn't get an IVC filter in place. The clot could break off and go to my heart, and then . . . game over. It was a ticking time bomb. I could see the concern on my parents' and friends' faces as we awaited the surgery scheduled for later that evening.

The outpouring of love and support overwhelmed me—there must have been twenty-five visitors that first night. A palpable sense of optimism pervaded the room. According to my mom, my father and the nurses thought it was too much, but she believed it was a good distraction. She was right. Though the pain of talking, coughing, burping, or hiccupping caused a severe shooting sensation through my back (as if I were being stabbed), if I was going to go out, I wanted to do so surrounded by love.

We all nervously watched the clock, awaiting the arrival of the doctor who was called in on Christmas Eve night to conduct the procedure. There came a point when the meds stopped working, and the pain became so severe and breathing so difficult that I writhed in my bed. With my mom stroking my head, we all feared the worst. If the clot broke loose, that could be it. Time was of the essence.

After a successful procedure, where the IVC filter was placed in my vena cava, I faded in and out of consciousness. I spent Christmas Day in a virtual drug-induced state of unconsciousness. There were times that were bearable and others that weren't. I'd had what they call an infarction, which meant that part of my lung had died, and the pain from that was the worst. On multiple occasions, I coughed up a mouthful of blood that left even the nurses visibly uneasy. It was a sketchy, scary, and rugged seven days.

After rebounding on day three, I took a bad turn on days four and five. At one point, they feared a brain bleed, and I underwent more tests in the middle of the night.

I will never forget that night. They had me on so many drugs, I couldn't think straight. From the get-go, I told them I couldn't throw up, as I was afraid my insides would come out—so great was the pain associated with burping or hiccups. As they were gearing up to take me in for the CAT scan, my nightmare became a reality as the antinausea meds failed. Clots of blood filled the bedpan.

The next day was the first time I really began to question whether or not I was going to pull through. I was in *really* bad shape—weak, listless, and for the first time, unresponsive. At one point, I remember whispering to my mom as she held my hand.

"I'm scared."

"So are we, Sweety," came her response.

The plentiful visitors that the nurses tolerated for the first four days weren't allowed in the room on day five. Only immediate family was permitted. My mom, dad, and sister, who had abandoned her Christmas plans in East Glacier Park to rush to Bozeman, were all I remember from that morning. They were quiet, scared, and clearly worried. I'd never felt so sick, so weak—so lifeless. I wanted to battle, but I had nothing in the tank. I could only rest and let go.

Having tremendous difficulty talking, I began to rub my ring finger (eyes closed) as a message to my mom. She immediately said my ex-wife's name. I shook my from head side to side and wagged my index finger, urging her to continue.

"Kamiah," she said.

This time, I nodded.

"You want us to bring Kamiah in to see you?" she asked.

With a single tear streaming down my cheek, I nodded again.

As much as I wanted to believe I was going to pull through, I knew my condition was dire. And this brings me to an important BA concept about which I feel very strongly.

As he fought his battle with cancer, the great Jimmy Valvano, in the most powerful of speeches (presented at the ESPY Awards), said, "Don't give up. Don't ever give up." Though I absolutely believe in this sentiment, I don't think Jimmy V died because he stopped believing, or because he wasn't courageous or strong enough. This idea that those who make it through life-threatening conditions do so because they are battlers has some truth to it, but it's also a distorted view of reality. How many brave, strong, courageous fighters with a heart the size of Spartacus "lost" their battle with a disease? Far too many to count. And the idea that those who die have "lost" is absolutely absurd. Whether you are a fighter by nature or you take a Zen-like approach ("let it go and let it flow"), staying true to yourself in any struggle is what's most important—not the score of those who have made it through a life-threatening illness versus those who have not. So while I pride myself on being dogged and tenacious, and believe these qualities helped me endure the onslaught and ultimately endure the siege on my health, my wise mind knew that in this battle, my will to live didn't represent the be-all and end-all. My body was either going to adapt, adjust, and recover or it wasn't—a situation outside my control.

And teetering on that metaphorical cliff, I needed to see my daughter.

The entire week, they hadn't allowed Kamiah to visit me in my hospital room; so I knew their willingness to make an exception spoke to the gravity of my situation. With a mask over her face and dwarfed by a puffy pink jacket, I could sense her angst. Opening one eye, I reached out for her hand. She simply stood by my bed, her eyes wandering around the room and all the machines attached to her daddy. Having uttered only two words all day, my mouth was parched as I held her little hand in between both of mine.

There was a part of me that knew this could be the last time I saw my daughter. I opened both my eyes and peered into hers. I've always believed in the power of our tears, and they had begun to flow as I prepared to speak to my little shadow.

"I love you more than anything in this world. No matter what, Dadda will always be with you."

"I love you, Daddy."

And that was it. Short but powerful. Though the next several weeks would still be an immense struggle, that evening, hours after holding Kamiah's hand and soaking in her soulful spirit, I finally turned the corner.

AFTERMATH

Awakening the following morning to the sun radiating off the summits of the Spanish Peaks, I knew I was going to persevere. While it would be weeks before I escaped the danger zone—and months of recovery ahead—when I crutched out of the hospital two days later, I did so with an overflowing gratitude and sense of survival. With the cold, crisp December air slapping me in the face, I looked up at the banner of the Bridger Mountains and yelled to the heavens.

"*Aho*, Creator! *Aho!*"

For the first two months of 2014, I visited my team of docs at the hospital multiple times each week for blood tests and checkups. By late February, the decision was made to remove my IVC filter. Following the procedure, I journeyed down to Salt Lake City once more, this time for a visit with a blood specialist. I had returned to coaching, though each day felt like a gamble, as a piercing pain shot into my lung each time I raised my voice.

It was still a tough time for my family too. After the heart-wrenching period where she thought she might lose her boy, my mom stopped coming to our basketball games; the residual trauma from my hospital stay was too painful for her to even watch me on the sidelines, so deep were her fears that I would simply keel over during a game.

The specialist at the University of Utah made it clear that it was time for me to step away from coaching to allow my body time to recover and heal—it could take upwards of six months for my energy to fully return. He also helped me understand the extremely rare blood disorder I had been diagnosed with on Christmas Eve. It's a clotting disorder called factor V Leiden; and in my case, I'm factor V Leiden homozygous (a very rare form of the clotting disorder), which means I'm 80 to 120 times more likely to clot than the next guy or girl. Because of this, the doctor warned me that my margin for clotting is "razor thin" and joined my Bozeman doctor in recommending that I be on blood thinners for life.

While being on blood thinners presents a challenge to someone who climbs mountains, races cyclocross, rides road bikes, runs whitewater, and loves to ski (as hitting one's head could prove fatal), the doctor felt strongly that, if left untreated, my chances of throwing another PE were high—especially when combined with all the traveling I do, where sitting idly in a car or on an airplane can prove lethal for those prone to developing blood clots. He warned me that I probably wouldn't wake up from the next pulmonary embolism, should it happen again.

Following my appointment, while on one of my hourly breaks from driving (once you've clotted, doctors recommend getting out of the car every sixty to ninety minutes to stretch and get the blood moving), I received a check-in text from one of my good friends who lives some distance away, in Hamilton, Montana, and had no idea of what had taken place over Christmas. After texting him a brief synopsis about my Christmas saga, I followed up with an update on my trip to SLC.

A soulful man, Robert's from-the-heart response was classic RG: "Holy shit. . . . No wonder you have been off the radar, brother. I can't imagine. Some souls walk the Earth never to be given a struggle; never to be given the reality that every battle makes a human stronger . . . mind, body, and soul. You, brother, are the one—the one who will never take an ounce of life or a fraction of a minute for granted. You will be the strongest of us all. You will be the one who will grow the most, both physically and spiritually. With no say, you and you alone will fight for the very essence of life. There is not one individual that I admire more. . . . No person I have met that is as powerful as you, no individual has such a soul. You and the family are in my prayers. I think of you often, and will forever transmit positive love and energy to you. I love you, brother."

Robert has always been one of the most thoughtful people I know. Even through his own hardships, his loving spirit always overcomes with beauty and grace.

One night over dinner, not long after my return from Hawaii, he and his beautiful wife, Naomi, lectured me, insisting that I never give up on my dream. In Robert's words, "You are a game changer, my brother." These words, combined with Naomi's resolute confidence that I stay the course, have guided me through many days of doubt.

This is one of the great gifts of hard times: it brings us closer to those we love, admire, and cherish. Words are spoken during and after periods of crisis that are most often left unsaid when the sun is shining; and Robert's words were medicine for my tired and battered soul. The reason I share them here is simply because they are words that could be written to any and all of us who weather storms, endure hardship, and overcome adversity.

You will be the strongest of us all. You will be the one who will grow the most, both physically and spiritually. You and you alone will fight for the very essence of life.

My brush with eternity did indeed put this essence—what really matters most—in perspective: love, family, nature, character, integrity, kindness, gratitude, compassion, and courage. The rest is secondary.

LOVE, BALANCE, GRATITUDE

One bright bluebird day in March, months after my weeklong stint in the hospital, I stopped by Bozeman Deaconess to make a donation on behalf of the nurses who had taken such good care of me. As I sat with the head nurse on the floor where I had spent my Christmas holiday, she told me how concerned her staff had been about my pulling through. According to her, when she arrived on day three of my stay, the nurses met her with "white in their eyes" and expressed the nature of my precarious situation. She told me how lucky I was to be standing upright.

Weeks later, I ventured back to Salt Lake City for a follow-up visit with the blood specialist at the University of Utah. Looking over my scans and report, his intern raised her eyebrows, seemingly surprised that I was the patient whose records she was reviewing.

"He defied the odds. He's a survivor," my doctor said with a smile. Then he listened to my lungs and told me I had made it through the storm. It was time to start living "as someone who had overcome a major cardiac event."

I don't know anything about luck or the odds, but as I said earlier, it's less about the outcome and more about staying true to oneself. Through it all, I tried to simply focus on my breath and on meeting each day with as much love, character, courage, and grace as I possibly could. While I may have failed to meet some of the days with courage and grace, I could always greet each day with love and character. And that's the mission, my friend.

Even so, the words the doctor spoke hit me like a ton of bricks. I had heard them dozens of times before, but something about the way the doctor said them on this day resonated more deeply, slapping me in the face like a cold winter wind. As I headed back to the black spaceship-of-a-sedan I had rented for the drive down, my mind swam with the gravity of the situation I had endured and overcome.

Sitting in the driver's seat, door ajar, I looked up at the sunlight magnificently radiating off the rocky outcrops and snow-covered summits of the Uinta Mountains, and I cried the heaviest flow of tears I can remember. The magnitude of what I had experienced was overwhelming. An immense sense of gratitude made me thankful for the air that filled my lungs and thankful for the knowledge that, six and a half hours later, I would be reuniting with my beautiful little girl.

In the midst of the hurricanes—four surgeries, four months spent on crutches, three experimental treatments on my Achilles, three months spent in a wrist cast, over a year spent in a walking boot cast, a divorce, learning to navigate the waters of being a single dad, and a potentially lethal blood disorder that nearly took my life on Christmas Eve—my world seemed to be spinning out of control. But appearance and reality are two vastly different things. Through it all, I could only get through the adversity with the hope that I was building up my resiliency reservoir for the next one. What other choice did I have in my pursuit of living a life that matters?

The choice to be audacious is clear: keep your head up, eyes forward, and feet moving. That is the path to prosperity, personal growth, and ultimately, your legacy. But don't forget the importance of *balance* (the BA Balance wheel in chapter 1). If I learned anything from 2013 and 2014, it was the importance of timing—the time for fighting and the time for letting go.

One of my greatest challenges in life has been the work to find this balance. I've always struggled to pause and *give in* to the moment. Determined to accomplish something worthwhile no matter what the obstacle, I believed the only way to go about this was by battling, fighting, and pushing the envelope. Whenever someone spoke to me of the importance of finding balance, I saw it as an attempt to slow me down, marginalize my passion, and turn me into a Buddha. I had trouble appreciating the "soft-ies," or those who didn't have the fighter's spirit. But in this way, I'd missed the boat.

Clearly there is a time to have a strong voice—to fight for what matters most and to keep swinging in defense of our dreams. *But there is also a time to be still.* Hell, I couldn't write this book without being still to some degree. Only in stillness can we truly identify the path to our own personal place of enlightenment. There is a time to fight and a time to endure. Coming out swinging with your eyes closed is going to be more damaging than impactful. We have to learn the art of knowing when to fight and when to step back. As an instigator, I've had to learn balance from those around me who go about things in a different way.

In my personal life, I've always needed to go hard. I've struggled finding the balance between regulating my need to go and my body's need to rest and recover. But this is where a person, place, passion, or pursuit can help us to become *grounded*. My stabilizing forces have been my daughter, my parents, rivers, and wild nature.

Without balance, I'm not sure we can uncover passion and empathy in our life. There is so much posturing and ego in our world; we are charged with the task of countering that—the task of exhibiting compassion and love. Many of us don't find it challenging to have compassion for the underdog; I always strive to be there for them, a warrior willing to fight on their behalf. I would be doing you a disservice, however, if I let you walk away with the belief that to be audacious means *always* fighting. In truth, it's *easy* to say "fuck it" to someone we perceive to be ignorant or intolerant; what's hard is having compassion for them. Loving-kindness toward others—and, perhaps most importantly, *ourselves*—is essential for us to lead a life worthy of our legacy.

Remember, there are two ways to go about the problems and challenges in your life: fix it or accept it. This is the beauty of being grown—you get to make decisions regarding how you are going to cope with and overcome periods of hardship. I've had to learn the art of acceptance with many of the hardships in my life. But when there is an opportunity to change or fix things, I owe it to myself (and you owe it to *yourself*) to make the necessary changes.

Think back to when I talked about The Handful in the last chapter. One of the best ways I know to weather storms, learn acceptance, and create change is to develop a team of believers. I feel there is unmatched power in sport, for example, but the art of competition isn't the only factor; its greatest strength comes from the team itself. When a team comes together with a common goal and dream, they achieve a bond that transcends the sport they play. I think the same can be said for the team of supporters in our quest to do something meaningful with our lives. The idea of the lone ranger pulling himself up by his bootstraps and getting it done on his own is Americana fiction. We *all* need supporters when we are venturing into uncharted territory. Why walk the woods, ford the rivers, trek the deserts, and climb the passes alone? At some point, we are going to need a hand, a kick in the butt, or perhaps, just a little love—and in return we will provide the same for our Handful.

The key is to pick your Handful wisely and consciously. I'm a firm believer that the title of family/*ohana*, is something that is earned. As a mentor of mine recently shared, it's not about DNA, blood, or a shared roof, it's about upholding something reciprocal. If anyone (family or foe) fails to honor your personhood, path, and pursuit of happiness, do not change to appease them. Remove yourself from their presence. When striving to live life your own way—in accordance with your beliefs, core values, dreams, and desires—it's absolutely essential that you recognize the tremendous power you have to choose with whom and where you put your energies.

With that said, don't be a fair-weather friend yourself. Endure the others' storms—stand by those that you love. Be a friend of character and integrity. It's a cop-out to say, "Oh, this friend has so much drama. I can't deal!" If you are dealing with your own storm and simply can't provide the support you would if the sun were shining, that is one thing; but don't bail when things get tough just because they're tough. An audacious life is messy—there's no way around that. It's during the hard times that you truly discover who your people are. Who is willing to stand by you, and who are you willing to grind it out beside? This is yet another gift of going through hardship: it weeds out the pretenders and shows you who really has your back.

True love endures all things. While many palm trees are uprooted with the lightest of winds (nonnatives), there are others that are bomb-proof (natives), capable of weathering the gnarliest of tropical storms. These seemingly hurricane-proof palms bend but don't break, capable of withstanding winds in excess of 145 miles per hour. *These* are the types of friends and family we want to seek cover beside.

Only in the mind and in the presence of love (person, place, pet) can we find our Shangri-la. With passion and love, we can achieve much, but resiliency is the difference between reaching our personal mountaintop and giving up on the summit attempt. As you weather out the next storm of your life, I want you to reflect on the power of struggle. Without suffering, how can there be substance? To inspire meaningful change in our own lives and those of others, we must not only struggle but be willing to embrace vulnerability by sharing our experience. The greater the suffering, the more profound the potential for the impactful.

In the end, storms inspire transformation, metamorphosis, and catharsis. And our ability to redefine and rebuild is only limited by the size and scope of our imagination, and our capacity to endure the changing tides.

Practice Exercise:
A GRATITUDE JOURNAL

Just like a race or running a marathon, we must be tactical in the pursuit of fulfilling our highest potential. Sometimes that simply means weathering the storm. When we find ourselves in the eye of the tempest, it's important to remember the power in simply finding the courage to tread water. But we can only tread water for so long. With the storm and choppy seas threatening to drown us, we must ultimately find refuge and take cover, waiting out the raging winds and torrential downpours that come with living and leading from the heart.

During my recent storm-weathering saga, I discovered a refuge that can outlast any hurricane: *gratitude*. All of us will experience periods of tremendous hardship at some point in our lives, but for those who embrace the potency of gratitude, the suffering is much more tolerable. Of all the elements contributing to the glory and abundant nature of our wild world, when hardships arise, I can think of no two intangibles more important than love and gratitude.

To be grateful is an act of kindness that takes thankfulness to another level. There is no way to be in a place of hopelessness or despair when we focus our energy on gratitude. Appreciation for our loved ones, pets, friends, and the bounty of the natural world around us provides self-induced rays of sunshine. And focusing our attention on the beauty of our breath—the filling of our lungs, the rise and fall of our chest—helps us keep our situation in perspective. Remember, it's not what happens to us but how we *choose* to react to what happens that matters. And when we choose gratitude, we always triumph.

Choose to be fully present and grateful. No matter the task, do it with focus and love, and the mundane will become the meaningful. The more you practice the art of gratitude, the stronger its medicine.

For our closing exercise, I want to introduce the straightforward but mighty practice of keeping a gratitude journal. You can make this exercise as short or as elaborate as you choose; I'm not going to give you step-by-step instructions this time. But here are a few pointers:

- You may find it helpful to keep the journal next to your bed with a pen handy. Then, before you close your eyes each night, take a few minutes to reflect upon your day. (Consider combining this practice with the gratitude windows I discussed in chapter 2's exercise.)

- No matter when you choose to journal, focus on what you are grateful for in your life, as this mere act will wire you to look through a different lens at the events, interactions, and occurrences that unfold throughout your day.

- At a minimum, after giving yourself a few minutes of reflection, simply jot down five things you are grateful for. They can be things that occurred during your day or they can reflect more all-encompassing, big-picture gratitude. (This could take as few as five minutes—not a big commitment, especially when considering the impactful result.)

- The content isn't what matters here; like so much in life, it's the intention that counts.

- Give it a week and see if it sticks. Perhaps some of you will adopt the gratitude journal while others will simply recognize the transformative merits of living your life from a place of gratefulness.

Ralph Waldo Emerson encourages us to "cultivate the habit of being grateful for every good thing that comes to you, and to give thanks continuously." Eckhart Tolle says, "Acknowledging the good that you already have in your life is the foundation for abundance." And in her book *Celebrations: Rituals of Peace and Prayer,* Maya Angelou tells us to "let gratitude be the pillow upon which you kneel and say your nightly prayer."

Allowing gratitude to permeate our lives—not just when things are going well but also when we are grinding through the struggle that is inevitable to our human experience—serves as the wind in our sail, powering and guiding us through the rough waters to seas of balanced fecundity.

CLOSING THOUGHTS

This journey we are on—this adventure—is the greatest, richest, and most bountiful gift we will ever be given. It is full of heartache, loss, despair, and struggle as well as beauty, love, hope, and potential. Whether we are experiencing the high of a particular moment or the pain of a heartbreaking low, we must learn to be present with our emotions. It's essential that we live intentionally and honor our story—the good, the bad, and the ugly. The hard times that we weather ultimately morph our DNA to build the foundation of our character, integrity, and resiliency.

I want to remind you of the words my mom shared with me during one of my most challenging times: "People who haven't struggled bore me." In a world teaming with biodiversity, wonder, mystery, and endless possibilities, I can think of few adjectives more painful than "boring." To be audacious is to be bold, courageous, uninhibited, and unrestrained—especially in the face of fear and opposition. By nature, those of us who embrace the Be Audacious mantra will not lead boring lives. We may experience more heartbreak than those willing to simply accept the status quo, but in the cost–benefit equation, the potential for joy far outweighs the fear of sadness.

When we uncover the audacity to embrace the storm as an opportunity to strengthen our resiliency reservoir, we truly tap into our higher self, unleashing our ability to explore all that we may become. No matter how daunting the storm or how ominous the clouds on the horizon, we must remember that *the sun will shine again*. The question then becomes *What tools do I have in place for survival—how will I stay afloat during the battering of heavy winds and downpours?* And with this guarantee of a new day, beyond the storms, are we as willing to throw in the towel and cave to a life of conformity when we could choose a more daring and adventurous path?

I will always advocate for the latter course of action.

We only get one shot at writing our life story, so we might as well take risks, live and love from the heart, and blaze a trail unique to our individual personhood. But this means finding the courage to weather the storms.

Remember, in the end, our personal story is all we truly have. So make it count and tell it well.

In Conclusion:

Your Legacy—
A Life That Matters

When I began the journey of writing this book, I was overwhelmed by the magnitude of the task ahead. How was I going to help readers believe in their ability to inspire a legacy and live a life that matters? And equally worrisome, how was I going to craft a book worthy of your time while conveying the power of the Be Audacious message? I had no problem visualizing this book on the shelf or my speaking at schools, colleges, and conferences across the country. The end product was easy to see, but the path I had to walk to get there was evasive. I struggled mightily with the intimidation factor of starting a project of this scale. What if I couldn't find the material? What if I got stuck? It's safe to say that my fear of failure bubbled up like Yellowstone's enigmatic mud pots.

That is the funny thing about fear: we can use it as fuel or allow it to leave us high and dry. Fear is the emotion that leads us to believe that the pain and heartache associated with the potential for failure or rejection is unbearable, which then keeps us from embarking upon the very journey that fuels our desire to live a meaningful life. But once we slay the demons of fear by simply putting one foot in front of the other, we break out of the box and begin the walk that we are meant to travel. Never before has there been more urgency fueling my desire to inspire a legacy and live a life that matters than the period following my recent brush with eternity. I can still vividly remember lying in my hospital bed regretting the fact that I hadn't fostered the writing habitat necessary for my dream—writing this book— to become reality. I knew in that moment that if I made it through the storm assaulting my body, I wouldn't let this dream slip away. I would be on a mission.

I made the choice to start the process. And the daily morning writing sessions began.

I knew out of the gate that the BA way isn't for everyone. This book is for the free spirits—those yearning to throw off the shackles of our societal norms, refusing to be boxed in by a life of conformity. It's for those willing to take risks in pursuit of finding their true self while inspiring a legacy— one that contributes to the world around them and stays true to what lies in their heart. Though I don't expect everyone to embrace the Be Audacious message, I'm fully convinced that if enough of you do, our world will never be the same. And I, for one, can think of no greater legacy for all of us to be a part of than a groundswell movement ignited by people pursuing their passion and changing the world in the process: one step at a time, one day at a time—one game, one dream.

I recently sat down with a very audacious individual from the South who has relocated to Montana and now calls Bozeman home; he's my "office mate" of sorts. While there are many regulars who occupy the perch area at the café where I've spent four hours a day for the last nine months working on this book, Alan is here every morning hustling his own projects. Working as a consultant, he has traveled the globe pioneering his own path, making a living doing what he loves while living in a place that allows him to pursue his passion for skiing and sailing.

We spent a few minutes around the tea bar last week lamenting over the state of our society—a culture in which ego, entitlement, bickering, and greed run rampant. With our climate changing, our population booming, and the landscape reshaping at unprecedented rates, we discussed the need to cultivate core values that embrace stewardship, character, collaboration, and community. He (like so many other people I've spoken to of late) expressed concern for the future of humanity. Could there possibly be any better fodder for this book than someone I respect solemnly stating his fear for our future?

While there is no way to ignore the maladies plaguing our world, I can't help but remain optimistic about our future. Is it too late to change the tide of habitat loss, warming oceans, and species decline? Can our society ignore the chest pounding and posturing long enough to inspire greater empathy and a sense of togetherness? Is there still enough space out there for us to chart our own course and blaze our own trail professionally and spiritually? By now, you know the answers to these questions.

Together, we can inspire change—think of it as the BA Revolution. Armed with *core values* such as community, character, and courage; living and leading from the *heart* with love, passion, and gratitude; walking with the *swagger* that comes from confidence, conviction, and the right amount of chippiness; while building up our *resiliency* by learning the art of rest, recovery, and scrappiness, there are few things we can't achieve.

If you're still with me this far into the journey, you are now officially a part of my community, and I am a part of yours. And knowing that there are others walking the audacious path of authenticity, doing it *their* way— the BA way—should provide us with enough reassurance to be unwavering in our commitment to the core values that guide us through life's many storms and struggles.

Now is the time of your becoming. Now is the time of *our* becoming. It's time to go get what is waiting to be ours—to reclaim our independence and be bold, passionate, uninhibited, and unrestrained. Now, more than ever, we need people willing to be audacious—to be a voice for the voiceless, to promote a *we* culture (not the played-out *me* culture), and to help build durable and prosperous communities. But this transformation begins where all great change is born: *from within.*

Dig deep; live intentionally, purposefully, and courageously; unleash the power of *you.* Find love, discover passion, and come out swinging in defense of your dreams—what matters most. Remember, love isn't always easy, convenient, or practical; it's often hard, scary, and heartbreaking. But love is the magic that keeps the world spinning. When given the choice, choose love. When given the opportunity, fight for love. We only get one time to walk this Earth, and we never know when this journey is going to end; so *be audacious*, take risks—because the greatest risk of all is choosing to live by the code of others and not your own.

We've come to the end of this book's pages, my friends, but the river of life flows before you. May your journey on this big, wild, and watery Earth be filled with winding roads, open trails, flowing rivers, and mountaintop vistas; and the most impressive views and most rewarding of experiences. *Think big and dream even bigger.*

Head up, eyes forward, feet moving. . . .

With nothin' but love,
—Michael W. Leach

PS: Remember Amanda, that beautiful woman from chapter 5 that I met along the shores of the Yellowstone River? Three days and three restless nights after we stayed up all night talking story, I wrote her a note on Facebook expressing my inability to get her off my mind. Within an hour, she sent me a bomber and most audacious response that was full of vulnerability. She was clearly open to risk taking.

One week to the day after meeting for the first time, I scooped her up for our first date.

Three weeks after our chance encounter, I brought her to the Seattle wedding of one of my best friends. Standing with the rest of my childhood friends as a groomsman, we were just gearing up to walk down the aisle when Amanda walked onto the patio. It was a showstopping moment. Ignoring the wedding planners' cries to keep me in line, I walked up to the most electric woman I had ever seen, grabbed her hands, and without hesitation said, "Marry me?"

"What?" she responded.

"Marry me?"

"Anytime, any place," she replied.

Getting back to my spot in line before the precession began, I was overjoyed. Watching my friend's wedding proceed without a hitch, I had to be the happiest groomsman of all time.

Four months after meeting, against all odds and in spite of people who thought we were crazy, we put a massive bow on our most audacious love story. On winter solstice, with snow flying in Yellowstone National Park, in the ballroom where she first saw me do my thing as a presenter, I married the love of my life.

And that, my friends, is audacious. . . .

Acknowledgments

The power of community is witnessed each and every day across the globe as acts of kindness, compassion, courage, and audacity ripple like ocean swells, rolling into shore, changing the landscape one wave at a time. Some are big and some are small, but each wave leaves an undeniable mark on its surroundings, much the way those who hope to inspire a groundswell of a movement impact those whose paths they cross. They are the people doing the work that inspires a legacy. In my journey, I've had the honor of connecting with many such people—people who have profoundly touched my walk upon this Earth. These are the people who have become my community.

At the center of my community stand two pillars. Their selflessness, dedication, and confidence in my path have represented a constant beacon of hope. To my folks, April and Steve: without you, none of this would be possible. My gratitude for your unwavering support of this vision extends like the Tetons rising from the valley floor.

To my soulful, beautiful, and spirited little girl, Kamiah: we have shared quite a journey together. You are my source. You overflow with so much little person integrity, compassion, and kindness, and have a heart the size of Montana. You gracefully and boldly embody our core values, and you're the most resilient little person I know. I'm so proud to be your dad. *Mahalo* for inspiring me each and every day to be more, to be better. Providing you with love, goodness, and stability will always be my purpose.

To end 2014, we put a massive bow on our most audacious love story. To My Love, teammate, and electric wife, Amanda: you are my game changer. Thank you for always believing in me, for standing by me, for fighting for us, and for being my biggest advocate. Your graceful beauty, radiant spirit, and authentic nature light up my world on a daily basis. I will always be your biggest fan. I look forward to weathering storms and chasing dreams together for the next fifty-plus.

To Dr. John Wimberly, whose words of wisdom are peppered throughout this book: you truly are my guru, my Socrates. I can't thank you enough for all that you've taught me and I hope you take great and rightful pride in the ripple effect your legacy work inspires.

Living audaciously and from the heart in East Glacier, Montana, my sister Ashley, brother in-law, Ryan, and niece, Mirabelle, truly walk the path of the BA way, showering those around them (winged, two-legged, and four-legged) with humble grace while positively impacting that sacred corner of the world.

My love for the Desert Southwest was largely inspired by my five *Diné* sisters (Alicia, Chris, Claire, Valarie, and Colleen), Minnie and Freddie, and their entire Zuni Edgewater Clan. Thank you for embracing and welcoming me and Kamiah into your beautiful family. *Ayóó'ániinishní.*

We call him the Centa-man because he does the work of 100 men. My literary agent and audacious friend, Alan Centafonte, you truly are the Guru of Go, a masterful and skilled salesman of everything you believe in. Thank you for believing in me and helping to make this dream a reality.

I couldn't be more grateful to everyone at Graphic Arts Books. You are a dream team of everything publishing. To Doug, Kathy, Angie, and Vicki: you keep the Graphic Arts Books ship moving forward with bold vision and authentic love for your craft. To Vicki, for her willingness to keep refining the cover of this book until it was exactly what we had hoped for.

Publicist extraordinaire Angie Zbornik, you are indispensable. Working with you has been such a tremendous pleasure. I'm so thankful for all you do to keep spreading the word and message. Thank you for your goodness.

To my editor, Jen Weaver-Neist: I extend much gratitude for your dedication and commitment to this project. After working with you on *Grizzlies On My Mind*, I couldn't imagine teaming up with anyone else for this book; and once again, you did your thing. For that, I'm deeply grateful. You are a master of your craft, Jen. We make one hell of a team, and I look forward to keeping this train moving. Onward and upward.

My life has been richly gifted with the truest of friends. To Brad Bunkers, Scotty B Black, Wayland Coleman, Randy Ingersoll, Dan Claussen, Matt Larson, Nathan Varley, Mitchell Cloghessy, and Devon Kennedy: my gratitude overflows. You have stood by me and weathered the storms. I'm especially grateful to Brad for his creative talent and vision, and to Scotty B, whose audacious influence is felt throughout the pages of this book.

Never before have I met a grown-ass man as audacious as Tom Roy. I've said it many times, but I never believed in heroes until I met Tom. Thank you, Tom, for your support and friendship, and for being such a source of inspiration for what is possible.

Without mentors we are adrift in a sea of vastness. Tim Christie, I'm so grateful for your friendship, wisdom, and tutelage, especially during the hard times. Steve Hoffman, your passion for our natural world is a gift to us all. Thank you, Steve, for always believing in me and for encouraging me to write and speak.

To all my boys back in Seattle/Bellevue, you know who you are. Ya'll most definitely left your mark and helped make me the guy I am today. Much love, fellas.

I want to extend my heartfelt appreciation to those whose stories I share throughout the pages of this book. Thank you for being part of *my* life story and for allowing me the tremendous honor of being part of yours.

To the *mana*-filled landscapes that inspired so much of the prose in this book: Yellowstone, Kauai, and the Desert Southwest. Gratitude and love abounds.

To the beautiful Tiffany Lach and her top-shelf crew at Sola Café: thank you for providing me with the good cheer, the best tea bar, the tightest cuts, and the most delicious eats for my daily morning writing sessions.

Without the Gardiner School administration giving me the opportunity to coach, *Be Audacious* may have never been born. Thank you to the Gardiner school, to the parents whose kids I coached, and above all, to my boys. I will forever treasure the connections we forged

To my friends Jeff and Kari, whose time on this Earth ended far too soon. The legacies you inspired will be forever felt.

To the organizations and individuals who are tirelessly fighting on behalf of our wild planet in peril, I say thank you, and urge you to be audacious in your efforts to inspire the masses and create a more sustainable future.

And to all of those living audaciously, authentically, and from the heart: may your passion and courage float on the wind like the song of the meadowlark, signaling the passing of seasons, from the darkness of winter to the succulence and abundance of spring. May you pursue your passion, live a life that matters, and change the world.

Notes

Introduction

[1] Wilferd A. Peterson, TheQuotePedia.com, accessed March 10, 2015, www.thequotepedia.com/big-thinking-precedes-great-achievement-wilferd-a-peterson/.

Chapter 1

[1] "'More Complex than a Galaxy'—New Insights Into the Human Brain," *The Daily Galaxy* (blog), May 15, 2013, accessed March 10, 2015, www.dailygalaxy.com/my_weblog/2013/05/more-complex-than-a-galaxy-new-insights-into-the-human-brain.html.

Chapter 2

[1] Meghan Neal, "One in Twelve Teens Have Attempted Suicide: Report," *New York Daily News*, DailyNews.com, June 9, 2012, accessed March 10, 2015, www.nydailynews.com/life-style/health/1-12-teens-attempted-suicide-report-article-1.1092622.

[2] "Teen Suicide Is Preventable," American Psychological Association website, accessed March 10, 2015, www.apa.org/research/action/suicide.aspx.

Chapter 3

[1] Tim Worstall, "On the Malthusian Views of Carl Safina," Forbes.com blog, May 8, 2014, accessed March 10, 2015, www.forbes.com/sites/tim-worstall/2014/05/08/on-the-malthusian-views-of-carl-safina/.

[2] Brené Brown, "The Power of Vulnerability," TEDxHouston, TED.com, June 2010, accessed March 10, 2015, www.ted.com/talks/brene_brown_on_vulnerability?language=en.

Chapter 5

[1] Jaimal Yogis, *The Fear Project: What Our Most Primal Emotion Taught Me About Survival, Success, Surfing . . . and Love* (Emmaus, PA: Rodale Books, 2013): 166–68.

[2] Jason Ruiz, "A Drop In the Ice Bucket: Good for the Cause, Bad for the Drought," *Long Beach Post* website, August 18, 2014, accessed March 10, 2015, lbpost.com/news/2000004218-a-drop-in-the-ice-bucket-good-for-the-cause-bad-for-the-drought.

[3] "Water Facts" page, The Water Project website, accessed March 10, 2015, water.org/water-crisis/water-facts/water/.

[4] "US and World Population Clock," United States Census Bureau website, accessed March 10, 2015, www.census.gov/popclock/; "Table 1329. Total World Population: 1980 to 2050," *US Census Bureau, Statistical Abstract of the United States: 2012*, United States Census Bureau website, accessed March 10, 2015, www.census.gov/compendia/statab/2012/tables/12s1329.pdf.

Chapter 7

[1] Daniel Goleman, "A Feel-Good Theory: A Smile Affects Mood," The *New York Times* website, July 18, 1989, accessed March 10, 2015, www.nytimes.com/1989/07/18/science/a-feel-good-theory-a-smile-affects-mood.html.

CPSIA information can be obtained at www.ICGtesting.com
Printed in the USA
BVOW11s2224080915

416172BV00003B/5/P